The Church of God

The Church of God
A SOCIAL HISTORY

Mickey Crews

The University of Tennessee Press
KNOXVILLE

Library of Congress Cataloging in Publication Data

Crews, Mickey, 1950–
  The Church of God : a social history / Mickey Crews. — 1st ed.
  p. cm.
  Includes bibliographical references.
  ISBN 0-87049-634-4 (cloth: alk. paper)
   1. Church of God (Cleveland, Tennessee)—History. 2. Pentecostal
churches—United States—History. I. Title.
BX7032.c662 1990
289.9—dc20   89-38121 CIP

To my wife, Martha, who has given me her love, understanding, and patience, not only during the writing of this work, but for the last twenty years. Although the book consumed much time that I could have spent with her and our three wonderful children, she has been supportive of my work. In my eyes, Martha will shine as "the brightness of the stars and firmament forever and ever."

Contents

Foreword by David Edwin Harrell, Jr. / xi

Acknowledgments / xv

1 Populistic Religion: The Social Origins
of the Church of God / 1

2 Christian Democracy / 19

3 Come Out from Among Them / 38

4 With Signs Following / 69

5 Your Daughters Shall Prophesy / 92

6 Turn the Other Cheek / 108

7 From Back Alleys to Uptown / 138

Epilogue / 173

Notes / 179

Bibliography / 201

Index / 249

Illustrations

Ambrose J. Tomlinson / 4
Richard G. Spurling, Jr., and His Wife, Barbara / 4
Organizational Structure / 35
General Offices, 1912 / 36
Healing Service / 71
Snake Handler / 88
Alda B. Harrison / 102
Mrs. S. J. Woods / 102
Church of God Soldiers / 136
H. G. Poitier / 169
Storefront Church of God / 171
Church of God General Offices / 177

Foreword

The most striking success story in twentieth-century Protestant history is the worldwide spread of Pentecostalism. Less than a century old, the Pentecostal/charismatic family has become the largest grouping of Protestants in the world, including over fifty million Christians. Scores of Pentecostal denominations have matured in the past fifty years, and the charismatic movement has taken the Pentecostal belief in the miraculous presence of the Holy Spirit into mainstream Protestant denominations and into the Catholic church. Modern Pentecostalism also has spawned most of America's religious television celebrities, including Oral Roberts, Jimmy Swaggart, and Jim Bakker. In the United States, Pentecostal megachurches have reared huge modernistic sanctuaries in nearly every city, and in many nations of the Third World Pentecostals have become a numerous and influential minority.

These successes hardly seemed likely at the turn of the twentieth century when scattered bands of enthusiasts in the backwater of American religion claimed to have received the baptism of the Holy Spirit and documented the experience by speaking in tongues. Furthermore, their search for a deeper religious experience by no means ended with tongues speaking. Pentecostal subjectivism invited innovation, and talented men and women attained prominence by convincing their fellows that God had granted special gifts to them. Most Americans snickered at the bizarre rituals of the "Holy Rollers"—from snake handling to faith healing. Few imagined that their theology would ever make its way from the farm to the city. The yokels who voted for Populist politicians seemed downright dangerous to many urbane Americans; their fellows who opted for ecstatic religion were regarded as comical.

However, as Mickey Crews tells us, Pentecostalism did make it "from back alleys to uptown." His book reveals a good deal about how it happened. The Church of God is one of the sources of Pentecostalism. It was born at the turn of the century in the mountain isolation of eastern Tennessee and western North Carolina. The leaders of the Church of God were aware of the moving of the Holy Spirit in other places, but they developed their own version of the full gospel message. The Church of God became the second largest American Pentecostal denomination. Despite its historical importance, the Church of God has received much less public attention than the larger Assemblies of God. Partly, that neglect may be because the church produced none of the highly visible Pentecostal evangelists of the post–World War II period and thus escaped the fame and notoriety gained by the Assemblies of God. More important, the church's lower visibility, as well as its unwillingness to capitalize on the rampaging popularity of the charismatic movement, can be understood only in the context of the church's history. In the story that follows, Crews tells of the personalities and the choices that kept the Church of God on its more isolated course.

The most singular influence on the history of the Church of God was its development of a tight and authoritarian organization. During the church's first two decades that organization saved southeastern Pentecostalism from spiritual anarchy. But it also opened the way for the talented A.J. Tomlinson to establish a virtual dictatorship. After a bitter split in the 1920s that unseated Tomlinson, power passed into the hands of more stable but less charismatic administrators. Every Pentecostal denomination ultimately replaces founding prophets with ruling priests; the time comes when the fear of "wild fire" comes to outweigh a desire not to "quench the spirit." Nowhere in the Pentecostal movement were these transitions more traumatic, or the victory of bureaucracy more complete, than in the Church of God.

Crews's history of the Church of God is important at two levels. First, it is a general story of how the poor Pentecostals of the early twentieth century carved out a religion that satisfied the spiritual cravings of the alienated people of southern Appalachia. Equally as intriguing, and as generic, is the story of how their children and grandchildren refined Pentecostal theology as they moved into the middle-class suburbs of the New South. In short, this is the particular tale of the transformation of another Protestant church from alienated sect to a denomination comfortable with its American environment, a story repeated scores of times in the nation's history. For students of the South, the experiences of Crews's Pentecostals parallel those of other southerners who left the poverty of the farm in the twentieth century for the allurements of the city, all the while struggling to impose the values of their childhood on a new and hostile environment.

Like all histories, however, this is also a unique story. The twists and turns in the history of the Church of God smack of the isolation of Cleveland, Tennessee, and of the leadings of A.J. Tomlinson and other homespun prophets. Crews writes of earnest men struggling to hammer out a code of morality in a region where tobacco-raising was ethically more problematic than slum housing and where the KKK was far better known than the AFL. In the end, this is the story of a church that contributed to the birth of worldwide Pentecostalism but that has spent most of its history in its own world confronting its own problems.

Crews knows the Church of God well—both experientially and as a scholar. He has read the writings of the prophets; he has talked and sung with the true believers. All denominational history is controversial; no telling of it is likely to satisfy everyone. But Crews has written with fairness and restraint about a movement that could hardly have expected such respect twenty years ago. That is as it should be. Pentecostals have earned a place in history, and it is fitting that their stories be told respectfully. Having won such regard, it is fitting that Pentecostals listen to an objective accounting of their past.

David Edwin Harrell, Jr.
University of Alabama at Birmingham

Acknowledgments

In a work of this magnitude, the author is always indebted to numerous individuals. Simply to acknowledge the invaluable assistance of such persons seems inadequate at best. Nevertheless, it is with a deep sense of gratitude that I express my sincere appreciation for all the help that I have received in the course of my research and writing.

This work began as a doctoral dissertation at Auburn University, under the direction of the noted scholar J. Wayne Flynt. Professor Flynt offered excellent advice and guidance over a period of years. At the same time, Wayne became a close friend. It was his encouragement and scholarly example that at critical times inspired me to complete my work.

The staff of William G. Squires Library, Cleveland, Tennessee, headed by Francis Arrington, provided valuable assistance in locating materials contained there. Barbara McCullough, head of their interlibrary loan department, was especially helpful in sending materials to me at the Ralph Draughon Library, Auburn University. Special thanks go to Dr. Clyde Root, director of the Hal Bernard Dixon, Jr., Pentecostal Research Center, Cleveland, Tennessee, and his staff for opening their archives to me and helping me locate various materials. Julian Robinson, director of the Department of Business and Records at the Church of God headquarters in Cleveland, Tennessee, provided necessary statistical information. Ruth May provided materials on the black Church of God. James Marshall helped me meet and interview several individuals in Monroe and Polk counties, Tennessee.

Several individuals in the Church of God of Prophecy at Cleveland, Tennessee, provided valuable assistance. My thanks go to general overseer Milton Tomlinson for his help and cooperation. Wade Phillips was especially helpful in providing documented materials on the early Church of God. I offer special thanks to Norman Fontana, dean of arts and sciences, Tomlinson College, for his assistance and to the library staff at that college for opening their library to me.

I also owe special thanks to my close friends, Bill and Jan Snell of Cleveland, Tennessee. Besides allowing me to stay in their home during many of my trips to Cleveland, Bill and Jan were always there with assistance and encouragement.

The Church of God

CHAPTER 1

Populistic Religion: The Social Origins of the Church of God

It had been a typical hot summer day in the rustic mountain community of Cokercreek, Tennessee, located in Monroe County just two miles from the North Carolina border. On the evening of 19 August 1886, a minuscule band of people from Monroe and neighboring Polk counties converged on a rough log structure called Barney Creek Meeting House. Richard G. Spurling called the meeting to order. Although those present were oblivious to the religious and sociological implications of this backwoods assembly, it was a momentous occasion. From this humble beginning grew the Church of God (Cleveland, Tennessee), one of the oldest and largest Pentecostal bodies in the United States.[1]

Desperate economic and political conditions eclipsed events at Cokercreek. The infant Farmers' Alliance was setting in motion new political current that culminated in 1896 with the nomination of William Jennings Bryan for president. Through the work of the Farmers' Alliance, the Agrarian Revolt gained considerable influence in Tennessee politics. In 1884, the Agricultural Wheel—a small agrarian organization—appeared in the state, and three years later the Farmers' Alliance was established. Membership in the two organizations grew rapidly. While their greatest strength was in the central and western counties, many of the eastern counties also supported the agrarian movement and formed local chapters of the Alliance. The two organizations united in 1889 under the name of Farmers' Alliance, choosing

John P. Buchanan, a farmer from Middle Tennessee, as president of the new group. The agrarian movement reached its peak in Tennessee in 1890, when the Farmers' Alliance succeeded in dominating the Democratic Party and in electing Buchanan as governor.[2] Monroe and Polk counties were two of the few East Tennessee counties that helped to elect the new governor.[3]

Encouraged by this easy victory, the Alliance looked forward to a similar conquest in 1892. The rise of the Populist Party in Tennessee disrupted the Alliance, however. This disruption and the repudiation of Buchanan's leadership by conservative Democrats, called Bourbons, resulted in the restoration of the Bourbons to power in 1892. Voters in Monroe and Polk counties made a significant contribution to this renunciation of the Alliance by voting Republican. They gave Buchanan less than ten percent of their votes.[4]

In Tennessee, the Agrarian Revolt came to a grinding halt in 1896, when Robert Taylor, a Democrat, won the governorship. Several factors limited the revolt in the Volunteer State. The diversified economic interests of the state prevented a united political effort on behalf of the Populist program. The race question acted as a deterrent to divisions among white voters. Rural Democrats also were cautious about what they regarded as the vagaries of western Agrarians.[5]

The Populist party, which grew from the Farmers' Alliance, was primarily a movement of southern and midwestern farmers to promote the interests of the common folk. People joined the Church of God with similar goals. In a very real sense, the Church of God offered Appalachians an alternative to Populist ideology, another way to interpret a chaotic, rapidly changing world. Although not directly related to Populism, the Church of God clearly was a parallel movement. The characters and purposes of the two differed in important ways, of course. Although the Church of God addressed many of the same human concerns as Populism (feelings of crisis, insecurity, and isolation created by a society in transition), few of its adherents became members of the Populist party. For two reasons, few Church of God members were interested in being political activists. First, they suspected that politics would have a damaging effect on their

Christian testimony. Second, they were too busy following their heavenly mandate to become involved in political affairs.

Ambrose Jessup Tomlinson is a case in point. A former Quaker, Tomlinson was reared on a farm near Westfield, Indiana, and came to Tennessee in 1900. Sometime in the early 1890s, he had experienced a conversion to evangelical Christianity. Previously, during his late teens and early twenties, he had become politically active in the issues of the day. Tomlinson remarked, "I entered the campaign long before I was old enough to cast a ballot, and by my voice and influence put forth every effort I could, both day and night, for my party."[6] He even entered the political arena himself once in an unsuccessful bid to win election as sheriff of Hamilton County, Indiana, running as a candidate of the Populist party. Despite his early involvement in politics, by the late 1890s, all of this interest had disappeared.

After his conversion, Tomlinson became deeply involved in the rapidly spreading "holiness" movement, an attempt by more orthodox Protestants to restore primitive Christianity. Soon he received the "second blessing" or "sanctification." This event produced many changes in his life, but few so clearly illustrate the magnitude of such transformation as his complete withdrawal from politics. Tomlinson stated, "My interest in politics vanished so rapidly that I was surprised at myself when campaign year came around and found nothing in me craving the excitement of conventions, rallies, and public speakings."[8] Despite encouragement from friends and neighbors, he refused ever after to take an active part in politics, even refusing to cast another ballot. Tomlinson explained, "When I was sanctified my whole nature was changed, and my whole being was almost constantly going out after God."[9] The Holiness way of life, with its emphasis on the Wesleyan doctrine of entire sanctification or "Christian Perfection," offered the former political activist an alternative ideology which led him to rearrange his priorities and interpret reality in a different way. Tomlinson's experience typified the effects of sanctification on many Church of God members.

Like many Populists, most members of the Church of God came from the lower stratum of society and rural areas. Economic hardship led them to join the church in search of a transcendent

Ambrose J. Tomlinson.
(Hal Bernard Dixon, Jr., Pentecostal Research Center, Cleveland, Tenn.)

Richard G. Spurling, Jr., and his wife, Barbara.
(Hal Bernard Dixon, Jr., Pentecostal Research Center, Cleveland, Tenn.)

experience, but poverty alone did not determine who became a member of this sect. Nettie Bryant, one of the early members, remembered that "most of the people were farmers. None lived in the city."[10]

The Church of God sank its roots in the less populous region of eastern Tennessee and western North Carolina. Because of their geographical isolation, Church of God members tended to live outside the social and economic mainstream. Just as Appalachia was on the periphery of the South, they lived on the fringe of the dominant society. Most of the church's members lived in the rural areas of Monroe, Polk, Bradley, and McMinn counties in East Tennessee and Cherokee County in western North Carolina. Many lived in small cabins in remote mountain communities such as Threshing Branch and Owl Holler.[11] Cleveland, Tennessee, in Bradley County, was the only town of significant size where many Church of God members resided in the early years. Even Cleveland had a population of less than five thousand. The town's only importance was that it was the county seat and a regular stop on the Norfolk and Western Railroad. For many years the Church of God would continue to draw most of its members from the rural areas.[12]

The vocational status of ministers also reveals the class origins of the church. Most of the clergymen were in fact bivocational, preaching on Sundays and at night, while working during the day because the congregations they served were unable to pay an adequate salary. Many ministers were subsistence farmers. Others worked for railroad or lumber companies. Most of these preachers struggled economically. The majority had large families; some had twenty or more children. Food, clothing, and other necessities consumed all their money. Even maintaining a second job did not always enable them to provide properly for their families.[13] Ambrose J. Tomlinson noted that his wife and children had "gone to bed hungry more than once, and sometimes lived on potatoes and salt for days, and their clothes so scant that they were hardly fit to go to [church] meeting."[14]

Such deprivations were characteristic not only of clerical families but of the laity as well. Life was hard for these proud and independent country folk, who nonetheless were apparently satisfied with their rustic lives. Their immediate reward was the knowledge that they were doing God's will and experiencing the wondrous joy of bringing the Holiness-Pentecostal message to their fellow man, thereby adding souls to the kingdom of God.

Although the overwhelming majority of Church of God members and ministers came from the lower socioeconomic classes, their principal spokesmen did not. Like the Populists (whose leaders were professionals in the lower middle class—clergymen, rural physicians, schoolteachers, more prosperous yeoman farmers, journalists, and editors), early Church of God spokesmen were property owners, and most owned a substantial amount of land.[15] Richard G. Spurling, the founder of the organization, owned two tracts of land—450 acres in Polk County and 640 acres in Benton County, Tennessee. The average freehold in that state was less than 80 acres during the 1880s.[16] After the death of the elder Spurling, Richard G. Spurling, Jr., who assumed the position of chief spokesman, inherited a sizable portion of the estate.[17]

Like his father, young Spurling received only a limited formal education, but he was an intelligent man. He was well acquainted with the Bible, ecclesiastical and Reformation history, and the lives of notable churchmen. To complement his sermons, he made use of charts and pictures to clarify and explain church doctrine. When proper materials were unavailable, he made use of what he had. Spurling improvised by drawing visual aids on feedsacks. In 1897, he wrote a book entitled *The Lost Link*, containing a short autobiographical sketch, sermons, and poems.[18]

As a millwright, Spurling possessed considerable engineering skills. He built many grist and lumber mills in nearby communities. Using his ingenuity, he drilled the first area well, for Bachman School in Farner, Tennessee. He once was employed to build a flume line thirteen miles long in order to float logs down a mountain. It is quite possible that he built the first water turbines in that section of Appalachia.[19] Spurling was representative of the early Church of God leaders: men who owned a substantial amount of property, and who were literate, capable, responsible citizens. These attributes served them well. Church members who did not posses some of these characteristics looked to these men for leadership.

The stronghold of the Church of God, as of the southern Populists, lay in white counties—poor piedmont, piney woods, and mountain areas—rather than in the plantation belt. Although the sect later established churches in the plantation counties and lowland areas, as late as 1920 the majority of its congregations was located in typical Populist country.

The constituents of the early Church of God came primarily from Baptist and Methodist denominations. These people had been deeply concerned with the spiritual welfare of their respective churches. New forms of skepticism and unbelief had arisen in the period immediately after the Civil War period, however, creating anxiety among Baptists and Methodists. By the late 1870s, American scientists supported Darwin's theory of evolution. About the same time, textual or "higher" criticism challenged the authority of the Scriptures by subjecting the Bible to historical analysis. Some scholarship declared that the Bible was not an inspired work, but actually a collection of history, prophecy, folklore, and poetry which had been put together over a period of more than a thousand years. This new skepticism threatened Baptist and Methodist orthodoxy, and as elements within both denominations succumbed to liberal forces, these churches moved into the mainstream of middle-class Protestantism. Among the upper and middle classes, emotionally charged services and "fire and brimstone" sermons had declined by the 1890s.[20]

In the last two decades of the nineteenth century, southern Methodist and Baptist churches underwent significant changes. The denominations placed more emphasis on social Christianity and less on Holiness doctrine. Leaders relaxed austere dress codes and taboos against worldly amusements. Liberalization created fear in the hearts and minds of many conservative Methodists and Baptists who witnessed the deterioration of "old-time" religion. Some Baptists responded by reviving Landmarkism, which had arisen in the 1850s to save the denomination from liberalism. Similarly, Methodists formed Holiness associations.[21]

In the late 1870s, southern Methodist leaders announced that an interest in holiness pervaded the entire denomination and encouraged the movement. Their advocacy, however, ceased within a few years. By the early 1890s, clergymen such as Bishop Atticus Haygood not only repudiated the movement but exerted much effort to undermine it. Holiness advocates perceived this attack as a threat to their religious beliefs, producing a feeling of desperation. In short, conservative Methodists entered a new crisis. Echoing such fears, one Methodist leader lamented, "In many places the old theme of personal religion has been virtually banished. Into its place are put mere discussions of current issues. . . . We feel sure that the final outcome of this policy will be disastrous beyond measure."[22] Some would tolerate no further advances of liberalism. An intense introspection resulted from this crisis. For some it meant reconciliation, but for others it meant painful separation from Methodist and Baptist denominations. Alternative ideologies resulted, giving rise to close-knit new communities.

Not only Methodists and Baptists, but other Americans, too, faced rapid changes. Recent studies have argued that Populism offered its adherents an alternative means of interpreting their chaotic worlds. Populists used this new alternative ideology to create a cooperative brotherhood.[23]

As we shall see, a similar phenomenon occurred with the Church of God. This group was to base its theology on a conviction that the believer's Pentecostal experience came in three distinct stages. The first was regeneration, or new birth (John 3:3). When one experienced regeneration, the individual realized that he or she had been saved from a life of sin and had been born into a new life with Christ. This experience often produced feelings of relief and joy. The next stage of spiritual progression was sanctification (Romans 5:2, 1 Corinthians 1:30, 1 Thessalonians 4:3, Hebrews 13:12). This was the "second work of grace." Sanctification was different from regeneration. A person could be born again, but still the old Adamic or sinful nature remained. Sanctification eradicated this sinful nature. This experience always produced great emotion in the believer. After an individual was sanctified, he or she was expected to live a "holy" life. Unlike some old-line Pentecostal organizations, such as the Assemblies of God, which taught that sanctification was a progressive work of grace, the Church of God taught that sanctification was received through faith. It occurred instantaneously and was entirely a work of God's grace. This teaching led Church of God members to believe in Christian Perfectionism, or what they called the "way of Holiness." The way of Holiness was the pursuing of a lifestyle of self-denial, or asceticism. Believers lived according to a rigid code of morality. After the believer was "sanctified," and only then, was the individual a qualified candidate for the third stage of progression, the baptism of the Holy Spirit. The baptism of the Holy Spirit produced great emotional outbursts, with believers speaking in tongues, shouting, running, dancing, etc.

Such basic beliefs constituted a stable ideology around which the Church of God was organized. The founder, Richard G. Spurling, was an ordained Missionary Baptist preacher and, as we have seen, a man of some means. Like many of his contemporaries, he believed that the forces of liberalism had taken their toll on evangelical Christianity. According to him, the church had departed from the law of God to follow creeds and doctrines of men, resulting in "the blind leading the blind and falling into the ditch of apostasy."[24] For Spurling, this situation necessitated a major reformation. From 1884 to 1886, he committed himself to the task of helping to bring about this change. He was not alone in his determination. His son, Richard G. Spurling, Jr. (also a Missionary Baptist minister), and John Plemons, a fellow Baptist, joined with the elder minister to awaken others from their spiritual slumber. That their message fell on deaf ears did not stop these determined reformers.

By summer 1886, the trio had realized the futility of the task. At this point, the elder Spurling decided to call a conference to discuss the group's future. On 19 August 1886, he and his followers met at Barney Creek Meeting House. This small, unpretentious group decided that if they were to restore the principles of primitive Christianity, separation was the only answer. Spurling invited those who were willing to pledge themselves to this goal to step forward. Eight individuals responded. The members then chose the name "Christian Union" for the new organization.[25]

Within a few months, the elder Spurling died at age seventy-four. His son assumed leadership. For the next ten years, the young organization experienced very little increase in membership. Then, in the mid-1890s, some southern Appalachian Baptists and Methodists became interested in the Holiness doctrine and revivalism. The revival that the members of Christian Union had desired so eagerly finally came in 1896, although it did not come directly to this group first. In that year, three men from the Cokercreek area received the "second blessing" or sanctification. None of the three—William Martin, a Methodist; and Joe M. Tipton and Milton McNabb, both Baptists—was a clergyman. These laymen preached the Wesleyan doctrine of entire sanctification, or Christian Perfection. About the same time, another group from the Liberty Baptist Church in the neighboring community of Camp Creek, North Carolina, began holding meetings in the home of William F. Bryant. The three Holiness laymen went to Camp Creek, where a revival erupted. Spurling and the members of Christian Union heard about it and united with the Camp Creek group, merging to form a single congregation.[26]

After Martin, Tipton, and McNabb had departed, the enlarged group of Holiness believers continued the revival, earnestly seeking a deeper religious experience. People worshipped, prayed, and shouted the praises of God. In one of these emotionally charged services, members—both men and women of all ages—received the Pentecostal experience of the baptism of the Holy Ghost. Some demonstrated various types of emotional behavior, but they all spoke in tongues. Spurling estimated that more than one hundred persons received the Pentecostal blessing.[27]

Not much is known about the history of the new group from 1897 to 1902. It appears that the young church went through a stage in which many members surrendered to fanaticism. They believed in extreme asceticism and sought deeper mystical religious experiences. To no avail, Spurling and Bryant attempted to correct this trend. Eventually, these enthusiasms petered out, and on 15 May 1902, Spurling, Bryant, and the others who had avoided the excesses met and reorganized under the name of

Holiness Church. In 1907, the name was changed once again from Holiness Church to Church of God. The young organization soon began to grow at a rapid pace.[28]

In the years following 1902, the Church of God continued to appeal primarily to members of the lower classes. To understand this fact, one must examine the many ways in which the church ministered to its constituents. The church allowed people to become an important part of a close, supportive, orderly community. To enter this fellowship, the candidate testified to the "brothers and sisters" of her or his conversion experience, which usually was quite similar to that undergone by other members. Entry into the fellowship became a time of communal sharing that was important to the individual and the entire body.

Church fellowship bestowed comparative equality. Church of God members were convinced that all believers were equal in the sight of God. Thus, all believers were accorded equal spiritual opportunities. Each could receive the blessings and grace of God that were believed to come through the experiences of conversion, sanctification, and baptism by the Holy Ghost. Participation in worship services, where all were to feel the presence of God, reflected the community's egalitarianism. Equal opportunity also afforded members a chance for personal achievement. In many different ways, church membership enhanced participants' self-esteem and sense of personal worth.

The cohesiveness of Church of God members can be interpreted as a rejection of what they perceived to be the cold formalism and spiritual austerity of Baptist and Methodist churches. Examples of the community spirit and appeal of the Church of God are seen in the performance of its sacraments. The two most vivid examples were the Lord's Supper and washing of the saints' feet. It appears that the congregation held these celebrations quite often. By sharing communion elements, members were reminded not only that Christ died for their sins, but also that they were all parts of the body of Christ. In most instances, feet washing was held in conjunction with the communion service. This was a sacred ceremony for Church of God members. Taking Christ as their example, they followed Him in this act of humility. More importantly, they made this a time of spiritual healing, clearing up misunderstandings, and demonstrating genuine love to one another. Occasions like this resulted in experiences of flooding joy and sublimity, creating a sense of solidarity among members. Other rituals—laying on of hands, anointing the sick, testifying, extending the right hand of fellowship, and speaking in tongues—similarly contributed to group cohesiveness.

As Rhys Isaac has pointed out in his study of Separate Baptists, preaching can also be seen as a ritual. In the early Church of God, the minister's message affected listeners in various ways. Some "fell under conviction"; others received ecstatic release, establishing a close relationship between the member and the minister. The Church of God minister delivered his message with a dual purpose in mind: denouncing sin and encouraging the community.

Although a large portion of a clergyman's sermon was given over to denouncing sin, he routinely urged his flock to seek a deeper relationship with God. He constantly encouraged believers to seek holiness, and their conduct was expected to reflect rigorous standards of holiness. Upon presenting themselves for church membership, candidates promised to give up, "all their bad habits, such as using tobacco, dram drinking . . . and all worldly amusements, all memberships in lodges, and insurance of all kinds where they were under obligation to some secret lodge."[29] To make this kind of vow meant that a member separated from one community and became an integral part of a new community.

The Holiness standard placed Church of God members in direct opposition to the dominant culture; as a result, they condemned much of what they perceived as being wrong with society. They were not alone in their attack. Members of the Church of God, like Populists, were antagonistic toward the new order of American society which had arisen as a consequence of industrialism. They believed that the industrial trend toward depersonalization and reliance on profit in ordering social values would destroy Christian morality. It seemed to church members that society no longer valued people's moral characters and individual contributions, judging people instead according to their accumulation of money and material possessions. These churchmen detested this "gospel of wealth," considered it anti-Christian, and regarded it as the basis of all that was wrong with society and the institutional church. Analyzing problems within the modern church, one Church of God spokesman lamented that too many of its members "love honor and money."[30] The leaders pointed out that the Scriptures clearly taught that love of money was the root of evil, and that when people made money their first priority, sin and personal degradation would result. The task of the Church of God, leaders felt, was to promote the gospel of Christ, as providing the only means of moral emancipation, not only from personal sins, but also from worship of the "almighty American dollar." The Church of God did not reject American industrial society totally; members appreciated the advantages of industrial and technological advancement, but they disliked the *impact* of industrialism upon personal morality and collective community.

The Church of God also demonstrated animosity toward middle-class Christianity. In the view of those who articulated Church of God policy, as urban, middle-class churches grew in number and affluence, close, personal relationships seemed to disappear. The churches became so large that the individual believer somehow got lost in a depersonalized world. Richard Spurling observed, "It is no wonder the once powerful [spiritual power] Methodist Church has lost so much power with God and man."[31] Church of God believers believed that this was not the way Jesus had intended his church to be; after all, He had enjoyed a close relationship with his followers, and Church of God members believed that they were to follow his example. From its inception, the Church of God placed strong emphasis on the personal worth of the individual and the close relationship of the believer to the group. This emphasis fortified church members and instilled in them loyalty to the institution.

Church of God theology, too, created enmity with mainstream Christianity. Church of God believers were both Holiness and Pentecostal in their religious experience. They held to an Arminian theology which was inherited from the Holiness antecedents of the late nineteenth century. Arminian believers opposed Calvinistic predestination and claimed complete faith in the ability of the individual to choose redemption by his own faith in God and by adopting a moral behavior based on the doctrine of perfectionism.

This emphasis on personal experience was another characteristic shared by Populism and the Church of God. For the Populists, the only decent social relationship was between individuals, not between people and impersonal institutions. "As a result," contends one historian of Populism, "the Southern Populists sometimes argued that America did not need structural, qualitative modifications of the country's social, economic, or political organization, but a change in people's behavior."[32] Because the Populists used religious and moral metaphors, they developed what one historian has called a double vision of how to solve social ills.[33] One vision, which Populists pursued most vigorously, depended upon the alteration of society through reform. The other goal, which Church of God folk shared, was a change in human behavior through salvation. In accord with their personal, redemptive vision, Church of God members regarded specific injustices as evidence of social and moral decay. The solution was to defeat universal evil and, by so doing, to restore God's moral order and thereby establish a near perfect community.

This emphasis on the personal relationship, in that it led church members to make moral judgments on society, made the church resemble Populism in yet another way. Church of God members believed that the only decent society was one in which people assumed responsibility for each other. In short, such religion resulted from the desire to produce a more egalitarian society.

The attack on urban middle-class churches was only one component of the Church of God's larger assault on the city and the new middle-class values associated with it. Close examination of extant written materials yields much evidence that churchmen condemned urban values and morals. Worse, moreover, in their view, urban Protestant churches themselves had succumbed to "worldly" corruption: some churches owned pool tables and card tables and participated in worldly entertainment. To Holiness Pentecostal believers, such activities constituted blasphemy and sacrilege.[34] Perhaps part of this Church of God rejection of middle-class Christianity and its values can be attributed to the fact that Church of God members felt that middle-class Christianity had rejected them. Larger denominations such as the Baptists and Methodists frowned upon the Church of God because of its emotional excesses and Holiness-Pentecostal doctrine, especially the practice of speaking in tongues. Many of these "respectable churches" denounced Holiness believers, disparagingly calling them "holy rollers." Such rejection only caused Church of God members to seek a more exclusive fellowship within their own community. Some sociologists and psychologists interpret Holiness-Pentecostal theology as essentially escapist: church members, unable to cope with contemporary realities, regressed to the days of primitive Christianity. Some historians have also viewed Populism as regressive. They argue that Populists were looking backward, nostalgically seeking a simpler, more innocent Jeffersonian world.[35] Like the Populists, however, these churchmen in fact did not want to return to an earlier time.

At the inception of the Church of God, the chartering group of believers was not attempting to establish a new church. The preamble of the first Church of God Assembly reads: "We hope and trust that no person or body or people will ever use these minutes, or any part of them as articles of faith from which to establish a sect or denomination."[36] Members of the Church of God did *not* want to return to the past and withdraw from society. They desired to recapture what they perceived to have been the spiritual standards of the past. By doing this, they could enjoy the benefits of modernity, while, at the same time, their religious practices would give order and meaning to their lives. In short, their attempt to recover lost standards provided them with an alternative ideology which they used to construct a new community.

Both Populists and the Church of God looked not to a past but to a future utopia, although Populists never really stated how its realization was to come about. While both Populists and the Church of God used the same terminology and eschatological language, there was a major difference between the two groups.

Populism was not a millenial movement, whereas the Church of God certainly was. Populists used the terminology only to give them a framework in which to cast their ideas.[37]

Most Populists were postmillenialists, while Church of God members were premillenial futurists. Both eschatologies are predicated upon the belief that there will be a long period of unprecedented peace and righteousness, closely associated with the second coming of Christ. Postmillenialists believe that Christ will return *after* the church has established the millennium through its faithful and spirit-empowered preaching of the gospel. Premillenialists expect Christ to return *before* the millennium in order to establish it by his might. Both believe that chaos and disaster will precede a utopian state. For Populists, utopia was to be brought about by gradual reform; for the Church of God, it was to be brought about by sudden divine interruption of history—by the second advent of Christ, who would establish his kingdom on earth. Church of God believers looked eagerly to the future, when their faith would be proved to have been justified, by the consummation of their salvation.

Whereas Populists used only positive millenial imagery, members of the Church of God used both positive and negative elements (divine wrath, judgment, and retribution) as means of justifying their evangelistic activities. Churchmen felt compelled to do whatever was necessary to warn people to repent and prepare for the coming of the Lord.

Even if Populists and Church of God members looked to the future and not to the past, later scholars have accused both of paranoia. Such charges resulted from allegations that both groups believed that their problems sprang from secret plots and conspiracies directed at them by satanic forces. Recent scholarship has shown that Populists in fact did not believe this.[38] Neither did Church of God members. Although both groups contained some people with conspiratorial beliefs, such individuals did not play a major role in shaping ideology.

In the same way that some Populists attributed their problems to sinister forces, some Church of God members did believe that the persecution they endured and the threats to their values came from an organized effort. To be sure, although persecution did not result from a conspiracy, it was nonetheless real enough in the early history of the Church of God. Persecution was not uncommon for new religious sects, and many early Pentecostal pioneers suffered intimidation and physical abuse at the hands of both outsiders and neighbors. Much of this abuse came in the form of intimidation by clandestine groups such as the Ku Klux Klan and "night raiders." Such terrorist groups vandalized the property of church members, destroyed church buildings, burned homes, polluted water sources, and ruined food supplies. Members, mostly males, suffered physical attacks from these self-proclaimed protectors of genuine Christianity and Americanism. During one service, Paint Broang was struck on the head and fell to the floor unconscious. Another member, a Brother Burris, was not so fortunate. The terrorists took him outside, where they stripped off his clothes and made him lie face down on the ground. One terrorist then gave him thirty lashes with a whip.[39]

Examples of harassment, destruction of property, and physical abuse were numerous. Although most opposition came in the form of ridicule and ostracism, physical attacks happened often enough to make church members wary. Church members' fears can be interpreted as paranoid, but they point toward legitimate concerns about religious freedom for unconventional sects. Community opposition, social ostracism, and occasional cases of physical abuse made the conspiracy theory credible to rational Church of God members.

Just as Populists and members of the Church of God both struggled with social persecution, both also provided new opportunities for women and blacks. Both organizations encouraged them and gave them opportunities for active participation. Such a stance was not synonymous with belief in sexual or racial equality, however.

Five of the eight charter members of the Church of God were women.[40] Women always constituted a majority of the sect's membership. During the early years, the ratio of female to male members was two to one. Women played a major role in the development of the organization, serving as evangelists, pastors, missionaries, teachers, Christian educators, and musicians, although the majority of female members filled less public positions. Females were allowed to preach, but they did not enjoy the same prominence as males or occupy equal status with them. The spotlight was on males; consequently, the importance of females to the movement has been underestimated, and they have not received the credit they deserve.[41]

Blacks constituted a small but growing percentage of the Church of God membership. At first the church was interracial, but, as it expanded, its idealistic policy was altered in conformity with the South's racial mores. Separating work among blacks from the general work of the sect began about 1912. General overseer Tomlinson attributed this to racial prejudice in the South.[42] Blacks, like women, were subordinated to an all-white male leadership.

Despite its various countercultural patterns, then, the Church of God was a product of its times. The sect originated in one of the worst depressions of the nineteenth century and in a period of religious upheaval. People already distressed by churches which seemed too secular, large, or compromising were buffeted by economic troubles and political protest movements. Populism and the Church of God offered their advocates an alternative ideology which they used to cement their new communities in a changing world. Participants in both movements generally came from the socially isolated lower class on the fringe of society. Both groups feared urbanization, but neither was entirely backward looking. Each contained paranoid members obsessed with irrational fears, but neither was an irrational movement. Although they thrived in the same areas and manifested some of the same attitudes, Populists and the Church of God chartered courses which took them in quite different directions.

CHAPTER 2

Christian Democracy

In addition to an alternative ideology, the Church of God developed a centralized form of government which it used to create a new community of believers. The bureaucracy grew from a representative body composed of twenty-one delegates from four local congregations, to a multitiered hierarchy. Today the leadership is composed almost exclusively of ordained clergymen, representing more than two million members from more than one hundred nations. In order to trace the growth of this highly centralized and somewhat authoritarian government, one must go back to its roots near the turn of the century.[1]

Following a Pentecostal revival in 1896 at Camp Creek, North Carolina, religious fanaticism threatened to destroy the new sect. Some leaders encouraged participants to seek deeper religious experiences which they described as "the baptisms of fire": holy dynamite, holy lyddite, and holy oxidite. The emphasis on emotionalism produced a chaotic situation which persisted for more than five years. The sect had no disciplinary body which might have prevented the disorder or at least curbed the fanaticism. After this period of spiritual anarchy, R.G. Spurling, Jr., and some twenty followers met in the home of William F. Bryant to restore order. The small group reorganized the sect on 15 May 1902 and christened it the Holiness Church.[2]

During the next three years, three new congregations were added to the young sect. These new churches were located in the Appalachian region of eastern Tennessee, western North Carolina, and northern Georgia. During this period of isolation, some members urged that the four congregations hold a general meeting for fellowship and to search the Scriptures for deeper knowledge and spiritual experience. As biblical literalists, these believers searched the New Testament for evidence of such a convention. They found in the Acts 15 that the leaders of the early Christian church held a conference in Jerusalem. This discovery convinced the Holiness-Pentecostal believers that a meeting was scripturally necessary.

The four ministers in the sect planned the historic event for 26–27 January 1906. From the beginning, they played the leading roles in the formation and maintenance of church government. They decided that the church ought to have a unified system of doctrine and practice. No congregation was to be allowed local autonomy; all were subordinated to the organization's central government. In the early years and while the sect was small, unity was maintained rather easily through member participation and discussion of issues at general meetings. The influence of the clergymen, however, was profound.[3] Their intent was to prevent excess democracy and the anarchy that had accompanied it. In this they succeeded.

Twenty-one members of the Holiness Church met in the tiny community of Camp Creek at the appointed time in 1906 and formed the first General Assembly, as the governing structure of the Church of God was later called. A.J. Tomlinson served as moderator, principally because he was pastor of the Camp Creek congregation. One of the main decisions made by the small group was that the General Assembly was to be neither a legislative nor an executive body, but merely judicial in character.[4]

At the close of the two-day convention, the participants felt that the meeting had been a splendid success. This historic conference marked the beginning of the centralization of the government of the Church of God. The group had created the nucleus of church government, taken care of all necessary business, and enjoyed a time of fellowship. The conference went so well that they decided that the assembly should convene annually.[5]

In subsequent assemblies, delegates made numerous decisions that were significant in the history of the church. For example, the 1907 General Assembly changed the name of the organization from Holiness Church to Church of God. Communicants agreed that this was the name that the apostles had used for the Lord's church.[6]

At each of these early conferences, participants chose A.J. Tomlinson as "moderator." From the beginning, the office of moderator was not a fulltime position. Tomlinson merely moderated the proceedings and kept the minutes of the business sessions. But in 1909, the General Assembly made the office of general moderator or general overseer, as it was later called, a fulltime administrative position. This person would have various responsibilities, including issuing clergy credentials, keeping accurate records, and promoting the general interests of the church.[7]

On 9 January 1909, the assembly chose A.J. Tomlinson as the first general moderator of the Church of God. Tomlinson, who had joined the church in 1903, was a popular leader. He was fairly well educated, persuasive, charismatic, and a dynamic speaker. There is no indication of any disagreement concerning the decision, although Spurling and Bryant had been the two primary leaders before Tomlinson's arrival.[8] The new general moderator was destined to become a powerful figure in the organization. Almost every year the church gave additional powers and responsibilities to the moderator; in some cases, he simply assumed such authority.

As in other Protestant organizations, the bureaucracy of the Church of God grew as membership rolls swelled. By 1911, the organization included fifty-eight churches containing more than 1,800 members. The number of clergymen with credentials had increased to 107. The leadership realized that some type of regional administrative position was needed to help supervise the growing church. With all of the responsibilities that the general overseer had, he could not manage the churches alone. To help alleviate the problem, the sect instituted the office of state overseer in 1911. This creation, however, did not diminish the power or authority of the general overseer, for the state overseers were placed under his supervision. The church gave the state overseers responsibility for appointing all pastors, keeping accurate records of the churches within their respective states, and sending annual reports to the general overseer.[9]

At this same 1911 assembly, delegates approved a list of twenty-five teachings.[10] All reflected the church's Holiness-Pentecostal theology and its emphasis on personal morality. The codification of teachings placed all members of the various congregations under a unified system of theology and doctrine. Although the leaders believed that this unification was desirable, it was nonetheless idealistic.

In the early years of the Church of God, unity prevailed for the most part. If a member departed from the official teachings on any point, church leaders dealt with the offender with methods ranging from mild chastisement to expulsion. Through the years, as the church grew and moved into geographical areas outside of the traditional "Bible Belt," compliance with the unified system of doctrine eroded. Members from different parts of the country and different social and economic classes brought with them cultural baggage much different from that of their southern coreligionists. Many of these nonsoutherners felt they need not comply with church teachings that had been developed because of conflicts within southern culture. In the post–World War II period, disagreements ensued. Because of cultural diversity, church leaders found it difficult to deal with recalcitrant members who did not conform to church dogma in every jot and tittle. In the years prior to the war, erring members were often expelled from the organization, but in the postwar period, few individuals were expelled unless they had committed some serious offense. In recent times, the power of church leaders to excommunicate has been utilized less and less.

The decline in number of expulsions does not mean that churchmen did not have the requisite authority. The power of officials continued to expand in the early years. In 1914, the assembly apointed A.J. Tomlinson general overseer for life. Tomlinson, a very capable spiritual leader and a tireless worker, had served in the office since 1906 and had been chosen for the position every year.[11] The precedent was to prove unwise, not because of the choice of Tomlinson, but because the office became a lifetime appointment.

During the years of World War I, the Church of God continued to grow at a significant pace, reaching converts outside its stronghold in the Southeast. The church recruited members from as far west as New Mexico and the Dakotas. In 1916, to help supervise and promote the work of the organization, the Body of Elders was added to its already growing bureaucracy. Twelve prominent ordained clergymen comprised its ranks. The Council of Twelve, as it was later called, had authority regarding "all questions of every nature that may properly come before them, their actions and decisions to be ratified by the Assembly in session."[12]

The dozen members of this group were the church's most popular and powerful ordained clergymen. The body had broad powers and played a leading role in the development of the church. The Council of Twelve had several duties and responsibilities. It met periodically with the general overseer between the annual General Assemblies and discussed all business matters relating to the Church of God. The council also prepared an agenda for the annual assembly.[13] Although the council could not make policy without the approval of the General Assembly, ratification usually proved to be a formality. Only on rare occasions did the assembly reject recommendations of the council. The assembly began as the nucleus of church government, and technically it remains that; over the years, however, the power of the hierarchy and church administrators grew until the General Assembly became a powerless entity that simply endorses recommendations proposed by the ordained clergymen.

In 1920, the General Assembly passed an unfortunate recommendation concerning a revision of the financial system. Previously church members had paid tithes into local church treasuries. Clerks at each church sent 10 percent of these receipts to the general headquarters in Cleveland, Tennessee, and 10 percent to the respective state headquarters. The remaining 80 percent were used to help support the local pastor and church. At the 1920 assembly, the council and general overseer recommended that a general treasury be set up in Cleveland, to which all tithes would be sent. A committee of seven men, including the over-seer, was designated to handle the collection and disposition of funds from the account. Pastors no longer would be paid from local church treasuries, but instead would receive salaries from the general headquarters in Cleveland. Inexplicably, the com-mittee was never organized, and Tomlinson took responsibility for distributing funds. The general overseer rationalized, "They had put upon me the handling of the money against my will, but I submitted."[14]

Problems with the new system soon arose. Apparently there were numerous pastors who believed that they were not receiv-ing their fair share of pay, and a small number who did not re-ceive any pay. The inequities persisted for months, generating increasing discontent with each passing pay period. Despite re-quests by Tomlinson and other church leaders for patience and understanding, nerves were on edge and tempers ran hot.[15] To make matters worse, the Church of God was heavily in debt. It owed more than $20,000 on a new auditorium, and the record books of the publishing house showed a deficit of more than $30,000. Despite mounting discontent and financial difficulties, most church officials defended the financial system, arguing that any new program would have wrinkles to iron out.[16]

The church continued to operate with a mounting deficit. Although the 1921 General Assembly did little to solve these problems, it passed three significant recommendations from the Council of Twelve. It created another administrative body, sepa-rate from the Council of Twelve, called the Council of Seventy. This group of ordained clergymen was elected and served a ro-tating term of office. This group constituted a powerful ecclesi-astical body until its dissolution in 1929. The 1921 assembly also instituted a Court of Justice, consisting of seven ordained minis-ters called "supreme judges." The purpose of this judicial board was to hear and judge cases by former Church of God members who had been expelled but who desired to appeal their cases to a higher authority. The court would hear such cases and make a final decision.[17]

The assembly also passed another measure that proved to have enormous consequences. Prior to the meeting, a special three-member committee had been appointed to write a constitution. The committee had drafted a document that contained a preamble and eight articles. General overseer Tomlinson introduced the document in his annual address to the assembly. He and numerous officials maintained that the constitution contained no new doctrine or man-made creed but was simply a written record of those policies that the church had always followed. One of the most important provisions of the newly-adopted constitution was the right to impeach any church official who was found guilty of malfeasance or misdemeanor. Another allowed new administrative positions to be created and added to the growing bureaucracy. Although the General Assembly adopted the constitution, the document became an extremely controversial subject in the following months.[18]

In summer 1922, the church abolished the new financial system and reverted to the original practice. But discontent with the way Tomlinson managed church finances did not diminish. Many leaders and other churchmen questioned the general overseer's ability to handle the financial affairs of the organization. Records indicated to them that various departments showed reductions in funds when they should have shown increases. Such discrepancies caused many of Tomlinson's fellow clergymen to suspect him of wrongdoing.[19]

Anger and tension continued to rise, climaxing at the 1922 General Assembly. At this meeting, the church split into two warring factions. One group of churchmen decided to put an end to the financial problem, regardless of what measures were necessary to do so. Tomlinson viewed the constitution as the source of all the problems and asked that it be abolished. He also asked the assembly to abolish the elected Council of Seventy and give him authority to appoint all members of the Council of Twelve. Before and during the meeting, the two factions accused each other of failures, and Tomlinson made the critical mistake of publicly accusing some of his opponents of conspiring against him.[20]

The general overseer did try to relieve the minds of those who suspected him of financial mismanagement.[21] Tomlinson explained to his audience that the church's severe debt crisis had forced him into an impossible situation. If he had not used part of the tithes to pay bills, the church might have lost its publishing house and auditorium. More importantly, he said, if he had failed to pay these bills and foreclosure had ensued, the credibility and reputation of the church might have been damaged irreparably. The only way Tomlinson could prevent the possible ruin of the organization was to use money from the tithe fund. He knew that if he used any money from this source, he would probably incur opposition, he explained, but he never had dreamed that this action would cause him so much grief.

Tomlinson's explanation reassured many, but others remained unconvinced and were determined to deal with the problem in a more severe fashion. An ugly power struggle that probably had been brewing for quite some time surfaced at the assembly. The general overseer's requests for constitutional revision and power to appoint the Council of Twelve were referred to the Committee on Better Government. It rejected both requests, and retaining the constitution and the process of electing council members.[22] As a result of the struggle for power, during the assembly J.S. Llewellyn, an outspoken critic of Tomlinson, proposed an amendment to the constitution that called for the creation of two new administrative positions, a superintendent of education and an editor of church publications. Both these positions were to be filled by ordained churchmen, who, together with the general overseer, would form an Executive Committee. This committee's responsibilities would include collecting, appropriating, and managing all funds coming to the general headquarters. The committee also would have the power to appoint all state overseers, a power formerly exercised by the general overseer alone. The Executive Committee would meet with the Council of Twelve at least once a year or whenever it became necessary. These two combined bodies would form the Supreme Council (later called the Executive Council), the church's highest administrative board. Llewellyn's amendment, which was adopted by the assembly, also called for elections of all church officials, including the general overseer, each year. This office had not been voted on in the previous eight years, since the assembly had made Tomlinson overseer for life.[23]

Perhaps these major changes were designed to give the general overseer some administrative help, but it seems more likely that they resulted from the desire of Tomlinson's opponents to reduce his power and authority. Prior to the 1922 General Assembly, Tomlinson had held numerous offices, including general overseer, editor and publisher, publishing house business manager, superintendent of the Bible Training School, and superintendent of the Orphanage and Children's Home.[24] The church evidently had made a grave mistake in granting so much responsibility to any one individual. The changes wrought by Llewellyn's amendment were designed to reduce Tomlinson's power greatly. Revealing his displeasure and hurt, Tomlinson responded by announcing his resignation. Although a few favored accepting it, the majority of the General Assembly refused. Tomlinson then consented to remain as general overseer.[25]

While for a time things seemed to be working out, soon the situation grew much worse. Prior to the meeting of the General Assembly in November 1922, the Council of Twelve had appointed a three-person committee to investigate all departments of the church. Three leaders constituted this investigative body: F.J. Lee, J.S. Llewellyn, and J.B. Ellis.[26] The latter two were Tomlinson's most vocal opponents. Regardless of the committee's findings, appointing Ellis and Llewellyn as committee members had been an unwise move. Their participation certainly did not help to defuse the explosive situation, but instead made it worse. When Tomlinson discovered that these three men were conducting an investigation, he became indignant and uncooperative. Showing his stubbornness, he refused to work with the Executive Council. Even worse, he refused to cooperate with other members of the Executive Committee (Lee and Llewellyn) to handle financial affairs. Tomlinson apparently continued to deposit church funds into his personal account at a local bank. Upon cursory examination, the investigative committee suspected that the general overseer had mismanaged funds; consequently, the committee engaged a public accounting firm, Lee H. Battle Company of Chattanooga, Tennessee, to audit the church's financial records. The company concluded that approximately $31,000 had been misappropriated, but an additional $14,141.83 could not be accounted for from existing records. The auditor admitted that the available records were incomplete and that it was impossible to ascertain with any certainty what had happened to all of the money in question.[27] The committee delivered a copy of the auditor's report to Tomlinson. A short time later, he met with the committee and the auditor in an attempt to clear up the confusion. The general overseer offered an explanation, but it did not satisfy the committee members. After the meeting, the auditor advised Tomlinson that he should submit proper records and any other available information that would show what had been done with the money.[28]

A few weeks later, Tomlinson and the investigative committee prepared for a confrontation at the regular meeting of the Council of Twelve during 12–21 June 1923. When the conference convened, the Council of Seventy and all ordained clergymen who wanted to attend were there—approximately two hundred in all. The council forced Tomlinson to relinquish his position as moderator to Efford Haynes, member of the council. The meeting continued for about a week, with Tomlinson trying to defend his actions. After a few days of testimony, ten members of the council filed a total of fifteen charges against the overseer, and the Court of Justice called for his removal from office. This decisive move was the last in a long series of events that led to a major split in the Church of God. The council also charged George Brouayer and S.O. Gillaspie, two fellow members of that body, as accomplices of Tomlinson. The council found all three clergymen guilty and impeached them.[29]

Tomlinson believed that his critics had accused him falsely. He considered the actions of the June council unjust and illegal. At the conclusion of the meeting, still convinced that he was general overseer of the Church of God, he called another meeting of the council for June 24, for the purpose of concluding unfinished business. Ten members of the council associated with the Lee-Llewellyn faction, refused to attend what they considered an invalid meeting called by a former official who had no authority. Tomlinson and two council members, Brouayer and Gillaspie, nevertheless met and conducted business as usual. They proceeded to impeach the other ten members, declaring the offices vacant. Before adjourning the meeting, Tomlinson called a special session of the council, to meet in Chattanooga 8–10 August.[30]

On 27 June, after the council meeting concluded, A.J. Tomlinson and a small group of supporters wrote a statement that declared the constitution null and void. In this document Tomlinson also invited church members "who want to remain in the Church of God and to worship our Lord Jesus with freedom and a pure heart and remain true to the Scriptures" to support him.[31] Tomlinson advised those who did not agree to withdraw their memberships from the Church of God.

On 26 July, the Court of Justice met and supported the decision of the Council of Twelve that called for the impeachment of Tomlinson, Brouayer, and Gillaspie. On that same day, the Supreme Council swiftly elected F.J. Lee to serve as interim general overseer. The body also chose J.B. Ellis as superintendent of education. Lee, Ellis, and Llewellyn, who conducted the investigation against Tomlinson, also joined the ranks of the new Executive Committee.[32]

On the afternoon of 8 August, Tomlinson and thirty-eight believers met in the home of H.A. Pressgrove, former state overseer of Mississippi. After a three-day conference, Tomlinson and the two former members of the Council of Twelve, Brouayer and Gillaspie, chose ten clergymen to form a new council. They also appointed other officials and established policies regarding the operation of their own church.[33] Confidently Tomlinson wrote in his journal that he and the others had "started a revolution to save the Church of God from wreck and ruin. Some day this act of loyalty to God and the Bible will be regarded as a heroic act."[34] By taking this course of action, Tomlinson and his followers started another Pentecostal organization.

The Lee-Llewellyn group dealt with business as usual. At the meeting of the General Assembly in November 1923, the ordained clergymen nominated Lee as general overseer, Ellis as superintendent of education, and Llewellyn as editor and publisher. More than 1,600 members at the assembly elected these men to their respective positions.[35]

In spite of the action taken by the General Assembly, trouble persisted. Tomlinson and his group remained in Cleveland and established their headquarters under the name "Church of God." Neither side would admit that a split had occurred in the organization, and the fact that both factions used the name "Church of God" resulted in mass confusion. During the next few years, this episode caused the organization much humiliation.[36]

Throughout the entire year of 1924, the factions censured each other, each insisting that it was the true Church of God. When the Lee faction asked Tomlinson to change the name of his organization, he flatly refused. Some individuals from the Lee faction accused the former general overseer of receiving mail containing tithes and donations which belonged to the Lee group.[37] By February 1924, the Lee faction had had enough. It brought suit against the Tomlinson faction in the Chancery Court of Bradley County, Tennessee.[38] In a case that lasted several months, the court declared that the group represented by Lee was the original Church of God and was authorized to use the name and all assets of the organization.[39]

Lee and the members of his group thought that they had won a great victory, but their celebration was premature. Tomlinson appealed the case to the Tennessee Court of Appeals in July. The higher court overturned the lower court's decision and ruled that the Tomlinson faction was the original Church of God.[40] The Lee faction responded quickly, appealing the case to the state supreme court. Months later, on 15 July 1927, the court decided that the original judgment of the Bradley County Chancery Court was correct, giving Lee and his followers exclusive rights to the name Church of God and to all assets of the organization.[41]

Two years later, the courts once again had to intervene. The Tomlinson group had continued to use the name Church of God for its organization. The court ordered the group to use a different name, and "Tomlinson Church of God" was adopted.[42] The group continued to use this name even after the revered leader's death in 1943, so the 1929 action of the court had not solved the problem. The court again ordered the Tomlinson organization to change its name. In 1953, after a decade-long legal battle, this group adopted the name "Church of God of Prophecy."[43]

During the years of litigation in the mid-1920s, the Church of God made significant changes in its governing structure. In 1926, the Council of Twelve recommended repeal of the constitution which had been unanimously adopted in 1921 and thereafter had caused so many problems.[44] The motion carried by a unanimous vote. The assembly approved other recommendations which added to the growing bureaucracy of the church. Three standing boards were created: missions, education, and publishing. Each of these had five ordained clergymen as members. These boards governed various departments of the organization, and each had its own duties and responsibilities; but they were all under the direct supervision of the general overseer, who served as *ex oficio* chairman of each board.[45] The Council of Twelve made two other significant recommendations that the assembly ratified. They gave the general secretary the duties of treasurer, so this official became known as the "general secretary-treasurer." They also changed the method of choosing members of the Council of Twelve. Previously the general overseer had appointed these members. From this time on, the council of ordained clergymen (General Council) elected them during the meeting of the General Assembly. The Council of Twelve was given the authority to relieve any church official of his position if it found him guilty of any wrongdoing. The final decision on such a matter would be made at the next meeting of the General Assembly.[46]

In 1928, the church created another executive position, assistant general overseer. In summer 1928, General Overseer Lee became critically ill. The Council of Twelve recommended that the new position of assistant general overseer be instituted. The assembly approved, and S.W. Lattimer, who at the time was serving as editor and publisher, was chosen to fill the office. F.J. Lee was reelected as general overseer but died a few days later, leaving the office vacant. The assembly, which was still in session, then elected Lattimer as the organization's third general overseer.[47]

At the meeting of the General Assembly the following year, the administrative structure was revised. The Council of Seventy was abolished; in its place, the church instituted the Bishops' Council or the General Council, as it was later called. This body, composed of all ordained clergymen, met annually just a few days prior to the regular meeting of the General Assembly. After debating issues, the General Council passed or rejected proposals by a simple majority vote.[48] Technically, the General Assembly still had the power to reject any measure, but it rarely opposed any recommendations coming from the General Council. Obtaining the assembly's vote of approval became a mere formality; decision-making rested firmly in the hands of the ordained clergymen, a relatively small group. Authority to conduct day-to-day church business and other affairs was vested in an even smaller group of officials. Laymen had little or no voice in matters of church doctrine or business.

In 1936, the Church of God created a new department, the Ladies Willing Worker Band. The church leaders recognized the potential of this female auxiliary, which was organized in Electra, Texas, by Mrs. S.J. Wood, wife of the state overseer.[49] The wife of the general overseer was to occupy the office of president of the national organization, by virtue of her husband's office rather than because of her own qualifications. The same was true for presidents of state auxiliaries. Except on a local level, women were not allowed to elect their own officers. Policy was made for them by a male-dominated hierarchy. Local bands could not even disburse funds that they had raised, without the consent of the pastor.[50] In spite of such subordination to an autocratic, male-dominated agency, the Department of Ladies Ministries (as it was renamed in 1982) made a tremendous contribution to the Church of God.[51]

In the Depression years of the 1930s, most American denominations experienced little or no growth in membership. Some rolls even declined. Church of God membership, however, more than doubled during this period. The church gained converts in many areas outside the South, especially in the Far West and the North. Many members also joined local congregations in foreign nations. With such prodigious growth, the church hierarchy also expanded.

In 1941, the General Assembly created the office of second assistant general overseer and elected Earl P. Paulk, state overseer of North Carolina and member of the Council of Twelve, to this new office. Growth put greater demands on the time of the general overseer and his first assistant, so the church hoped that the second assistant would provide much-needed aid to the other two executives.[52] The official *Minutes* do not indicate whether the two positions of first and second Assistants were created to prevent one man from ever again exerting the degree of power that former general overseer Tomlinson had, but this must have been a consideration. Although the *Minutes* contain brief records of most issues which were debated, they do not contain the entire story. Church officials edited out some controversial items before publication.

Another crisis occurred during the World War II years. The 1944 General Assembly proved to be one of the most innovative in the church's history. Because of travel restrictions, a relatively small group of participants met in Columbus, Ohio, for the Thirty-Ninth General Assembly. Despite poor attendance, the church made numerous changes at this historic meeting. Some changes were permanent, and others were merely experimental and temporary. One of the shortest-lived was the abolition of the two assistant general overseer positions and the creation of six regional ones. The change called for the division of the United States into six regions, with an assistant general overseer for each section of the country. The church repealed this measure the following year.[53] The experiment may have been a response to some who wanted to see the church's national headquarters moved to a more central location in the United States, but it also could have been a response to charges that the church hierarchy was becoming too autocratic.

The decision to place a four-year limitation on the tenures of all general officials, including members of the Council of Twelve, certainly reflected this latter concern. A case for limited tenure had been growing since 1935. In that year, a controversy had erupted with respect to the reelection of the general overseer, S.W. Lattimer. He had been elected to the office each year since 1928. In spite of his obvious dedication, devotion, administrative talent, and energy, many of the bishops (as the ordained clergymen were called) accused Lattimer of political "wheeling and dealing" to keep himself in office. According to Frank W. Lemons, a member of the Bishops' Council, Lattimer did this by appointing cronies to key positions. Lemons charged that these "muscle men" were appointed by the general overseer to head every important board and committee, as a means of making certain that

Lattimer's wishes were followed.[54] State overseers from the Lattimer camp allegedly were rewarded for their support by various methods, including substantial pay raises and promotions. According to Lemons and other opponents, the general overseer, acting as a type of political boss, had created an efficient political machine and used it to run church affairs, not just on a national level but on the state level as well.[55]

Opposition to the Lattimer machine had been growing for quite some time. It did not reach a volatile state, however, until the Bishops' Council meeting in summer 1935. At this conference the problem exploded. A vote for general overseer was taken; Lattimer received the most votes, and assistant general overseer R.P. Johnson received the second highest number. One of Lattimer's opponents then stood and argued that the vote had been "unfair" and should not be accepted. Immediately others made similar complaints. Chaos ensued, and tempers flared. One bishop described the situation as one which produced "hot speeches and red faces."[56]

The event which precipitated this crisis was the reading of the report of a special committee which investigated alleged discrepancies at the general headquarters in Cleveland, Tennessee. The committee's secretary, Paul H. Walker, who was a Council of Twelve member and state overseer of Montana, read the report prior to the election of the general officials. Among other things, the report revealed that "some had raised their own salaries but neglected to raise the salaries of certain department heads."[57] This report substantiated the case against Lattimer. Because of the chaos and dissatisfaction that followed Lattimer's apparent reelection, one council member proposed that both Lattimer and Johnson step down and a general overseer be elected from among the other bishops. The body then elected J.H. Walker as the new general overseer.[58] Walker served as the church's highest official until 1944, when the assembly limited the tenure of all general officials.[59]

In spite of the limitation on tenure, a small group of older ordained clergymen still held the highest positions in the Church of God from the 1950s until the late 1980s. At the end of tenure in one office, they simply moved into another.

Organizational Structure

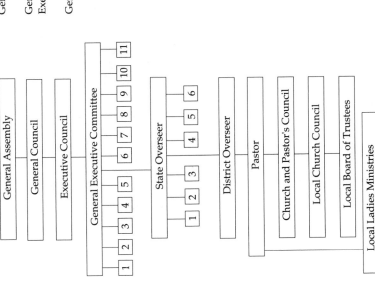

General Assembly—composed of all ministers and laymen who wish to attend.

General Council—composed of all ordained ministers.

Executive Council—composed of the Executive Committee and the Council of Eighteen.

General Executive Committee—composed of the General Overseer, the three Assistant General Overseers, and the General Secretary Treasurer.

First group of boxes:
1. World Missions Department
2. Youth and Christian Education Department
3. Evangelism and Home Missions Department
4. Department of Benevolences
5. Department of Media Ministries
6. General Board of Education
7. Lee College Board of Directors
8. West Coast Christian College Board of Directors
9. Publishing Department
10. Department of Ladies Ministries
11. National Laymens Board

Second group of boxes:
1. State Ministers Council
2. Board of Education
3. Youth and Christian Education
4. Evangelism and Home Missions
5. Department of Ladies Ministries
6. State Board of Trustees

General Offices of the Church of God, 1912.
(*Hal Bernard Dixon, Jr., Pentecostal Research Center, Cleveland, Tenn.*)

As the organization grew in the post–World War II period, many new departments and agencies were created. For example, in 1968 the church instituted the General Education Department and in 1980 a Stewardship Department. Each department has a standing board or committee, and an administrative executive to supervise the department's operation. In 1987, the Church of God had more than a dozen departments. Each was under the supervision of a director and usually an assistant director. The departments all had standing boards comprised of seven or more members.[60]

The Church of God also added to its hierarchy on the highest levels. In 1964, the church created the office of third assistant general overseer. This ordained clergyman completed the powerful five-member Executive Committee.[61] In 1984, the organization added six more members to the Council of Twelve, to create a Council of Eighteen. This change automatically increased the size of the Executive Council (Executive Committee and Council of Twelve), from seventeen members to twenty-three.[62]

The development of Church of God administrative agencies and procedures took place in two distinct stages. In the first stage, from 1902 to 1944, the church created new administrative positions in reaction to crises such as the fanaticism that pervaded the infant church around the turn of the century, the 1923 split involving A.J. Tomlinson, and the conflict over S.W. Lattimer and his "muscle men" politics of the 1930s. In the second stage of development, membership grew along with the social and economic status of the organization. The church created and implemented many new boards and committees and even increased the number of top administrators to cope with this growth. This second stage of bureaucracy formation reflects both the Church of God's move into mainstream conservative evangelicalism and its evolution into a middle-class Protestant denomination.

CHAPTER 3

Come Out from Among Them

No aspect of the Church of God better demonstrated its dedication to radically fundamentalist Pentecostalism than its austere, puritanical code of personal morality. The Members were required to abstain from alcohol, tobacco, secret societies, labor unions, church bazaars, carnivals, dancing, movies, chewing gum, and certain styles of dress.[1] A member who indulged in any of these practices was considered a backslider. Discipline was rigidly enforced in the early Church of God, and members were subject to expulsion if they strayed from narrow church standards. "Backslidden" individuals were expelled in order to retain group purity. The biblical basis for such action was Galatians 5:9: "A little leaven leaveneth the whole lump."

Churchmen saw their mission as two-fold. They furiously denounced personal sin, while at the same time pointing souls to Christ. After the individual's conversion, the minister encouraged prompt separation from worldly pleasures. By following a legalistic prescriptive code, members demonstrated that they were sanctified. Conversion plus adherence to puritanical mores guaranteed them eternal security.

This moral asceticism reflected a rejection of middle-class values and lifestyles. Even so, the austerity demanded by the church was not unrelieved. Activities such as dancing and spirited singing and playing of musical instruments, although condemned for the ungodly, could be "sanctified" by the Holy Spirit's direction. Such spirit-directed, physical manifestations compensated for the austere Holiness code.

To the Pentecostal mind, holiness was the product of sanctification, understood as a separated life. Following conversion, ministers encouraged believers to seek the experience of sanctification. Only then could they be true Holiness-Pentecostal believers. Most received this experience immediately after being saved. If not, group members pressured the new convert until he or she testified to receiving this second work of grace.

Most scholarship has been unsympathetic toward Holiness-Pentecostal religion. Scholars tend to stereotype Holiness doctrine as placing too much emphasis on external behavior. This conclusion, however, severs the rigorous external code from its inward theological source.[2]

In Church of God thought, outward change was the result of a sacred union with Christ. The transformation of the unethical into ethical, the immoral into moral, came from within the believer. External adherence to the Holiness code was simply a product of an internal experience. Without this inner realization, ascetic observances were meaningless. While some Church of God preachers did not emphasize the inward-to-outward continuum, most did.

The Church of God advised members to avoid all worldly pleasures. Clergymen agreed that all worldly recreation and amusements were a "dangerous progression" from an inward malady. F.J. Lee outlined the dangers in what he believed to be a natural sequence:

1. Late night parties
2. Late night beach parties
3. Improper dress
4. All night dances
5. Physical contact
6. Sexual immorality
7. Shame and disgrace
8. Expulsion from the church
9. Ruin[3]

The sexual implications of dancing concerned church leaders. When two people of opposite sexes came into intimate physical contact, sexual arousal, however subtle, occurred. Church of God churchmen, like some Baptist and Methodist clergymen, concluded that such activity ended in promiscuity. In view of this logic, it is not surprising that members who persisted in attending dances were excluded from church membership.

Similar logic caused churchmen to condemn church bazaars and festivals. Church fairs were considered illicit money-making schemes. Churchmen argued that it would be wrong to hold a bazaar and "invite those that hate Him [Christ] to come and pay their fifty cents for merchandise and thus compel them [sinners] to support the gospel."[4] Church leaders believed that true believers should not depend on the finances of sinners for the building and maintenance of Christ's church. In I Corinthians 16:1–2, Paul had instructed believers to "give of their own resources as God had prospered them." When Christians obtained money by staging "worldly" bazaars, they robbed themselves of the privilege and duty of giving.[5]

Such arguments were predicated as much on lower-class prejudices as upon scriptural proofs. Objections to "necktie socials" and "fancy costumes" obviously reflected economic and social deprivation. Church of God members, aware of their lower-class status, concluded that the middle-class churches exchanged true Christian faith for a cheap imitation. Most Church of God members felt that by condemning fairs and bazaars, they had been true to the faith. As one church member summarized, "A thin congregation, a small salary, no parish, the world's hate with Christ are infinitely to be preferred to a flourishing church at the expense of Christianity."[6]

Church officials designated people who participated in worldly recreation and amusements as "lovers of pleasure" and not lovers of God. Those guilty of seeking pleasure had misdirected their affection, since the Scriptures taught that the true child of God should have his affection centered on things above, not on things of the world. One churchman noted, "We are confident He] [Christ] would not participate in these things if he were here; therefore we are trying to be like Him. . . ."[7] Much of the other-worldliness associated with Holiness-Pentecostal religion stems from such rejection of secular culture.

Most spectator sports—boxing, horseracing, auto racing, football, and baseball—came under attack from church leaders in the

South. Following their lead, the Church of God classified sports as expensive, frivolous wastes of time, and linked them to gambling.[8] Clergymen consistently reminded members that gambling was a spiritual parasite. If the addictive, malicious practice was not completely discontinued, it would lead a person to eternal doom and destruction. Churchmen also warned that gambling would rob family members of a decent living; children would go hungry and without proper clothing, and the family soon would become destitute, shamed, and disgraced because of a gambling husband and father.[9] Ministers often told sad stories of gamblers whose lives ended in ruin.[10]

Most Americans saw no harm in the spectator sports which thrived in the 1920s. Although thousands of other church leaders and members attended sporting events, the Holiness codes prohibited Church of God partisans from attending, lest they became "partakers of evil deeds." Church of God leaders also objected because such recreational activities were sometimes held on Sunday. In the minds of most clergymen, this frivolity served to draw people away from the house of God, where decent individuals ought to be. Desecration of the "Sabbath" was a serious offense.[11]

It was not until after World War II that members began to dissociate sports from gambling, profanity, and the consumption of alcohol. By the 1950s, many of the younger generation were attending or even participating in sports ranging from golf to football. Because of the war's economic consequences, many Church of God families moved into the middle class. They had money to spend on recreation. Americans of the postwar period turned to recreational sports for entertainment and tension relief in the face of society's faster pace. Many church members found enjoyment in recreational diversions. By the 1960s and 1970s, sports participation, which had been forbidden by the early church, had become a vital part of members' normal life.

The trend toward pleasure-seeking disturbed some of the more conservative Church of God leaders. In his address to the General Assembly in 1960, general overseer James A. Cross informed his audience that, for many members, witnessing to lost souls was yielding place to the pursuit of pleasure. The concerned official noted that both ministers and laymen were going to places and doing things that Church of God loyalists never would have considered in the "old days." Cross acknowledged that "golf courses claim many hours of the ministers' time. Baseball diamonds are frequented by our ministers and church membership. Bowling alleys are absorbing a lot of time preachers spend in pleasure."[12]

Only the most conservative Church of God members still adhered to the old rulings. In the mid-1960s, conservative or traditionalist denominational leaders called sports participation and other accepted practices "borderline things." In 1966, general overseer Wade H. Horton told delegates to the General Assembly that "a Christian cannot go to places, act like or say and do things like the worldly crowd . . . this is a day of conformity . . . very few are willing to suffer the reproach of being different or peculiar for Jesus' sake."[13] Members paid little attention to such admonitions; the message landed on deaf ears, and the number of Church of God members who engaged in such activities continued to increase. By the latter part of the decade, many leaders realized the futility of simply telling members that such things were wrong, so they developed a new strategy. Some maintained that, in itself, going to ballgames, golf courses, bowling alleys, and other similar places was not wrong. The danger lay in the non-Christian atmosphere that one found in such places. When asked by one interested party about bowling lanes that served alcohol, James Cross informed his inquisitor that an individual placed "his Christian testimony in a position where his sincerity may be questioned."[14] Cross's explanation became the standard line for traditionalist leaders in the following years.

"Picture shows" also drew the fire of church leaders, even in the early days of the industry. The leaders believed that movies played an active part in corrupting the morals of the American public. Church of God members categorized movies either as mere foolishness or as pornography. Comedies were frivolous. Sober Christians had more important things to do with their time than to watch such nonsense. Clergymen believed that most films were pornographic. Things that ought to be seen and done strictly in privacy were put on display for all to see. Churchmen felt that lurid films were the norm, and they objected furiously.[15] These Pentecostal purists evidently were evaluating the merits of films they had never attended. It appears that they based their opinions on second-hand information.

Church of God members also shunned theaters because of their presumed debasing influence. Pentecostals envisioned theater houses as disreputable, dark, secluded dens of iniquity which bred all manner of sin. People went to these "love nests," not to watch the movie, but to engage in illicit sex.

The teachings of the Church of God prohibited members from going to the movies, one of the nation's fastest-growing pastimes. Throughout the 1920s and 1930s, churchmen attacked movies and the persons who operated theaters. In 1933, the church went so far as to declare that "parties operating moving picture shows be considered ineligible for membership in the Church of God." [16]

By the following decade, a number of clergymen realized the potential of movies as a training aid. Some more liberal or progressive pastors started showing "Christian films" to their congregations. These shepherds apparently believed that, since members of their flock insisted on going to the movies, they should show them acceptable ones at church. A pastor could regulate the type of movies viewed, and members could watch them in a wholesome environment instead of the non-Christian atmosphere of movie houses. The practice of showing movies in local churches worried some Church of God leaders, however. At the meeting of the Council of Twelve in summer 1940, officials were divided over the issue. Some saw spiritual benefits from showing movies, but the traditionalist councilmen were skeptical.[17] In the postwar period, some Church of God leaders continued to condemn movies. Riding a wave of anti-Communism in the late forties, the editor of the *Evangel* proclaimed that communism had invaded the motion picture industry; Hollywood producers, nearly all of them alleged to be communists, were said to be poisoning the minds of gullible Americans. Condemning the subject matter of films, the editor stated that the latter were filled with the "eternal triangle of lustful love affairs, where the third person wrecks the home; the perpetual display of every known kind of crime; and now Communism plants its seeds of destructiveness."[18] Despite such warnings, members continued to attend movies.

During the 1960s, producers made and released motion pictures containing sexual scenes far more graphic than in earlier decades. Risque films caused many churchmen to ask for a formal church ruling prohibiting members from attending movies. The subject came up for discussion at almost every top-level church meeting. At the Executive Council meeting in May 1970, council members voted to recommend "that any member who attends a public moving picture show, including any kind of drive-in theater, be considered disloyal to the Church of God and that this be a test of membership."[19]

It was not until 1974 that the church added a similar ruling to its list of teachings. This measure may have deterred some, but many other members continued to attend movies. Although the Church of God *Minutes* in the mid-1980s still contained a teaching against members going to movies, attendance was no longer a controversial issue.[20] The reason that the teaching remains in the *Minutes*, probably, is that most members feel that it is either outdated or not worth fighting over, especially in view of the fact that the church does not attempt to enforce compliance.

Television constitutes another factor deterring the organization from forcing members to comply with the ruling. In the 1950s, most middle-class Americans bought television sets. When Church of God members began purchasing them and watching movies and "questionable" programs, television became a target of sharp criticism from church leaders. Some clergymen even wanted the organization to pass a ruling that would prohibit members from owning a set. In summer 1952, the ordained ministers discussed the subject of television. A few of the older, conservative churchmen argued that no members should be allowed to have one, even in the privacy of their own home. One unidentified minister made a motion that church officials appoint a special committee to draft a measure to "stop the use of television in the homes of Church of God ministers and members."[21] The motion was defeated.

Despite this defeat, many clergymen continued to worry about the bad influence of television on members. A few Church of God preachers considered the device a thief which robbed church members of time which should be spent in service to Christ and the church. J.C. Vore, from Clarksburg, West Virginia, wrote that the money spent for television shows should have been given to the church or to pastors. According to Clark, "TV sets have been bought with money that should have gone into the tithe envelope. . . . What that 'little' theatre costs would buy for him [the pastor] a fine suit." [22]

Although numerous Church of God leaders were critical of television during the early 1950s, by the latter part of the decade, some critics had changed their minds. Alda B. Harrison, a leading female member and founder of the Church of God youth publication, *Lighted Pathway*, stated that there were some good programs aired on television fit for any Christian to see. There were news programs, educational features, and family-oriented shows. "The task is to select the worthy programs," explained Harrison.[23] Undoubtedly many church members bought television sets, and, for some, program selection was important. The issue of television ownership divided the church. As the organization accepted the idea that television was going to be a permanent fixture in most homes, a few sharpeyed members discovered a contradiction in church dogma. The Church of God condemned movie attendance, but, by the late fifties, the church approved of members who owned television sets. One young parishoner wrote to a staff member of the *Lighted Pathway*, pointing out the apparent contradiction. Avis Swiger, a regular contributor to the periodical, addressed this topic in the May 1958 edition. She wrote that it was really a personal matter and that each person had to make his own choice as to whether to own a television set or not. Comparing movie theaters with television, Swiger argued that "there is a difference between attending a movie house and seeing a film in your own home." [24]

Some Church of God ministers came to view television as a useful evangelistic tool. A few innovative pastors of large urban congregations even considered using cameras and other video equipment to televise their worship services. Apparently the first to do so was Earl P. Paulk, Jr., pastor of the Hemphill Avenue congregation in Atlanta, Georgia. The local church's first televised Sunday morning service was broadcast in 1953, with good results. Paulk reported that many people who had never attended a Church of God service called the church offices to ask for further information about the organization. The jubilant minister stated, "Many have come to our regular services as a result of seeing the television service."[25] The potential was enormous. Thousands of people from distant towns and communities could get an inside look at the Church of God and see people worshipping God in a Pentecostal service.

In the 1960s and 1970s, most Church of God members, like other Americans, owned television sets, and hardly anyone condemned members for having them. Church leaders did remain highly critical of television programming. Officials argued that television was playing a leading role in the moral collapse of American society, and that Satan used this insidious device to destroy traditional values and morals. In 1973, general overseer Ray H. Hughes wrote that "when TV became the way of life for the vast majority, the devil struck a devastating blow at the heart of morality and righteousness. A filth factory now operates within the confines of the home."[26] One year later, the General Assembly passed a ruling forbidding members to attend ungodly amusements. Included in this dictum was a warning "that extreme caution be exercised in viewing and in the selectivity of television programs."[27] By the mid-1970s church leaders advised members to strike back at objectionable television programs by switching channels, turning sets off, and writing to networks and sponsors in protest. In 1976, a committee which was appointed to study the problem suggested to the Executive Council that the Church of God join forces with other conservative organizations to protest objectionable programming. The committee further suggested that the church send a written statement to the Federal Communications Commission, insisting that it use its influence to pressure producers and sponsors "to present programs of higher moral quality."[28]

In 1977, the Church of God initiated a four-phase protest. The first phase declared that the week of 11–18 April was a "nonviewing" period when members should turn their television sets off. In the second phase, church leaders encouraged families to decide how much time they would allot for viewing and which programs they would watch. Phases three and four came in autumn 1977. Church members rated television programs in two categories, according to the ten highest and ten lowest. The denomination sent information on the ten lowest ranking to sponsors and informed them that if they did not respond favorably, church members would boycott the sponsors' products beginning in January 1978.[29] In summer 1978, Church of God officials believed that this multiphased protest had made an impact on the industry. At the General Assembly in August, the ordained ministers passed a resolution calling for an extension of the protest. The measure also asked "that families participate in a week of non-viewing in order to re-evaluate the impact television is having upon their family life."[30]

In the 1980s, Americans were introduced to new technological innovations in video equipment. Cable television brought numerous types of programs, including "adult" movies, into the homes of those who subscribed. Many families purchased satellite dishes to receive the same wide programming without having to subscribe to cable television. During the eighties, the habit of viewing rental movies through videocassette recorders (VCRs) took the country by storm. Such electronic devices made it possible for individuals to rent movies of all types and view them in the privacy of their own homes. These new, more sophisticated gadgets caused Church of God leaders renewed concern. In spring 1982, the Executive Council issued a statement urging members to use extreme caution in the selection and viewing of these movies and programs.[31] But their protest had moved a long way from the categorical attacks of earlier years on movies *per se*. Now the issue was selection and self-discipline rather than blanket condemnation.

A number of Church of God pastors and their congregations bought satellite dishes and subscribed to religious broadcasts, which members watched in classrooms and other designated areas in the church. These members believed that religious broadcasts were a blessing to the congregation, but many church officials believed otherwise. According to them, local congregations which subscribed to satellite networks were exposed to erroneous doctrine. To help curb this trend, the Executive Council issued a proclamation which strongly encouraged that "all local churches subscribe to and support only the Church of God 'Forward in Faith' satellite program."[32]

Consumption of alcoholic beverages was an area of personal morality where church policy changed more slowly. Church of God members, like many Christian fundamentalists, were staunch prohibitionists. In its early years, the organization even forbade consumption of soft drinks such as Coca-Cola. This particular beverage gained the misnomer of "dope" almost immediately after it was developed in 1886, but it became ever more popular in the 1920s and 1930s. Coca-Cola contained an infinitesimal amount of cocaine until about 1905, when the makers of the soft drink removed the drug additive; nevertheless, the bad reputation of the product lingered.[33] A Church of God regulation which forbade the making, selling, or consumption of any "dope" drink was passed in 1917. Coca-Cola was at the top of the church's "most despised" list of nonalcoholic bottled drinks.[34]

Church of God leaders regarded "dope" drinks as detrimental to personal health and Christian reputation. One anti–Coca-Cola spokesman explained:

> We are to shun the appearance of evil. Someone may see you drinking from a bottle and would not know but that you were drinking whiskey or some other strong drink. Every minister who wants to especially guard his influence will not be found at these cold drink stands drinking, though it may be a harmless drink. The boys and girls standing near would not know but that you were drinking coco [sic] cola or some other dope.[35]

Erring members were subjected to the usual severe disciplinary action. If any relaxation of this rule were allowed, "the Church will gradually drift back to the world."[36]

The widespread consumption and popularity of Coca-Cola and other soft drinks forced the church to soften its position regarding the beverages. In 1930, the ordained ministers decided only to discourage members from consuming "Cokes." By 1935, the organization had concluded that the attempt to discourage consumption of soft drinks was futile, and most leaders realized that there was no harm in drinking them anyway. At the General Assembly that year, the ordained clergymen voted to repeal the ruling concerning bottled drinks.[37]

The Church of God, however, has never repealed its ruling against the consumption of alcohol. From its inception, the church has taken a strict prohibitionist stand. Ministers warned that "liquor or intoxicating drinks" were as hazardous to health as drinking deadly poison. Not only did alcohol constitute a health hazard, but churchmen attributed all manner of social maladies to its consumption. General overseer Tomlinson cautioned, "To use whiskey in any form or for any purpose is intolerable and sinful."[38] Churchmen employed numerous scriptural citations to substantiate this prohibitionist position, including Proverbs 20:1, Romans 14:21, Ephesians 5:18, Galatians 5:21, and I Corinthians 5:11 and 6:9. Any member caught using alcohol for any reason was severely reprimanded.

It was not until 1910 that clergymen codified the prohibition of alcohol, along with twenty-four other teachings. The General Assembly officially adopted these in 1911.[39] Even though Pentecostals were staunch prohibitionists, written evidence on the subject is surprisingly scant. References are few and appear only in scattered accounts within church literature. Neither did Church of God members participate in the National Prohibition Movement. Perhaps this restraint was part of the social noninvolvement of the "sanctified." Members of some southern churches avoided being too vociferous on the alcohol issue because bootleggers gave sizable monetary donations to local churches. Available evidence indicates only one occasion when such charity occurred within the Church of God. M.P. Cross, a Church of God preacher, described the lucrative relationship: "At this time it was not unusual for those closely associated with the bootlegging business to be very friendly toward religion in that part of the country [North Carolina], so long as they did not think there was danger of you 'spying' on their business. One man who lived, and lived well, from the trade had largely financed a revival for us, and his wife was blessed in the meeting and became a good Christian worker."[40]

Consumption of alcohol was not a major issue in the Church of

God until the repeal of the Prohibition Amendment in December 1933. The action of federal and state governments legalizing the sale and consumption of alcohol worried some church leaders. In 1935, the state of Alabama placed the alcohol issue on a referendum. J.B. Ellis, the Church of God state overseer, urged members to vote against the proposition. Ellis pointed out that since the repeal of the Prohibition Amendment, the number of saloons had increased rapidly in states which voted to allow the sale of alcohol. Worse than that, alcoholic beverages were available in grocery stores, restaurants, gas stations, pharmacies, hotels, and other public places. The overseer was convinced that alcohol would bring nothing but misery and trouble. Besides liquor, saloons also would provide "upstairs rooms, hidden peep holes, concealed basement bars, and above all, the every-ready women for sale."[41]

When the United States entered World War II, there were many religious conservatives who believed that in order to win the struggle, American soldiers should be prevented from consuming alcoholic beverages. Church of God leaders were convinced that soldiers could not perform at peak level while under the influence of alcohol. This opinion moved church officials to action. In 1942, the Supreme Council recommended that the organization "ask the President of the United States to ban the sale of alcoholic drinks to our soldiers."[42] During summer 1942, one congressman sponsored a bill (the Shepard Bill) to make it illegal for soldiers to consume intoxicating beverages. At the meeting of the General Assembly in August, the ordained ministers passed a resolution in support of the Shepard Bill. The measure also called on the government "to pass such other legislation as is necessary to stop the manufacture and sale of liquors during the present emergency."[43]

In the immediate postwar period, the Church of God continued its attack against alcohol. According to some leaders, the liquor traffic was uncontrolled throughout the nation. Alcohol was a deadly enemy, the major cause of crime and broken homes in America. This type of thinking led one clergyman to state that "the liquor traffic . . . has no right to exist in our civilization."[44] Many Church of God ministers felt powerless to do anything about the problem; others appeared indifferent or not terribly concerned. Attempting to motivate apathetic members, the editor of the *Evangel*, J.H. Walker, advised his readers to support antialcohol organizations like the old Anti-Saloon League, the Women's Christian Temperance Union, and the National Temperance Movement. The editor's main suggestion was to vote for prohibition candidates. Denying that he was attempting to instruct members how to vote, Walker in 1948 strongly suggested that Church of God voters support the National Prohibition Party.[45]

In the 1950s, it appeared that the United States had a significant problem with alcoholism. Sociologists, psychologists, and members of the medical profession concluded that alcoholism was a disease; consequently, the alcoholic should not be condemned for his actions. Paul H. Walker, state overseer of Ohio, called this conclusion a "half-witted, sickly, sentimental, mussy, nonsensical idea being promoted and advocated by the liquor interest and *accepted* by thoughtless, careless, indifferent people."[46] Church of God clergymen like Walker believed that if alcoholism was a disease, there was only one cure—the blood of Jesus Christ applied to the heart of the alcoholic.

In the fifties, the alcoholic beverage industries experienced prodigious growth. Breweries and distilleries conducted mass advertising campaigns through television, radio, magazines, and newspapers. Church of God members deeply resented the bombardment. Clergymen felt that it was an unwarranted invasion of their privacy. The church objected vociferously. In 1958, leaders passed a resolution "to prohibit by law advertisements for intoxicating drinks appearing in magazines, newspapers, on television and radio, highway billboards, and other media."[47]

In the 1960s and 1970s, the denomination's struggle against the "liquor traffic" dwindled. Drug abuse had captured the interest of the church during the Vietnam War era. This is not to say that the church was any less concerned about alcoholism. In the 1980s most Church of God members were teetotalers. The teaching calling for total abstinence from all liquor or strong drinks remained listed in the official *Minutes*. But the emphasis had softened.

Another issue of personal morality offensive to Church of God adherents was the use of tobacco. Church leaders attacked it for three major reasons: it was injurious to health, filthy, and a waste of money.[48]

The most common objection to the use of tobacco was that it was unhealthy. Many clergymen believed that it produced physical ailments ranging from nausea to blindness. One antitobacco churchman, Howard Juillerat, attributed an increased death rate in the 1920s to habits of reckless living, notably the excessive use of tobacco. He further stated that the use of tobacco was prohibited at the Naval Academy and West Point because it created a "thirst for alcoholic stimulation, increases propensities and induces secret practices, impairs the vision, blunts the memory and interferes with mental effort."[49] As a climax to his argument, Juillerat noted that a Russian scientist had discovered that nicotine was too powerful a poison to be consumed by human beings.[50] Juillerat's reasoning was that if an atheistic Communist knew this, then surely Christians should put away the practice.

But churchmen found other objections as well. Like other antitobacco proponents, they linked unemployment and crime to tobacco use. What they detested even more was that the "noxious weed" produced spiritual lethargy, laziness, and inactivity.[51] Clergymen believed that the survival of the church depended on a zealous and hardworking membership. Anything that made church members "lazy" could not be tolerated. Church of God leaders also objected to the use of tobacco because they considered it a filthy habit. Many Protestant churches located in the South considered the practice amoral, and some even provided worshippers with cuspidors. This was not done, however, among Church of God congregations. One clergyman admonished, "Let us cleanse ourselves from all filthiness of the flesh and spirit."[52]

At the first General Assembly in 1906, the ruling body denounced the use of tobacco as immoral.[53] Charles Conn, Church of God historian, states that although the denunciation of tobacco became commonplace in the 1970s, the early Church of God was among the first organizations to protest against it.[54] In fact, although churchmen opposed the use of tobacco, other antitobacco forces were already at work.

Although the Scriptures did not literally condemn the use of tobacco, which was not known in biblical times, Church of God ministers interpreted such Scriptures as Isiah 55:2, 2 Corinthians 7:1, and James 1:21, which refer to cleansing oneself from the filthiness of the flesh, as a biblical basis for their denunciation. But in order to sound more convincing, clergymen occasionally misquoted or misrepresented the remarks of a well-known individual. Juillerat wrote, "Reduced to an ultimatum, tobacco is worthy of no less an anathema than Shakespeare applied to alcohol: 'If thou hast no other name, I will call thee devil!' "[55]

Not only did the clergyman misquote the line from *Othello*, but he fashioned it to appear that Shakespeare, who apparently did not seek to launch a moral crusade against alcohol or tobacco, was the one who made this remark.[56] General overseer Tomlinson added, "It is not considered that a person is really saved if he uses tobacco and thus he is not fit for membership in the beautiful and glorious Church of God."[57] Ministers were advised never to "take a person into the church, knowingly, who uses tobacco in any form or retains [sic] a member who persistently refuses to abstain and clean up."[58]

There were a few members who felt that the tobacco habit was not immoral, but these were rare. Tobacco-using members were often sought out by local pastors. A disciplinary board met with the accused, and, if the defendant was found guilty, the erring member was given an ultimatum: stop the practice altogether or face expulsion.

This was the usual means by which traditionalist church leaders handled worldly opponents. Opposition to church dogma was limited by the discipline imposed by the organization. The Church of God incorporated an authoritarian rule, and church leaders were swift to point out that "those who reject the counsel [of church leaders] . . . will sooner or later meet with a complete downfall and ruin. Prov. 1:23–31."[59] This type of discipline was apparently effective in maintaining group homogeneity.

Church of God ministers also viewed the use of tobacco as a terrible waste of money. Church leaders castigated the American public for its exorbitant spending on the "noxious weed." One prominent leader decried: "If fifty men had lived from Adam until now [1916] and received a salary of $3,200 per year, they would during these 5,920 years have labored long enough to earn as much as the American people have smoked, chewed, snuffed, and spit in a single year!"[60]

Pentecostals felt that hard-earned money should be spent on life's necessities. Clergymen often quoted highly questionable statistics in an attempt to substantiate their arguments. One preacher confidently stated, "The amount spent for tobacco in one year would have bought bread for the whole United States population and would have left every person $3.49 cash."[61]

The most common complaint against foolish spending for tobacco was that this money should have been used to promote teaching of the Gospels. Such vast sums would have financed revivals and camp meetings, dispatched missionaries, and led to the conversion of thousands of souls.[62]

In 1915, the church passed a ruling which not only prohibited members from using tobacco but also forbade them "from growing and selling tobacco, [or being] either owners, renters or clerks in stores [that do]."[63] If members violated this dictum in any form, they received warning. If they persisted in the violation, church officials expelled them from membership. The organization strictly enforced the ruling in its early years. It was not uncommon for members to be "disfellowshipped" for smoking, chewing, dipping, and other such offenses. Church officials even defrocked a few ministers for violating the tobacco ruling. Taylor Shanks, an ordained minister and farmer in East Tennessee, apparently helped his family raise tobacco as a cash crop. Someone informed church leaders of his activities. Officials asked Shanks to stop, but he refused, informing his superiors that raising tobacco was part of his livelihood. The church revoked his credentials.[64] This measure posed serious problems for Church of God families who lived in areas where tobacco was the basis of the local economy; numerous church members had grown the crop for years. In order to comply with the tobacco ruling, these people had to find other employment, and sometimes this forced families to move, causing bitterness between members and the organization's leadership. To prevent such impasses, some church leaders wanted to drop the portion of the ruling concerning the growing and selling of tobacco. At the meeting of the General Assembly in 1933, the ordained ministers modified the ruling. They lifted the rigid restriction from persons who grew and sold tobacco only "if it is absolutely necessary for our people to do so in order to earn a living."[65]

Most Americans believed that smoking tobacco was harmless. This belief continued to be a pervasive attitude until the late 1950s and early 1960s, when scientists and physicians announced that smoking was extremely hazardous to health. Cigarette-smoking was understood to cause numerous health problems, including heart disease and cancer. Some members of the medical profession warned that smoking was a form of suicide. This announcement pleased leaders of the Church of God, who believed that the church had been vindicated. For years the organization had warned people about the terrible consequences of using tobacco. Leaving no room for doubt as to his feelings, William J. Krutza explained, "Scientists and doctors are right where they should be on this smoking issue—backing up with statistics what Christians have proclaimed by faith all their lives."[66] In May 1962, Charles W. Conn, the editor of the *Evangel*, spoke for many Church of God members when he wrote, "I like the suggestion of one of our congressmen who wants a measure passed requiring cigarette manufacturers to print on their packages a clear warning . . . that continued use of their product may result in heart disease, lung cancer, or death."[67]

In the decades following the 1960s, church leaders reiterated arguments that the early Church of God had employed. Clergymen maintained that anything a Christian did should glorify God. One minister, Cecil Burridge, asserted that "surely no Christian believes in his heart that he is glorifying God as he puffs away on his pipe, cigar, or cigarette."[68] The church's most common scriptural argument came from I Corinthians 3:16–17. Church of God ministers believed that the body was the temple of God and that anyone who harmed it with cigarette smoke was contributing to her or his physical and spiritual end.[69]

Although the tobacco taboo applied to both sexes, a rigid dress code was aimed primarily at females. Clergymen during the 1920s worried about the moral implications of women's dress.

They warned females that the new fashions appearing in the years immediately following the First World War were designed to appeal to the "lower passions" of mankind. Moreover, leaders charged that these seductive styles originated in "Paris (a modern Sodom) in houses of ill fame" and that the overexposure of the fair sex was "positively indecent."[70] Churchmen were shocked that a woman would "wear her dress above her knee or six inches below her throat or her sleeves off at her shoulders."[71] Church leaders admonished female members not to dress in a manner that would attract people's attention. The wife of a leading clergyman asserted, "Women who want to please Jesus, who love Him with all their heart, will never make their clothes so attractive as to draw the attention of men."[72]

But the apparel that disturbed Church of God members most was the swimsuit.[73] The thought of "half naked" females parading their bodies in public before the eyes of lustful men horrified Pentecostals. Many considered this lewd behavior as the main cause of "an appalling increase in criminal immorality."[74]

By classifying certain modes of dress as immoral, Church of God leaders joined a cultural conflict between rural and urban values. For example, two church leaders, Zeno C. Tharp and E.L. Simmons, made a business trip to New York City in summer 1929. While in the city, they went to the beach at Coney Island. As they walked down the boardwalk, they were aghast at the sight of half-naked men and women running on the beach or participating in amusements. Tharp and Simmons were shocked at such public sinfulness.[75]

In other instances, dress codes became a focus of conflict between the church and members of other cultures. As the organization expanded outside the United States, church leaders insisted that foreign members conform to the same rigorous standards as their American counterparts. Ignorant of African culture, F.J. Lee severely criticized the attire of the African sisters. He wrote with obvious perplexity, "It may be that you haven't advanced far enough from heathenism to know that you should dress modestly."[76] He continued with the familiar warning that "you are going to have to put on a dress or be given over to your reckless ways to suffer the consequences of disobeying God, also you will be debarred of membership in the great Church of God until you learn to be modest."[77] As he later discovered, changing a culture hundreds of years old was much easier said than done.

A few leaders recognized the nature of rural-urban conflict. L.G. Rouse, a rural preacher who moved to a congregation in Knoxville, Tennessee, faced opposition when he "preached against women wearing spider web clothes."[78] Church members complained to the state overseer, J.S. Lewellyn. Recognizing that the problem was rooted in culture, Lewellyn told Rouse not to preach to city dwellers in the same way he preached to country people. According to the rural preacher, his overseer advised him to return to the mountains "where the people didn't know much."[79]

Such relativistic insight was uncommon among early Church of God leaders. Fashions in women's clothing troubled generations of Church of God leaders. One expression of concern was voiced in fall 1928 at the meeting of the Elders' Council, in a debate over a motion that would have made dress length a test of membership. Most elders believed that such a ruling was needed because many Church of God females were wearing the fashionable shorter dresses. The clergymen passed a resolution stating, "It is the conviction of this body that it is a violation of the law of modesty for our sisters to appear in public with a dress exposing her knees either sitting or standing."[80] The council made this recommendation to the General Assembly, but the assembly did not adopt the resolution on dress. Apparently paying little attention to the male leaders, many of the younger females and those who lived in urban areas continued to wear the latest fashions. In response to this lack of conformity, Church of God officials often had some of the more prestigious older women deliver exhortations to their younger sisters. In 1931, Myrtle Whitehead wrote, "The Devil is trying to get pride in the Church and it grieves my heart to see our people dress like the World."[81] She noted that the Bible left no room for doubt: a Holiness woman should dress plainly, and she should never buy expensive clothes. Such appeals, consciously or unconsciously, pressured younger members and often made some feel guilty. But other women continued to dress as they pleased.

In 1933, the General Assembly adopted a measure requiring female members to wear dresses that came to the elbow and ankles. Anyone who wore dresses that exposed legs or upper arms was to be considered immodest.[82] The resolution did not mention possible expulsion of guilty members, a fact which worried some males. In the next meeting of the assembly in 1934, some ordained ministers proposed that the ruling be redrafted to include an enforcement clause.[83] Supporters managed to persuade a majority to vote for the new ruling. The prohibitive measure did not solve the problem, however. On the contrary, as new fashions became popular, Church of God women, like many American females, bought and wore dresses that were shorter and more revealing. Recalcitrant women infuriated some churchmen, especially males of the older generation. Stubborn preachers retaliated by delivering sermon after sermon criticizing female fashions as ungodly and suggesting "that the dress question . . . be enforced more strictly."[84]

In the early 1940s, the church was at an impasse on the question of whether to enforce an unpopular ruling or to relax the dress code. The church chose the latter course. At the Bishop's Council meeting in fall 1940, clergymen discussed this highly controversial issue. A committee recommended adoption of a new statement on dress which simply called for female members to dress according to New Testament guidelines concerning modesty. All former rulings would be deleted from the *Minutes*. The council was divided on the issue, and a storm of controversy erupted. Traditionalists believed that modest apparel should be defined, so that all would know how to dress. This faction argued that if a definition was not issued, there would be lack of uniformity, and women could do as they pleased. Progressive churchmen suggested that the former ruling be deleted and no ruling issued. Most council members agreed that the Bible really did not define what constituted modesty. One clergyman surmised that the church could not make females conform if they did not want to. Another progressive minister made a motion that the issue be referred to a committee composed of males and females. This proposal resulted in another controversy. The motion went down to defeat because traditionalist council members objected "to [the] inclusion of five women on the committee, or the committee consulting with women."[85] The council finally passed the original motion that females should dress according to New Testament standards.[86]

As fashions changed in the 1950s and 1960s, many women in the Church of God desired to keep up with the times and wear the latest styles of clothing. Few were willing to lag behind the times and don outfits they considered outdated. This was especially true of the younger women and the more affluent ones who had money to purchase current fashions. The younger members desired not to be identified as old-fashioned. Many of the older traditionalists in the church, however, simply could not understand why stubborn females insisted on following fashions that, year after year, were condemned as immodest or obscene. These elders questioned the spirituality of women who dressed fashionably. In an article entitled "Be Not Conformed To This World," assistant general overseer Earl P. Paulk wrote in 1958, "I tremble when I see so-called holiness people being enticed away from real Bible holiness to the extent that the fashions of this world become predominant in their lives."[87] Such attacks intensified existing animosities.

The definition of modesty was the root of the problem. Some Church of God leaders failed to realize that not all members defined modesty in the same way; they wanted all female members to meet their own personal standards. It was simply unrealistic for them to think that all Church of God women would live according to one standard dress code devised by an all-male ecclesiastical hierarchy.

Some female members accepted the standards that the male leaders had established. Probably they were content with their roles as wives, mothers, and homemakers. Such women often encouraged and cajoled recalcitrant females to comply with the dress codes. In the early 1960s, numerous articles written by women appeared in the church's periodicals. A large percentage of these were not condemnatory in nature, but instead attempted to convince young females to accept their definition of a beautiful woman. The latest fashions, cosmetics, jewelry, and other finery did not make a woman pretty. Rather, argued one Church of God author, Hazel Brewer, people "see the beauty of holiness displayed in her face. Her husband will honor and adore her as the queen of the home. Her children will love and respect her."[88] Brewer's concept was that a beautiful woman adhered strictly to the traditional female sex role. In the view of many younger females, this definition was outdated and confining.

The revolt of the younger generation of female members of the Church of God was a microcosm of the broader Women's Liberation movement that swept America during the 1960s. In the years following World War II, the number of women who held white-collar jobs increased significantly, and traditional sex roles became blurred. Led by middle-class females, women emerged from homes, burned their bras in protest, and promised to obtain equal rights. Many "Women's Libbers" started wearing less traditional clothing, including slacks and blouses that resembled men's attire. Soon fashion designers made a complete line of women's slacks, shirts, and suits. The militancy of "Women's Libbers" and their revolutionary ideas threatened traditional values and frightened both male and female traditionalists within the Church of God.

Whether Church of God females should wear slacks was one of the most controversial and emotional issues concerning standards of dress. Church leaders consistently condemned the wearing of pants by female members because of such Old Testament scriptures as Deuteronomy 22:5—"The woman shall not wear that which pertaineth unto a man, neither shall a man put on a woman's garment." Traditionalist clergymen believed that God intended there to be distinctions between the sexes. James A. Cross, former general overseer, voicing an opinion typical of the traditionalists, asserted that "any attempt to obliterate the distinction between man and woman appears to be a violation of God's order and purpose."[89] In summer 1968, the church's Executive Council issued a statement on modest apparel. This body declared that low-cut, sleeveless dresses, miniskirts, shorts, slacks, and jeans were unacceptable. To soften the proclamation, the council noted, "In view of the fact the present day dress fads for men include the wearing of shorts and going shirtless, we also appeal for modesty in dress among male members."[90]

Despite these prohibitions, the new styles in women's clothing became popular among Church of God women. In the fifties and sixties, only younger women wore the newer styles, but by the 1970s, women of all age groups were purchasing and wearing the most up-to-date clothing. In the mid-1970s, the church adopted, in addition to the normal prohibitions, new tactics in its fight to discourage female members from wearing "immodest" apparel. Clergymen began to categorize female members into new groups, "dedicated" Christians and "non-dedicated" Christians,[91] a practice that increased tensions between traditionalists and progressives. Traditionalists vilified progressives as compromisers who lived "anything goes" lifestyles. Progressives stereotyped traditionalists as anachronistic old fogies.

Other issues pertaining to personal morality also divided the church. More "mature" church members discouraged their spiritual sisters from wearing "jewelry and useless attire."[92] Such articles had not presented a major problem in the church's early existence, but as prosperity increased and wearing jewelry became a popular social custom, church leaders felt that the practice detracted from the spirituality of the church; consequently, preventive measures were taken. The 1915 General Assembly passed a ruling "against members wearing gold for ornament or decoration; such as finger rings, bracelets, earrings, lockets, etc.: Isa. 55:2, I Pet. 3:3."[93]

Churchmen believed that Christian women did not need superficial adornment to make them appear more attractive. Women who resorted to such frivolous decorations, the leaders felt, attempted to improve on God's creation. Women should not be concerned with outward appearances but only with inward, spiritual qualities. A female member explained simply, "God says he will 'beautify the meek with salvation.'"[94]

Churchmen sounded the familiar argument that purchasing extravagant garments or ornaments was a waste of money that was needed elsewhere. One minister pleaded, "Many souls are dying and going to hell who have not the privilege of hearing the gospel. So if you love Jesus with all your heart, would it not be better to take the money that you spend for jewelry and useless attire, and help to send the good news of Jesus and his love to some dying soul?"[95]

Nor were male clergymen exempt from reprimands from their superiors concerning the attire of family members. The general overseer scolded one preacher who apparently had found it difficult to finance his travel because a young daughter was "decked with gold bracelets and rings."[96]

In 1930, the General Assembly passed a ruling which prohibited members from wearing jewelry for decorative purposes.[97] Aimed primarily at females, this prohibitive measure called for the expulsion of guilty parties. Like the rulings on modest clothing, the church's stand on jewelry was unpopular with younger females. But, in the midst of the Depression, most women probably accepted it because they did not have money to buy such luxuries anyway.

In the mid-1930s, the question of wedding rings arose. It appears that the customs and laws of some foreign nations required all married persons, including Church of God missionaries, to wear a wedding band. This requirement resulted in controversy among Church of God members. Some favored lifting the ban against jewelry and allowing wedding rings to be worn by all married members. Others only wanted the existing ruling modified to allow foreign missionaries to wear rings. In 1936, the General Assembly recommended that the church allow wedding rings to be worn by missionaries in "certain foreign countries where social laws or customs governing society require it."[98]

In the early 1940s, more and more Church of God members wore jewelry. Church leaders faced a dilemma. If they attempted to enforce an unpopular teaching, it might cause a deeper rift in the organization. If they relaxed the ruling against jewelry, it might lower standards. Even the leadership was divided on the controversial subject. At the meeting of the Supreme Council in 1942, some members wanted stronger measures implemented. Others favored a much more liberal policy. Although it did not pass, the body discussed a resolution allowing "married women to wear wedding bands and the engaged girls to wear engagement rings."[99] In a stormy debate, traditionalist members of the council prevented passage of the resolution.

In 1945, the Supreme Council debated another motion concerning jewelry. Previous rulings had been aimed primarily at

females, but on this occasion the motion included a section ap-
plying to clergymen. The committee on the ring question stated,
"We believe that wearing of gold wrist watch bands, chains, and
tie clasps by ministers is contrary to the spirit and intent of
the rule."[100] It appears that the traditionalists wanted to restrict
both females who were guilty of wearing immodest clothing, and
progressive pastors and husbands who not only allowed such
permissiveness but supported the women in their revolt against
church teachings. The measure failed.

In the 1950s the organization continued to grapple with the
ring issue. The General Assembly in 1958 amended the ruling
on jewelry to allow married members, both male and female, to
wear wedding rings.[101] The assembly's action pleased many members, but some traditionalists felt that it was a terrible mistake
and that the standard of Holiness had been betrayed.

Another fashion issue that captured the attention of church
leaders was "bobbing" of hair by females. Short hairstyles, part
of the "flapper" image popular during the 1920s, appealed to
Church of God women. As with other fashion trends, clergymen
thought short hair was sinful and indicative of foolishness and
human pride. After World War II, the church relaxed its strict
stand on short hairstyles for women, as it did on so many issues
of dress.

In the mid-1970s, in response to rapidly changing customs
and values in American society, the Church of God adopted
a number of practical commitments. In 1976 the organization
added another regulation aimed at females. This measure required that "our members conform to the Scripture relative to
outward adornment and to the use of cosmetics."[102] Unlike other
controversies concerning personal morality that had their roots
in the period before World War II, the use of cosmetics did not
really become an issue until after the war, mainly because until
then many Church of God women could not afford them.

Among the areas of personal morality that concerned the
church most were divorce and remarriage. In the early years of
the Church of God, in order to insure group solidarity, parents encouraged their children to choose marriage partners from within
Pentecostal ranks. Concerned parents warned young adults not

to be "unequally yoked together with unbelievers." Scripture prohibited the marriage of a Christian with an unbeliever, and church leaders defined anyone who was not a member of the Church of God as an unbeliever. If a Church of God member married an individual of another faith despite such warning, the person was expected to convert the spouse to the Holiness religion. If the conversion was unsuccessful and the marriage ended in divorce, churchmen were swift to point out that the individual had been forewarned that divorce was probable.[103]

Articulating an official position on divorce was one of the most vexing problems that clergymen faced. After debating the subject for long hours at the 1908 General Assembly, church leaders reached no decision. The majority of churchmen agreed merely "that there was only one cause granted for a divorce that would leave either party innocent and at liberty to marry again, and that was fornication or adultery."[104] Church leaders advised that unless an individual was the innocent party in such a divorce, church membership was impossible. Prospective members who were divorcees were told that the safest course was to remain unmarried.[105] Church minutes reported that divorcees should not present themselves for church membership until they had first explained to the minister the circumstances of their divorce. Only upon completion of a pastoral investigation and recommendation was the individual to be granted membership.[106]

Church leaders continued to grapple with the problem of divorce and remarriage long after 1908. In fact, it remained the most explosive family issue that the organization encountered. Traditionalists argued that although the Scriptures made an allowance for divorce, remarriage should not be permitted under any circumstances. Progressives argued that remarriage was perfectly acceptable in the case of widows, widowers, or persons who had divorced their spouses because of adultery. The 1915 General Assembly again failed to reach a decision. The general moderator stated that he wanted to table the issue for another year. One of the assembly delegates immediately declared that he was unwilling for the question to remain unanswered, arguing that the ruling body had a responsibility to settle the problem once and for all. This spontaneous response caused a stir. Pro-

gressive forces called on general overseer Tomlinson to cast the
deciding vote. Refusing to do so, Tomlinson offered to abdicate
his position as general overseer. The official church minutes recorded: "A few brief messages [in tongues] and interpretations
followed. 1. Be careful little children, tread softly. 2. My doctrine
shall fall as the due [sic]. 3. When the veil is taken away we will
see clearly. 4. If you will walk in the light I will lift the veil and
you can see eye to eye." [107]

After the "move of the spirit," Tomlinson contended, "God may
not want it settled yet. It is wonderful what the Lord has been
doing without this question settled." [108] The problem of divorce
and remarriage remained unresolved. It was not until 1925 that
a ruling against divorce and remarriage was added to the official
list of church teachings.

During and following World War II, the divorce rate in America
increased. This trend, resulting in part from greater affluence
and personal freedom, disturbed church leaders. Some Church
of God ministers believed that "a few cases of divorce in some
instances might be tolerated, but when it comes to wholesale
divorces and for trifling causes, the example is of a ridiculous
nature." [109] In 1950 the General Assembly passed a resolution
reaffirming its opposition to divorce.

During the 1960s and 1970s, the Church of God offered advice to its single members. The organization exhorted them to
choose marriage partners who were of the same religious faith,
race, and class. [110] It was important that members never marry an
unbeliever. As one churchman argued by strained but colorful
analogy, "Do not put an ox and an ass together!" [111] The organization continued to oppose wholesale divorce, but church leaders
recognized the reality and permanence of the problem.

Membership in secret societies was another area of concern.
The Church of God followed the lead of other conservative denominations in disapproving of such clandestine organizations as
Freemasonry. The church inherited this sentiment from its Holiness antecedents. Although antimasonry was a moribund issue
by the 1870s, Church of God leaders strongly opposed fraternal
orders of any kind. During the 1908 General Assembly, delegates
decided that "no member that belongs to a lodge [secret orga-

nization] is eligible to membership of the Lord's Church."[112] In 1916, the ruling against members belonging to lodges was added to the official church teachings. Clergymen argued that in John 18:20, Jesus provided a model suggesting that one should never say or do anything in secret. Here too they warned members not to be "unequally yoked together with unbelievers," although this text was cited more commonly in reference to marriage.[113]

The Church of God included the Ku Klux Klan among its list of prohibited secret orders. In a survey of church literature and extensive interviews with surviving members, no instances of a Church of God member who was a member of the racist organization were found.

In the minds of Church of God members, secret societies and labor unions were inextricably connected. At each General Assembly, officials discussed the two topics in juxtaposition, concluding with the same decision: "The Assembly stands against the members of the church being members of lodges and all oath-bound organizations and labor unions."[114] Social and economic reality moderated this doctrine. Acknowledging that many church members worked in coal mines and had to become members of the United Mine Workers to retain employment, the church granted "the privilege of paying dues to labor unions as a tax to purchase a right to work in the mines, . . . but members should not attend their meetings."[115] This exception did not apply to ministers, who were forbidden union membership under any circumstances.[116]

Many Americans attacked labor unions after the 1917 Communist coup in Russia. Like their fellow citizens, Church of God ministers suspected that the United States government was in danger of being overthrown by a violent Bolshevik revolution. Tensions were heightened when an epidemic of violent strikes shortly after World War I eventuated in the "Red Scare" of 1919–20. Church leaders were convinced that labor unrest and violence were Red-inspired and Red-led. Church of God leaders equated labor unions with Communism, radicalism, and anarchism. As far as these churchmen were concerned, these three were anti-Christian and anti-American. A prominent clergyman stated that Bolshevism was the enemy of Christianity because it was an atheistic ideology and because the Bolshevik government in Russia had suppressed the church and all religious doctrine.[117]

Bolshevism and labor unions often were lumped together in the apocalyptic thought of the Church of God. Bolshevism represented the spirit of the Antichrist. The nickname "Reds" was associated with apocalyptic Biblical names ("rider of the red horse" and "red dragon") of the Antichrist. In the minds of clergymen, these colorful names were linked with "pillage, bloodshed, torture, and mutilation."[118] Churchmen characterized Bolshevism and the Antichrist as atheistic, bloody, and terrifying. According to church leaders, both Bolshevism and labor unionism had the same goals: the overthrow of Christianity, democracy, and American capitalism. Many Church of God adherents believed that labor unions served the Bolsheviks as a means of accomplishing this task. Characterizing Bolshevism, F.J. Lee wrote, "The 'red dragon' will soon be making his slimy trail through this world."[119] Church of God members saw violent secular events such as strikes and labor disorder as a "sign of the times," an indication that the "end time" was at hand.

Some Church of God leaders continued to be very suspicious of labor unions long after the turmoil which followed the end of World War I. Violent labor-management strife increased in the South during the 1930s, especially in the mining and textile industries. Harlan County, Kentucky, and Gaston County, North Carolina, were scenes of bloody confrontations. As the Church of God spread into regions such as these, its converts included those who worked in coal mines and textile mills. When union leaders established locals in these areas, church members found themselves in a dilemma. Because of the union's closed-shop principle, they could lose their jobs if they did not join the union. If they joined, they would be at odds with the church. Church of God rulings regarding union membership reflected an attempt to alleviate the problem. In 1928, the organization lifted its restriction on labor union membership, allowing it, however, only for those who needed membership to "obtain or retain employment."[120] With the increase in violent strikes in the early 1930s, the Church of God modified its ruling, stating that members, "in the event of labor troubles will refrain from acts of violence."[121]

As with other issues of personal morality, time and new realities brought alterations in church policy. Although church minutes in the 1980s officially prohibited members from belonging to secret lodges, unions were no longer included in this category. Many Church of God loyalists had become active union members; some had even become union leaders. In the mid-1970s, Tracy Ingram, a member of the Church of God in Ohio, served as president of the largest union in Cincinnati, United Auto Workers Local 863. Ingram stated that he became involved in union activity because decisions concerning wages, hours, and benefits were made without his input. Although an active church member, he wanted to be a part of the decision-making process.[122]

In the years following World War II, a young and more progressive generation joined the ranks of the Church of God. Many had little knowledge of or link to the Holiness tradition. The moral rigor which had so pervaded the early church began to dissipate. Many of these new members were from more affluent social classes. The influx of these new urban dwellers helped to soften the clash between urban society and the old Church of God, whose members had been largely rural. These new members spent money on the latest fashions and amusements and believed that there was more to life than just going to church. Consequently, as they conformed to the dominant urban culture, they laid aside many of the old distinguishing marks of holiness and decreased the traditional emphasis on "separation from the world."

CHAPTER 4

With Signs Following

No single characteristic of the Church of God was more important than its insistence upon a literal interpretation of the Scriptures, an emphasis which led to eccentric practices among its early constituency. Based on their reading of Mark 16:20 ("And they went forth, and preached everywhere, the Lord working with them, and confirming the word with signs following") and Acts 5:12 ("And by the hands of the apostles were many signs and wonders wrought among the people"), churchmen argued that miraculous signs should follow true believers. Their exclusive attitude often led to the denigration and alienation of those who believed differently. Such exclusivism was a recurrent theme in sermons and organizational literature. A 1917 article in the *Evangel* put the issue directly:

> The Church of God is the Bible Church, and the only church God has honored with the signs following. . . . Since there is but one church named in the Bible we can't be mistaken. . . . I never saw any other church that ever made a pretense of being holy or sanctified. The Church of God claims both. . . . Well amen, hallelujah! I am a member of the great Church of God. Are you?[1]

It appears that the author regarded the Church of God as having exclusive rights to spiritual signs. This hauteur caused friction with members of other churches. Since Church of God people could not fully understand such resentment, they simply attributed it, as they did most things they did not understand, to the workings of satanic powers. Such rationalization allowed them to ignore the fact that other Christians, who were just as dedicated and sincere, might believe differently, and that God's approval could extend to people outside the Church of God.

Although biblical literalism bred an exclusive theology, a better known by-product was divine healing. As a belief inherited from the church's Holiness progenitors, divine healing was a cardinal doctrine in the early history of the church. During the General Assembly of 1907, the communicants discussed the subject of divine healing at length and passed a resolution which stated, "Shall we use drugs in case of sickness or take Jesus alone? This was discussed in the power and demonstration of the Spirit, the decision being reached that we should take Jesus as our Physician."[2]

The clergy and laity alike adhered tenaciously to this decree. Some even carried an identification card to convey the name of their personal physician:

> Name: F.J. Lee
> Name of Firm: Church of God
> My Physician Is: Jesus
> Address: Heaven
> Phone: By Way of Prayer[3]

The Church of God based its theology of divine healing on a literal interpretation of such scriptural passages as Isaiah 53:5, Exodus 15:26, Psalms 34:19, Psalms 103:3, Matthew 8:17, John 15:7, and I Peter 2:24. The favorite and most often quoted passage was James 5:14–15: "Is any sick among you? Let him call for the elders of the church; and let them pray over him, anointing him with oil in the name of the Lord: And the prayer of faith shall save the sick, and the Lord shall raise him up." Churchmen believed that healing (physical, mental, and spiritual) was provided in the Atonement. It was not only the duty but the privilege of the saints to ask and expect the Heavenly Father to confirm his Son's atoning work with healing grace. All the petitioner had to do was ask and have the appropriate faith.

David Edwin Harrell, Jr., in *All Things Are Possible*, his excellent study of healing and charismatic revivals, indicates that the most crucial factor in the reception of divine healing was an appropriate faith on the part of the individual who wanted this

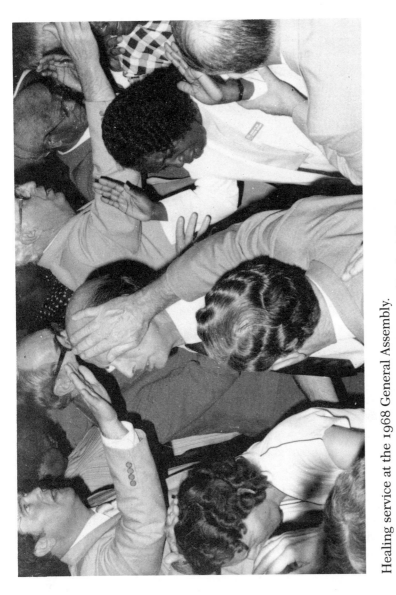

Healing service at the 1968 General Assembly.
(Hal Bernard Dixon, Jr., Pentecostal Research Center, Cleveland, Tenn.)

blessing. Harrell contends that it took the preacher to help create this faith, and that the minister alone seemed to possess the "gift of healing."[4] Church of God people, however, did not believe that the ministry of healing was confined to a few select individuals. They concluded that all spirit-filled Christians were eligible not only for this gift but for all nine spiritual gifts (I Corinthians 12:8–10). Pentecostals took Mark 16:18—"Believers shall lay hands on the sick and they shall recover"—at face value. If the Scriptures stated that all believers could pray for the sick and expect recovery, Pentecostals would do just that.

Although faith was the foundation of divine healing, the means to create that faith varied. Sometimes when the person who was ill was not physically able to attend religious services, other members anointed cloths (such as handkerchiefs) with oil and took them and placed them upon the sick. They performed such an act in obedience to Acts 19:11–12, which states that sick persons were healed when anointed cloths were placed upon their bodies. Another way to minister to shut-ins was simply by agreeing through faith ("prayer of agreement"—Matthew 18:19) that the individual would be healed. For those who were able to attend services, Church of God members preferred the "laying on of hands" (Mark 16:18) as the mode of prayer. Usually the minister called those who were ill and desired prayer to come to the altar. He anointed the sick with olive oil, and fellow believers laid their hands on the petitioners and offered intercessory prayer.[5]

Participants acknowledged healing miracles by an assortment of reactions. Many spoke in tongues or prophesied; others demonstrated outward manifestations: shouting, running, leaping, dancing. One manifestation, "the art of being slain in the spirit," when a believer fell unconsciously under the power of God, was taken as a sign to believers that the power of God was present. After the ecstatic mood calmed, the minister usually asked the individual who was divinely healed to give a testimony. The sharing of the healing experience was the culmination of the entire ritual.

In Pentecostal thought, illnesses were inextricably linked to the total depravity of man. Pentecostals believed that one of the consequences of the fall of mankind (Genesis 3) was that the physical body became susceptible to mortal decay. In addition, the malevolent activity of demonic powers caused sickness. Unlike contemporary Pentecostals, who believe that illness is a sign of demonic possession, biblical scholars in the Church of God concluded that, at least in the case of Christians, it was the result of demonic *oppression*. They felt that it was impossible for a Christian to be possessed by a demon. But, for the sinner, illness very well could be the result of demonic possession.[6]

There were hundreds of reported healings among early Church of God members. Their illnesses covered a broad spectrum from headaches to removal of cancers. An editorial entitled "Marvelous Healings" advised:

> There have been some remarkable cases of healings reported throughout the press for many years but since the falling of the "latter rain" in Los Angeles eight years ago, these reports have grown more numerous.
>
> During this period of time a large number of Pentecostal Papers have been circulating throughout the world. The contents of these papers have been principally reports of great meetings, healings, miracles, and wonders performed by the power of God. Almost everything that is recorded in the Book of Acts has been reported, from the slightest pain to the most stubborn diseases of long standing. Broken bones, . . . burns have been instantly healed. . . . Many kinds of incurable ailments have yielded to the power of God in answer to the prayer of faith.[7]

Matching the hundreds of reported healings were as many or more who were not healed. Individuals who apparently had been healed somehow "lost" their healing. One possible explanation is that the person's recovery was psychosomatic. Many people received apparent healing in an ecstatic worship service. Suggestion, in the hands of an experienced evangelist, became a powerful tool. In an atmosphere of expectancy, the capable leader encouraged those who were ill to come forward and receive God's blessing. The man of God then offered a prayer of intercession. Many went away feeling better but without real healing. Others who suffered from psychosomatic illnesses no doubt were "healed."

Many Church of God members attributed the failure to receive healing to a lack of faith, either by those who prayed or by the individual who was ill. Many times believers attributed such a failure to the refusal of the person who was ill to "accept" his healing. They also attributed failures to neglect by the individual to exercise authority over diseases through the name of Jesus. Some churchmen used James 5:16 to insist that faith to receive healing depended upon confessing one's sins. One clergyman explained, "If you are sick and desire to get through to God you should not leave a single fault unconfessed. . . . if it isn't done, God is not under any obligation to hear the prayers. . . ."[8] If there were hidden sins, the person was not in a right relationship with God or "was not on speaking terms with God." When neither of these explanations was applicable, God must have permitted sickness as a means of divine purpose. According to such reasoning, an illness could strengthen the individual's character and teach a valuable lesson.

From its early years, the Church of God maintained an extreme position on divine healing. The church's extremism produced suspicion and skepticism among many members concerning physicians, an attitude rooted in traditional Appalachian culture. Remote mountain people had limited access to doctors and compensated by developing folk medicines or relying on divine healing. When a parent or child became ill or was injured, the adult usually refused medicine and medical assistance. Sermons which demanded submissiveness and obedience to church dogma reinforced the organization's extreme position. A typical sermon declared that "Jesus has never intimated that the members of the Church of God should use them [medicines] as remedies, but tells us just what to do if any among you are sick. He does not say call for the doctors or apply any remedy."[9] Churchmen felt that it was perfectly acceptable for someone who was not a Church of God member to take medicine or seek medical attention; but God required more of Holiness believers because they had been entrusted with the "full gospel." Many considered any member who fell short of this expectation to be weak and immature. Furthermore, any minister who advocated taking medicine certainly could not be an example to others.[10]

Such extremism led to tragedy on several occasions. Legal authorities arrested and charged Walter Barney, a member of the Church of God at Foster Falls, Virginia, with involuntary man-

slaughter because he allowed his desperately ill child to die without calling a physician or administering medicine.[11] After hearing
evidence, the Wythe County Circuit Court jury rendered a ver-
dict of guilty and fixed punishment at six months in the county
jail. Counsel for the defendant requested a new trial, but the motion was denied. Judge A.A. Campbell sentenced Barney to hard
labor on Virginia public roads for a period of six months.[12]

Barney did not appeal his case to the state supreme court. He
apparently decided to serve his time. The Church of God member's incarceration left his wife and five remaining children with
no means of support. Their desperate situation prompted the
Church of God general overseer, A.J. Tomlinson, to petition for
Barney's release. The overseer commissioned Flora Trim, wife
of the Virginia state overseer, to obtain the required signatures.
She persuaded approximately sixty people from the Foster Falls
community to sign the petition asking the state governor to release Barney.[13] The governor granted the request and pardoned
him. Authorities released Barney from custody after serving four
of the six months to which he had been sentenced.[14]

There were other cases in which parental neglect resulted
in the death of a child. The most publicized was that of James
Bradley of Brandon, Florida. On 26 April 1918, his fifteen-year-
old daughter, Bertha, fell into an open fireplace during an epilep-
tic seizure and was burned severely over approximately one-third
of her body. The girl remained under the care of her parents until
31 May. On that day, law officers took her from her home by court
order and transported the young girl to the State Hospital for the
Insane at Chattahoochee, Florida. She remained there until her
death on 22 June. Physicians declared that the immediate cause
of death was septicemia, commonly known as blood poisoning.[15]

After the death of the child, the local sheriff arrested the girl's
father and placed him in the Suwannee County jail. He was tried
on 22 May 1919 in the Circuit Court of Suwannee County, convicted of manslaughter, and sentenced to ten years' hard labor in
the state prison.[16] Bradley appealed his case to the state supreme
court, which in May 1920 overruled the lower court decision by a
vote of two to one. Judge Whitfield, speaking for the higher court,
stated, "There is no statute in this state specifically making the

failure or refusal of a father to provide attention for his child, a felony." [17]

Such cases posed serious questions for many church members. Were they to obey laws which demanded that medical treatment be given to children? Although there was some dissension among members, general overseer Tomlinson stated emphatically that there was not one instance where Jesus or the disciples consulted a physician when a person was desperately ill. Moreover, he asserted that "the Church of God will not compromise. Some individuals may wear the white feather of cowardice and compromise, but the Church as a whole will not do it." [18] He advised members to obey civil authorities and the laws so long as they did not conflict with the teachings of Jesus or the Apostles. But how could they do both? Members could obey authorities by submitting to the penalties of the law. [19] Some church leaders considered anything less to be disloyal. Confronted with this unfortunate dilemma, members either accepted religious extremism or faced condemnation and ostracism by their church. Under these circumstances, it is not surprising that parents sometimes stood by and watched sick children die, while refusing professional treatment.

Intimidated parents and those who shared the beliefs of their general overseer instilled extremism in their children at a tender age. When five-year-old Edna Samples of Cleveland, Tennessee, became seriously ill, an adult asked her if she wanted to take medicine. She responded, "I am holiness. I don't believe in it." [20] She died a few days later and was buried on 26 February 1917.

As authorities arrested more parents and sent them to jail, church members and leaders became less certain of what they would do if their own children required medical treatment. Prior to the reversal of the Bradley case, the church appointed a five-person committee to study the issue and present its findings at the annual General Assembly. The report not only reflected skepticism on the part of the leadership, but indicated a possible willingness to take a more moderate position. The committee chair stated, "This is a serious question in these days. We can't be too radical on this. It must be decided individually. I can't be a martyr for you, you must be a martyr for yourself. I can't tell you what to do." [21]

These cases might have compelled the organization to modify its stand, but for the fact that the Florida State Supreme Court handed down its decision overruling the lower court in the Bradley case a few months after the assembly met. Church leaders interpreted the higher court action as vindication and legal justification of its position. General Overseer Tomlinson took great pleasure in announcing that "there is no penalty for refusing medical aid in such cases and this will give our people more of a restful feeling at such times." [22] He encouraged them to trust God for their healing.

Through the 1920s, many church members tenaciously clung to their convictions. Rebecca Dixon's beliefs were put to a test when her young son contracted diphtheria. The local sheriff brought a doctor to treat the lad, but his parents refused the medical aid. They informed the sheriff and doctor that they were trusting the Lord to heal their son. The determined parents stated that "the Lord gave him to us and [if it was his will] He could take him." [23]

Some church members believed in divine healing regardless of circumstances or consequences. Such beliefs often brought tragic results. C.W. Cole of Kissimee, Florida, related that he and his wife trusted God for the physical healing of themselves and their children. He testified that he and his wife had four children and had never given them a single dose of medicine. All four of his children died because of a lack of medical attention. Cole explained that "He [God] has taken them to a better place than this, but we trusted Him with them to the end." [24] During the Great Depression, many Church of God parents continued to trust God for the healing of their sick or injured children. In early 1930, the infant of the Reverend and Mrs. B.L. Hicks, the state overseer of Alabama and his wife, died after the pair refused medical treatment and trusted the Lord for the baby's recovery. When the child became ill, the parents prayed for healing, but, sadly, the infant died. In April, Hicks was arraigned on charges of parental neglect. The court found him guilty but fined him only the minimal amount of twenty-five dollars. [25]

If the case of James Bradley and similar cases in Arkansas and Tennessee had not been decided in favor of the defendants, the Church of God might have adopted a more moderate position on divine healing.[26] This is exactly what happened much later. As states enacted more stringent laws, they forced the church to modify its position regarding parental responsibility. Such laws did not take away the Pentecostals' right to believe in divine healing, but they did protect the rights of minors. They prevented children from having to endure intense pain and suffering because parents were unwilling to provide proper medical care. To most Americans, it seems absurd that parents would allow their children to suffer agonizing deaths without medical care, but to Church of God members it was a matter of religious conviction.

Most Church of God members were rural people who came from the lower social stratum. Many of these joined the movement because it gave them a sense of identity and meaning. Divine healing gave them a direct experience of God, the ultimate source of meaning. It enabled them to face an uncertain future in a changing society and, by placing control in the hands of an omnipotent deity, it relieved believers of responsibility for their own destinies, even the loss of life.

Church of God members also followed the instructions of a popular charismatic leader, Ambrose J. Tomlinson. A man with great powers of persuasion, he exuded self-confidence. An examination of church literature and the minutes of church procedures reveals the extent of Tomlinson's influence. His views on divine healing were extreme, and it may have been that most members simply followed the example of an admired and respected leader.

In all cases involving children who died as a result of parental neglect, the parents were poor and had little or no education. There were no cases involving parents who were from the higher ranks of Church of God leadership. This would tend to support the observation that economically deprived parents were following a charismatic leader. Whatever their reasons, their sincerity and determination cannot be doubted.

Church of God members not only were extreme in their belief in divine healing for their children, but many trusted God to heal their own bodies as well. Taking Job, an Old Testament character, as her example (Job 13:15), Celia Mahan declared, "I mean to trust the Lord though He slay me."[27] In 1928, general overseer

F.J. Lee, who had trusted God for his healing since he joined the Church of God, died of cancer following a long illness. According to numerous persons who were with Lee until the end, the general overseer refused all drugs and medical treatment, even though he suffered a painful death.[28]

Such determination was common in the early church. Some members were so thoroughly dependent upon divine healing that they proclaimed that physicians and medicine were useless, and that if more people would trust God for their healing, doctors would soon be driven out of business. Such statements brought the Church of God bad publicity and increased the hostility of the general public toward the church. To lessen this negative image, church leaders passed a resolution asking members to refrain from making such remarks.[29]

By the 1940s, many church members, especially adults of the younger generation, no longer held to a strict belief in divine healing. Some young parents did not refuse medical aid for their children, and most no longer "trusted the Lord" for their own bodies. Undoubtedly, some young parents knew of children who had died because of lack of medical attention. Sensitive parents were unwilling to see their children suffer when they could be relieved by the use of doctors and medicine. Others were unwilling to be imprisoned for such an unpopular belief.

The relaxation of such standards distressed traditionalist Church of God clergymen. One minister, Sam Holcomb, surmised that "the reason people are not getting healed today is because they won't do what God wants them to do. There are certain conditions to be met."[30] The churchman testified that he himself had trusted God for over twenty-five years, and God had cured him of medical problems ranging from appendicitis to a broken arm. The Lord had healed all his ailments either instantly or gradually. He encouraged all to "practice it [divine healing] and see how much better you get along."[31]

Like-minded Church of God members sought to encourage their fellows to return to past standards. The church reemphasized the need for trusting God instead of medicine. One member, Glenn Eason, explained that the purpose of such trust was "to strengthen our faith in God, also to prove to the unbelievers and sinners that our God is the true and living God."[32] Eason also noted that healing services which had good results drew large crowds; consequently, more sinners could be converted and won to the church.[33]

In the post–World War II period, most Church of God members still believed in prayer for the sick; but the new, more progressive members did not hesitate to seek medical attention. This attitude troubled older traditionalist churchmen. They felt that younger members had compromised the faith and sinned by seeking medical aid. One clergyman, Merle H. Greene, represented a middle-of-the-road position. He believed that trusting God for healing was better than resorting to medicine; but if individuals sought professional help, there was nothing wrong with that. They had not sinned. The minister stated that "to say that medicine does no good at all is fantastic [fanatical], if we would only use common sense and acknowledge that medical science has done wonders in the medical realm."[34]

In the 1950s, the issue of divine healing continued to divide the organization. More affluent and better-educated Church of God members insisted that it was not necessary to rely on prayer alone; God used doctors and medicines to heal the body. They saw no need for the church to retain the teaching of divine healing. Such opinions puzzled many of the new Church of God converts, who wondered if the organization still believed in healing through divine intervention. This kind of doubt produced a flurry of articles in the mid-fifties. W.E. Johnson, state overseer of Tennessee, asserted that "the Church of God is just as strong today as it has ever been on these cardinal doctrines. I believe that Jesus Christ has the same power today that He had when He was here on earth."[35]

Adding to the controversy was the healing revival movement of the 1950s. Healing evangelists hit the sawdust trail throughout the nation. They erected huge gospel tents and preached to large audiences. Evangelists like Oral Roberts prayed for those who were afflicted with all manner of disease and ailments, creating great excitement and enormous publicity. It appeared to some that the old-line Pentecostal churches' emphasis on healing and miracles was being supplanted by the healing revivals. Although

the Church of God taught divine healing and many of its adherents attended the healing campaigns, such attention irritated
some Church of God leaders. Numerous churchmen believed
that the organization needed to renew its belief and leadership
in divine healing, both in doctrine and practice. Clergyman J.E.
Devore stated emphatically that "we have stood for divine healing for many years. From the beginning it has been in the articles
of faith. Let us pray and seek God fervently lest greedy wolves
destroy the flock; let us preach and practice the message of faith
in God and in His power to deliver."[36] Such concern caused the
church to pass a resolution in 1954 reaffirming its belief in divine
healing and other healing-related doctrines, such as signs following believers and gifts of the spirit.[37]

In their prayers for the sick, the healing revivalists emphasized the need for faith. It was this virtue, most evangelists declared, which moved God to heal the afflicted. The role of faith
was the subject of disagreement among some healing evangelists and Church of God officials. At the peak of the movement
in 1956, Charles W. Conn, editor-in-chief of all Church of God
publications, wrote a lengthy essay regarding the role of faith
in the healing process. Stating that the evangelists were faith
healers, he maintained that faith healing was based upon the
presupposition that illnesses were only psychological. The therapeutic value of faith activated the cure. In divine healing, by
contrast, "faith was only the vehicle which releases the healing
power of the Lord," argued Conn. "He performs the healing."[38]
Most of the healing revivalists in fact agreed with Conn on the
proper role of faith. Only a few of the more radical revivalists
believed differently.

Although the healing revival had virtually ended by the late
1950s, a few evangelists, such as Asa A. Allen of Miracle Valley, Arizona, continued to conduct healing campaigns into the
next decade. Some opportunistic revivalists ascribed healing to a
"gift" which they possessed. Believing that most of these persons
entered the ministry for economic gain and self-aggrandizement,
Church of God officials heaped them with scathing criticism.
Wade H. Horton, assistant general overseer, noted that shenani-
gans by such evangelists caused terrible embarrassment to those

individuals who believed in divine healing. "It has also resulted in some honest-hearted men," lamented Horton, "who have long felt a burden and passion for sick and afflicted humanity, hesitating at times to forcibly present the healing message for fear of being accused of having ulterior motives."[39] Church leaders feared that such hesitancy eventually might lead to a total neglect of the doctrine. The solution was simple. Convinced of the doctrine's validity, one churchman urged, "Let us preach the Word with power, and I believe that God will confirm the word with signs following."[40]

In the late 1960s and 1970s, the doctrine of healing received a boost from the outbreak of the Charismatic Revival. Thousands of members within the Protestant denominations accepted and practiced divine healing. This acceptance helped to make the doctrine more palatable to affluent Americans. Some of these converts joined the Church of God. One such individual was Gale V. Moffet, a medical doctor from Wisconsin. Moffet, a member of a traditional Protestant denomination, had been a practicing physician for more than twenty years. In 1965, Moffet and his wife received the Baptism of the Holy Spirit. Sometime later they became Church of God members, and he obtained a minister's credentials. The doctor and parttime clergyman combined his two occupations into a unique practice. Moffet explained, "Now I can no longer be satisfied to see only the bodies of men healed while their souls perish."[41]

In recent years, many Church of God members have attempted to analyze the phenomenon of divine healing. All agree that the doctrine was provided in the Atonement, and all Christians who ask God can be healed. The decay of the human body and physical death are a result of man's depravity. Illness comes to all people eventually. After conversion, a Christian believer remains susceptible to sickness because of this natural law, not because of sin in the convert's life. Not everyone who prays for healing receives it, nor does every minister who prays for a sick person see that individual recover. Church of God clergymen continued to offer the same reasons why healing did not occur: lack of faith, the need of a recalcitrant believer for discipline, to teach patience and maturity, and a host of other reasons.

A few individuals believed that God was not obligated to heal in cases such as terminally ill persons. In an article that appeared in the *Evangel*, Joseph Bayly discussed several problems relating to divine healing and praying for the terminally ill. The key was the realization by Christians that all human beings have a limited life expectancy. If the person who is ill and those who pray realize this fact, then positive results, such as tranquility and a sense of divine control, can be attained. The author points out that there can be some negative effects of prayer, if those involved believe that only a lack of faith prevents healing. If a person who is ill believes that he or she remains in that condition because of "lack of faith," this conviction can produce depression, guilt, and emotional stress, causing great harm. Bayly concluded that "if such praying obscures the reality of heaven and its joyful prospect for the person who is ill, making it appear that only in prolongation of life on earth may satisfaction be found, it is less than Christian."[42] Donald B. Gibson, a doctor and a Church of God member, wondered if praying for a terminally ill patient did not prolong the patient's misery and suffering. The physician suggested that, after exhausting all means of helping the sick, "we should prepare ourselves to let the dying pass on."[43]

Many Church of God members continued to believe in divine healing and testified that they had been healed of ailments ranging from the common cold to cancer. But by the 1980s, most members tempered their conviction with the practicality of seeking medical attention when they contracted an illness. For many, the combination of prayer and medicine had become a satisfactory compromise between religion and the secular world.

Divine healing was not the only eccentric belief of the Church of God. Snake handling was regarded as even more bizarre. A former Baptist, George W. Hensley, actually initiated the practice. Hensley lived in a small, remote community called "Owl Holler," located not far from Cleveland, Tennessee. After he and some neighbors accepted the Pentecostal message, Hensley handled his first snake in the nearby community of Grasshopper Valley, Tennessee.[44] In 1910, he received his call to the ministry. Soon afterward, general overseer A.J. Tomlinson invited the novice to preach in Cleveland, although Hensley was not yet a member of the Church of God. The snake-handler from "Owl Holler" went to the small town and conducted a worship service. During his sermon, some mischievous individuals interrupted by bringing in a rattlesnake in a box and challenging the preacher to handle the poisonous viper. Hensley took the snake from the container and handled it without any apparent harm. Other worshippers, including the general overseer's young daughter Iris, also handled the snake several times without any injury.[45] This incident introduced the practice of snake-handling into the Church of God. In 1912, Hensley joined the Church of God, and so gained access to pulpits across the Southeast. The ritual spread throughout the sect, with some clergymen and laymen practicing it and others denying its validity.[46] The rite was based on a literal interpretation of Mark 16:17-18: "And these signs shall follow them that believe; In my name shall they cast out devils; they shall speak with new tongues; They shall take up serpents; and if they drink any deadly thing, it shall not hurt them; they shall lay hands on the sick, and they shall recover." Once again, a literal interpretation of the Scriptures had placed the sect in a precarious position, but opponents could hardly deny the biblical basis of the practice.

James B. Ellis recorded an early case of snake handling in his autobiography. Although he himself did not handle snakes on this occasion, his first experience with snake-handlers occurred in 1912 at Straight Creek, Alabama. Members accepted the challenge of outsiders to handle three large rattlesnakes.[47] Before members handled the poisonous reptiles, the orgiastic service reached a climax of intense excitement. Some spoke in tongues, while others gave interpretations. Simultaneously, other saints began "shouting" and "dancing in the Spirit." When the excitement reached a peak, clergymen removed the serpents from a box and passed them among the believers. Ellis reported that a few were bitten, but that no harm came to the victims.[48]

Believers never handled snakes before the climax of an emotionally charged service, because only at this time did the "anointing and power" of the Holy Spirit fall. It was considered extremely dangerous to attempt this activity before the correct moment. Believers also viewed any individual who attempted such a thing as being "in the flesh"; that person would be outside God's protection and so subject to harm.

In summer 1914, George Hensley conducted a revival at the Church of God in South Cleveland. The evangelist preached each night, urging sinners to repent of their sins and seek the Holy Ghost's baptism. Under the "anointing," he preached on the subject of signs following believers. During the revival, some curious outsiders who had heard of Hensley's reputation as a snake-handler brought a rattlesnake and dared the preacher and others to "take up the serpent." They were not disappointed. Hensley and several others handled the serpent without harm. One Church of God leader, however, was not so fortunate. The viper bit Tom L. McLain, but he refused medical aid, relying on God to heal him. The minister recovered. A few nights later, the Church of God folk fondled a poisonous copperhead. Finley Goodwin, one of the members, received a bite on his left hand. Exercising his belief in divine healing, he refused to see a doctor or take medicine.[49]

Throughout Hensley's revival at the Cleveland church, numerous communicants, men and women, handled poisonous snakes. These handlers ranged from the humblest members to some of the most prominent Church of God leaders. W.F. Bryant and his wife Nettie were among those who handled snakes.[50]

Apparently the members in southern Cleveland who handled serpents were all adults. It was not long, however, until children also were among the saints who took up serpents. In September 1914, Hensley erected a big tent and held a revival in the small community of Ooltewah, just a few miles from Cleveland. The evangelist introduced the congregation to the practice of "taking up" serpents. One night, when the power of the Holy Ghost fell, a young girl only ten years old handled a rattlesnake for some time with no apparent harm.[51] The practice of snake handling by children apparently was not widespread in the Church of God. Most handlers were adults, males and females of all ages. Although the practice began in the Appalachian region, it spread within the sect among local congregations from Ohio to Florida and as far west as Texas. L.G. Rouse, a Church of God preacher, handled snakes numerous times. His first opportunity came during a tent meeting outside Maryville, Tennessee. Challenged by mischievous youth, Rouse told them that he would not handle a serpent for their entertainment. He instructed the young men to return with the poisonous reptile the following night, and, if God granted him the power, he would handle it. Next evening, they returned with the snake, and Rouse took the serpent out of a box and let it coil around his hand. The snake did not bite him.[52]

Rouse was not always so fortunate. A black rattlesnake bit the preacher during the time he was pastoring the church at Delbarton, West Virginia. Uncertain whether he would survive, Rouse recorded:

> I kissed my wife and babies goodbye. I thought I was going to have to leave them. I preached until I could not stand. . . . My muscles drew in knots as large as hen eggs. . . . on Monday [two days later] I passed from my kidneys blood just as black as that old snake, and when I mashed my gums with my lips, I spit a mouthful of blood just as black as ink. Every drop of blood in my body was as black as ink.[53]

Rouse survived the snakebite and gained the dubious reputation of "snake-eater."[54]

Snake handling captured the attention of outsiders. Critics denounced the bizarre practice as heresy and characterized serpent-handlers as fanatics. Still others accused handlers of defanging the poisonous reptiles or extracting their venom. Responding to such criticism, one Church of God minister, G.G. Williams, declared that this was not true. During a Church of God service in Dunn, Louisiana, he walked back and forth across the rostrum, revealing to his large audience of over four hundred persons that the snake he held was a poisonous cottonmouth moccasin with fangs. Although the reptile bit the preacher on his left hand, he suffered no apparent harm.[55] Some of the most virulent criticism came from clergymen of other Pentecostal churches. C.F. Noble, a preacher affiliated with the Pentecostal Holiness Church, argued that the dubious practice was a "crooked delusion" and a "heathenish practice."[56]

In spite of such criticism, Church of God members continued to handle snakes, and some leaders supported the practice. In 1922, general overseer A.J. Tomlinson argued that the disciples of Jesus handled serpents; therefore, Church of God members were following New Testament examples. "In the face of this plain analogy," warned Tomlinson, "I would certainly hate to be in the shoes of some who are so bitter against taking up serpents."[57]

By the late 1920s, the practice spread into areas far outside the southern mountains, generally following Appalachian migration patterns. D.G. Phillips, a member of a local Church of God congregation in Akron, Ohio, reported that on many occasions members handled snakes without injury. Some received bites, but all recovered. Phillips confidently affirmed that the members' success in handling poisonous snakes was a "stamp of real Christian Perfection."[58] Other Church of God ministers believed that snake handling was proof that the Bible was the infallible Word of God. P.F. Barnewall wrote a series of articles for the *Evangel* on the disputed text of Mark 16:18. Higher Criticism had declared that this text was a later addition to the New Testament canon and was not included in the best older manuscripts. Barnewall concluded that the handling of snakes by Holy Ghost–filled saints was more than ample proof of the validity of the text in question.[59]

Relating the performance of miracles to perfectionism only encouraged snake handling among believers. Moreover, a few zealous clergymen and members began to teach that unless a person handled serpents one could not be a true believer. This new idea brought sharp criticism from church leaders. S.J. Heath, a Church of God minister from Boaz, Alabama, observed that numerous snake-handlers had become fanatics, bringing the Church of God an avalanche of adverse publicity. Heath accused some preachers of using the church as a means of promoting their "snake shows." Although Heath rebuked such clergymen, he did not really repudiate the practice of taking up serpents. In fact, he concluded that "if snakes were handled to convince unbelievers of the power of God, that was something altogether different."[60]

In time, a complex theological rationale developed to explain the practice. Believers handled snakes, which symbolized Satan (Genesis 3:15), as a test of faith. The power of God enabled true believers to overcome imperfections of the flesh. Snake-handlers

Unidentified snake handler.
(Hal Bernard Dixon, Jr., Pentecostal Research Center, Cleveland, Tenn.)

in turn considered the spiritual development of brethren inferior if they succumbed to Satan's venom.

The blessed, who had demonstrated their spiritual amplitude in a miraculous manner, felt compensated for cultural, social, and economic deprivation. Because rich people generally avoided the excesses of religious sectarianism, they were scorned as ill-developed, uncommitted, or even pagan by those less fortunate materially but more daring in religious practice.

Many Church of God leaders realized that the eccentric practice of snake handling was wreaking havoc, and the reputation of the organization had become tainted as a result. The church became deeply divided over the issue. To help heal the division, the Church of God General Assembly passed a resolution in 1928 officially repudiating the practice.[61] This action did not prevent members who desired to handle serpents from continuing the practice. Ironically, the sect itself persisted in reporting stories of snake handling. Immediately following the assembly, in November 1928, an article appeared in a church periodical reporting a revival in Booneville, Mississippi, where members handled snakes.[62] In the early 1930s, Church of God communicants at Valdosta, Georgia, reported that God was blessing the saints with signs following believers, including handling two poisonous snakes. Mrs. Frank Dasher, a member of the Valdosta congregation, maintained that "if we wish to grow in wisdom and knowledge of God, we should never resist His power but give ourselves completely over into His hands that He might be able to use us for His glory."[63] Mrs. Dasher, who handled the two serpents, described the experience as "joy unspeakable and full of glory."[64]

Despite official repudiation by the 1928 assembly, some church officials continued to straddle the issue. In 1934, E.C. Clark, editor of the *Evangel*, maintained that when individuals handled snakes for the entertainment of others and were bitten, it brought shame and disgrace to the name of Christianity. Clark, however, stated that he believed in handling snakes but only "under the power of the Holy Ghost."[65]

As more practitioners were bitten and a few died of snakebite, the practice came under closer scrutiny. Most fatalities, however, seemed to have occurred with members of "independent" Pentecostal groups. Because of the growing number of fatalities associated with snake handling, in the 1930s several southern states passed laws prohibiting the dangerous practice in connection with religious services. Nevertheless, many "independent" Pentecostals continued handling poisonous reptiles, resulting in the arrest of those who violated the new laws. But attitudes within the Church of God were changing. In summer 1940, the new editor of the *Evangel*, E.L. Simmons, wrote an article praising a law that the Kentucky legislature had adopted. According to the editor, members of a congregation called the Pine Mountain Church of God, located at the remote community of Laurel Branch, Kentucky, had been arrested and were planning to test the law in court. Simmons carefully explained that "these Pine Mountain people who claim to be the Church of God are not the Church of God [of Cleveland, Tennessee] and their leader is a polygamist and a fugitive from justice and has no recognition from us."[66]

In the early 1940s and the years following World War II, the Church of God attempted to dissociate itself completely from the unpopular practice of snake handling. In the postwar period, the church denounced the practice and denied any connection with any snake-handling sect. Church leaders also chose to discount the practice in the early development of the organization. Church historian Charles W. Conn devoted a single footnote to the subject in his history of the church, *Like a Mighty Army*. He maintained that this "spiritual defect" had taken hold only briefly and in isolated sections of the South. Both contentions are incorrect. The practice of snake handling began in 1910, and, despite the church's repudiation in 1928, members continued to handle the poisonous reptiles well into the 1930s. Although this twenty- to thirty-year period is relatively short compared to the one-hundred-year existence of the denomination, it was a considerable span of time and an important period in the development of the early Church of God. Nor was the practice confined to remote sections in the South. In fact, Church of God members from Michigan to Florida handled serpents.

Conn again was mistaken when he argued that F.J. Lee, the

general overseer in the 1923–28 period, had discounted the practice among church members. If Conn based his opinion on a cursory examination of two letters that he cited, he may have thought his contention was true; but he did not explain *why* Lee had minimized the eccentric practice. The overseer had received a letter in 1926 regarding the possibility of amalgamating the Church of God and the Assemblies of God.[67] It is apparent from the related correspondence that Lee was interested in the possible union. The Assemblies of God had condemned snake handling, and Lee's attempt to minimize the extent of the practice within the Church of God served his efforts at union.

Later Lee refused to deny the practice of snake handling, when the material interest of the organization led in a different direction. In this instance, Jennie Crawford, who proposed to donate property upon which to build a Church of God, inquired about the sect's position on snake handling.[68] Lee replied by letter, "We do not claim that everyone had [sic] to handle them, but if any should handle them under the power of God, others should not rise up against them."[69] However discreditable we may think it now, the irrefutable fact remains that the practice of snake handling was a key element in early Church of God practice.

Like other new religious groups, this Holiness-Pentecostal sect developed some eccentric practices in its early years. These created an unfavorable public image. As a result, many Americans viewed Pentecostalism with suspicion or contempt. As the Church of God began its rise into mainstream conservative evangelicalism, the organization discarded many of these unusual practices; however, many years passed before the Church of God became a respectable middle-class denomination.

CHAPTER 5

Your Daughters Shall Prophesy

When the Church of God was organized, American society denied women many rights that it permitted to men. States prohibited women from voting. In some areas women were not allowed to own property. Although many women worked in mills and factories, prejudice denied them equal opportunity and equal pay. They were expected to abide by a double standard of morality. Such oppressive conditions spawned a crusade for women's rights. By the turn of the twentieth century, women had rebelled against social and economic handicaps as well as the Victorian stereotype of the helpless female whose "place was in the home." By 1900 legal disadvantages of women slowly had begun to disappear.

Church of God members, like many religious conservatives, refused to accept the demands of the new twentieth-century woman. Male members believed that woman's place was in the home and that she should take care of domestic matters, including the rearing of children. The instruction of Proverbs 22:6— "Train up a child in the way he should go: and when he is old, he will not depart from it"—was taken by Church of God parents to mean that they should instruct their children in the Holiness-Pentecostal tradition. All indications are that most of this parental responsibility fell to mothers, because fathers worked and spent much of their spare time on church activities.[1]

Although some male members felt that their female counterparts should serve only in the home, more progressive churchmen believed that women should have an active role in the church. One recent Church of God educator suggests that "because the Church of God was formed in an attempt to separate itself from the pulls of society, women were not restricted in its early days to the same extent that they were restricted in other denominations."[2] Unlike mainstream churches, the Church of God afforded women the opportunity for active service within most departments. The extent of this participation became an issue before the General Assembly in 1907. At this meeting, church officials learned that membership rolls contained more females than males. Enlightened by this statistic, churchmen realized that women workers could be a valuable factor in the church's growth and concluded that this source of strength had to be utilized.[3]

Consequently women played a variety of roles in the early Church of God, serving as ministers, missionaries, church clerks, teachers, musicians, and matrons of church orphanages. The first clergy was all male, but because evangelism was considered so imperative, the Church of God allowed female members who felt "the call" to preach. During this same time, most Protestant denominations banned women from preaching, arguing that Pauline injunctions (1 Corinthians 14:34—"Let your women keep silence") prohibited females from teaching or speaking in public assemblies. Although Church of God leaders were biblical literalists, they proved capable of accommodating theology to social reality. Departing from mainline Protestants on the role of women, they cited Acts 21:9, a passage which speaks of Philip's four daughters, who were prophetesses, as the biblical authority for allowing females to preach. They also argued that the prophecy of Joel 2:28—"Your daughters shall prophesy"—indicated that spirit-filled women could proclaim God's word.

By 1907, the Church of God was one of the few religious bodies to allow its female members actively to engage in a pulpit ministry. These women ministers were called female deacons and may have had the same rights as their male counterparts, although this is not certain. In 1907, the sect had three separate categories of ministers: bishops (ordained ministers), deacons, and evangelists.[4]

This apparent equality of female ministers ended abruptly

when the delegates to the 1909 General Assembly decided that there was no precept or example in the New Testament authorizing the ordination of women.[5] This decision restricted the ministry of women because it placed administrative powers and authority exclusively in the hands of male ordained ministers. The decision also marked a turning point in women's ministries. From this time forward, females gravitated into other fields of service.

Despite their subordinate role, Church of God women preached indefatigably. Although relatively few women pastored churches in the early years, there were numerous lady evangelists. Many evangelized locally, but others went on lengthy tours throughout the Southeast, risking abuse by opponents of Pentecostalism. Many men who emerged later as leading Church of God clergymen were converted and received the Pentecostal experience (the baptism of the Holy Spirit) in revival meetings that were conducted by female evangelists. In 1910, one of the best-known Church of God evangelists, J.W. Buckalew, received the Pentecostal blessing in a revival conducted by a female preacher in Boaz, Alabama.[6]

Lady preachers often established Church of God congregations in new areas. After receiving the Holy Spirit baptism, Lou Etta Lamb, a former Methodist, started a Church of God in Artesia, Mississippi, in 1917. She conducted the first meetings in her home. Feeling a stronger need "to serve the people," she devoted her life to fulltime evangelism. As a result, she started a dozen churches throughout Mississippi, Oklahoma, and Tennessee during the early years of the organization.[7] Life was difficult for these traveling female evangelists because, like Mrs. Lamb, many were widows who had to support families. These ladies assumed the multiple responsibilities of breadwinner, mother, father, and preacher.[8] Under such awesome burdens, they performed admirably.

Mrs. Lamb's ministry also demonstrated another quality of early churchwomen. When the pastor of a Negro church—the Black Free Spirit Church—in Artesia, Mississippi, resigned his pastorate, members of the congregation asked Mrs. Lamb to preach for them. A black man from this church told her that none of the preachers in town would help because they considered the congregation just a "bunch of niggers." Crossing the racial barrier, Mrs. Lamb accepted the invitation and preached on Sunday afternoons for two years until the black congregation obtained a pastor.[9]

Although female preachers made great contributions to church growth, the inaccessibility of ordination diminished their authority and precluded them from major positions in the church hierarchy. In 1913, the General Assembly further reduced the authority of women preachers when it denied them the right to perform marriages.[10] The creation in 1916 of the Body of Elders, which limited membership to ordained males, excluded female preachers and laywomen from all business transactions. Church of God educator Carolyn Dirksen points out that "only at the lowest level of this rapidly growing hierarchy were women encouraged to participate."[11]

Active in the pulpit ministry, women also served as foreign missionaries, introducing the Church of God into Egypt, Palestine, Grand Turk Island, China, Mexico, Costa Rica, St. Vincent, St. Lucia, St. Kitts, Cuba, Chile, Angola, Honduras, Rhodesia, and Tunisia. The overseas evangelistic impetus of the organization appears to have been directed by females, just as they dominated domestic evangelism.[12]

Lillian Thrasher, like most of the early Church of God preachers, paid for her own mission to Egypt in 1910. She had the distinction of being the first Church of God missionary who went abroad to spread the Pentecostal message.[13] Walter Hollenweger, in his excellent study *The Pentecostals*, includes Thrasher in the category of women with "theatrical talents," among whom Aimee Semple McPherson was the outstanding example. The Pentecostal historian explains:

> These are women preachers who by their dominating motherly personality, their beauty, and their outstanding and genuinely theatrical talents play the same role in the Pentecostal movement as great actresses in the rest of society. Women with such talents would, as members of traditional churches, take up careers as actresses or singers. But because

these callings are taboo for Pentecostals, the pentecostal "actresses" have no other course than to transform the calling of a woman preacher in such a way that it can be carried out by an actress.[14]

Thrasher founded an orphanage in Assuit, Egypt, in 1910 which served as home for many Egyptian children. She taught the children rudiments of education, at the same time introducing them to Pentecostal religion. Within five years, she had taken fifty-one orphans into her home. Operating on a slim budget, she wrote a letter in 1915 to the Church of God headquarters in Cleveland, Tennessee, asking for help; but she received very little assistance. By 1917, the orphanage contained eighty children and the monthly budget had increased to $250 per month. The Egyptians held Mrs. Thrasher in high esteem and indigenous friends, not her church, provided most of the financial assistance for the Assuit orphanage. Because of its lack of interest and financial support, by 1920 Lillian Thrasher had left the Church of God. She later joined the Assemblies of God and became one of the most celebrated missionaries in the world. Because of her work and her devotion, she was called "Nile Mother" by the Egyptian people.[15]

Another Church of God missionary, Lucy M. Leatherman of Green Castle, Indiana, preached the Pentecostal message to the people of South America. Leatherman had worked as a missionary in Egypt and Palestine before joining the Church of God in Valdosta, Georgia. After uniting with the sect, she went to Chile in 1916 and conducted numerous revival campaigns before going to Buenos Aires, Argentina. In Argentina she played an instrumental role in helping to establish the organization there.[16]

Even though the initial attempts of Mrs. Brinson Rushin to found a permanent Church of God congregation in China ended in failure, she worked tirelessly among the Chinese. Leaving her home in Valdosta, Georgia, she went to China in 1914 and worked in the northern province of Shantung. For almost ten years, her work seemed a prominent interest of the American Church of God. In 1916 she successfully opened two Pentecostal missions, but it was not until 1921 that a church was established in Tsinanfu. The church was short-lived, but Rushin had planted the Pentecostal message in the hearts and minds of a few converts.[17]

Although female Church of God preachers held a more exalted position and labored under fewer restrictions than lay members, they continued to work within a limited ministerial framework. Dirksen maintains that the church alloted females equality during the organization's formative years. She contends that "every member, including women, evangelized, attended business sessions, spoke and voted at the General Assembly and had a viable voice in the affairs of the Church."[18] Without offering documentary evidence, Dirksen suggests that women had voting privileges until the sect created the Body of Elders in 1916, which consisted only of ordained ministers. Because women could not be ordained, this excluded them from the decision-making process.[19] In an otherwise excellent unpublished article, she may be incorrect about this Church of God policy. The early *Minutes* of the organization do not indicate that women were given the right to vote on church business; on the contrary, there are numerous indications that women kept silent during these meetings. In fact, some evidence suggests that females were not even allowed to debate the issues during business sessions of the General Assembly.[20]

Most Church of God leaders interpreted 1 Corinthians 14:34—"Let your women keep silence"—to mean that females were not to take part in church business or to hold high church offices. A few Pentecostals outside the Church of God insisted that the Apostle Paul spoke of conditions that existed under Old Testament law, and that Christians no longer lived under law but under grace. These progressive churchmen argued that women should be assigned full equality with men. Some Church of God members agreed, but A.J. Tomlinson, reflecting the beliefs of the majority of clergymen, wrote, "I am frank to repudiate such erroneous teaching that will lead others who are innocent and unlearned and unthoughtful into gross error."[21] Churchmen instructed women not to expect such equality and considered any attempt to gain such power as scripturally-forbidden usurpation of authority over men. Tomlinson explained, "That is the very thing that got Adam and the whole human race into trouble."[22] Revealing his Victorianism, he maintained that woman, being the weaker sex, was easily deceived. He further asserted that "to get out from under the care and protection of men she is liable to be influenced into wrong teaching."[23] Tomlinson cited Mary Baker Eddy as an example of a woman who had been tricked into believing such false teaching as Christian Science, which he called "a menace to civilization."[24] While blasting women preachers who taught "false doctrine," Tomlinson conveniently ignored the fact that it was the fanatical teachings of a male that nearly destroyed the early Church of God, leading to a heavy loss of members and the 1902 reorganization of the denomination.[25] Church of God leaders often denounced the work of women preachers, mostly non-Pentecostals, with whom they disagreed, but praised female Pentecostal evangelists such as Aimee Semple McPherson.[26]

The exclusion of females from high administrative positions became apparent as the church grew. By the mid-1920s, the church hierarchy included officials on district, state, and national levels. It also included numerous permanent boards and committees. Ordained ministers, exclusively males, held all elected or appointed positions. Because the church refused to ordain women, it prohibited them from holding such positions. In 1926, the Church of God established a precedent when it allowed the Executive Committee—composed of the general overseer, editor and publisher, and superintendent of education—to appoint members of all boards and committees. This action further restricted the role of females.[27]

Church officials did encourage women to serve as church clerks, a secretary-treasurer position in the local church. By 1920, at least one-third of all clerks in the Church of God were female. This was by necessity, not design, since many of the early churches did not have a male member who was qualified or competent to hold the office. This position required keeping accurate business and membership records. As part of their responsibilities, clerks attended all business sessions (comprised exclusively of male members) and kept the minutes of such meetings but were forbidden to participate in the discussions or voting.[28]

Clerical leaders also encouraged women to perform other jobs for the church. As the nation drafted young Church of God men into military service during World War I, general overseer Tomlinson noticed a decline in the growth of the church. Believing that promoting the "Kingdom of God" was more important than the war effort, he urged women to participate actively in church work. Some Church of God preachers objected. In reply, Tomlinson wrote:

> I have heard of some of our men being very much opposed to women acting as Sunday School superintendents, or even teaching classes or having any active part in the church work, but it is time now for them to leave off such fanatical notions for if the men are taken away we will have the women to fill their places, because the work has to be done. . . . By saying this, I do not mean that the women shall have the pre-eminence and exercise authority above all of the men.[29]

Apart from the numerous achievements of women preachers, female members of the laity often played an instrumental role in founding new congregations. After hearing the Pentecostal message in Atlanta, Georgia, Emma L. Boyd and Ella Fry returned to Dahlonega and held religious meetings in their homes. A Pentecostal revival resulted, attracting increased attendance by local residents. To house them, the congregation built a small frame church. Along with prosperity came intense persecution, including harassment and destruction of church property. Undaunted, the two ladies continued to hold services. In 1910, the small congregation united with the Church of God.[30]

Women also took an active part in the formation of Church of God Sunday schools, as an effective means of teaching the gospel and a source of new evangelistic opportunities. Females served in leadership roles in these schools. In 1917, church members raised the question of whether women could serve as Sunday school superintendents. The church declared not only that they could serve, but added, "Sometimes they make the very best superintendents."[31] Females also were active on the district and state levels of Christian education work, at least until the organization created a national Department of Christian Education. Afterward, women continued to labor in the Sunday schools but only on a local level. Males held all state and national leadership positions.

Women also were prominent in establishing Church of God orphanages. After Lillian Thrasher founded the first successful home for children in Assuit, Egypt, in 1910, many other Church of God members tried to establish orphanages in the United States, but initial attempts failed.[32] Mr. and Mrs. William F. Bryant began an orphanage in their home in 1911. Later they rented a house and hired two ladies to care for fifteen homeless children. For unknown reasons, the orphanage closed within a year.[33] At the 1919 General Assembly, A.J. Tomlinson, in his opening address, reiterated the need for a Church of God orphanage and appealed to his audience for help. More than a thousand delegates responded to this need and pledged more than six thousand dollars toward the founding of an orphanage. Church officials rented a building in Cleveland, Tennessee, and opened Orphanage No. 1 on 17 December 1920. The church employed Lillian Kinsey of Pell City, Alabama, as matron and placed four young children under her care.[34] The responsibility of collecting funds for maintaining the orphanage fell upon the shoulders of two other women, Nannie Ruth Hagewood and Ella Hilsabeck, who had helped to establish the home. Although women helped create and maintain the home, when a supervisory committee called the Orphanage Board was formed in 1920, it consisted only of males. Female membership was prohibited.[35]

Although women were not responsible for creating the first Church of God school, its first instructor was female. As early as 1911, church leaders realized that the church needed a school for the training of young men and women. The loss to other Christian institutions of some young adult members who wanted a better education greatly disturbed church leaders. One churchman explained that "some of our young men . . . have gone to other schools, and as a result they have fallen into influence that opposed the Church of God and we have lost them entirely."[36] Delegates at each subsequent General Assembly discussed this pressing issue, but each time they concluded that sufficient funds were not available for the founding of a school. Finally, the Church of God opened its first Bible Training School on 1 January 1918, with twelve students, seven of whom were women. After much consideration, the church hired Nora Chambers, a former student at Holmes Bible School in Greenville, South Carolina, as the first instructor. She served in this capacity until 1920.[37]

Working with Church of God youth was another area in which women excelled. The female most responsible for this development was Alda B. Harrison. The wife of a Presbyterian minister, Harrison joined the Church of God, although her husband never did. The fact that her companion never became a member apparently did not handicap her work with Church of God young people. Nor did her age at conversion (fifty-four) hinder her enthusiasm or her ability to work with members of a younger generation.[38]

Beginning in 1923, Harrison organized a Young People's Band. This small group became the nucleus of the church's national youth organization, established in 1929. She also founded and published *Lighted Pathway*, a youth-oriented magazine. She published the magazine at her own expense for its first eight years, until the church took over in 1937 and began publishing it monthly. Then the church hired Harrison, who served as its editor until her retirement in 1948.[39]

Women's organizations provided females in other denominations, including Pentecostal ones, some of their first experiences in leadership. In 1928, Alda Harrison suggested that the Church of God organize the efforts of women. Workers then could care more effectively for the sick and needy, visit prospective church members, and raise funds for various projects. Harrison explained that the organization could be called the Dorcas Society.[40]

Another Church of God member, Mrs. S.J. Wood, wife of a Church of God minister then pastoring in Electra, Texas, founded a women's group that later became a department within the church administration. Because of her concern for church finances, on 16 November 1929 she organized the Ladies' Willing Worker Band to help raise money for the church. This idea spread rapidly, and local groups were organized.[41]

When the Great Depression struck in 1930, many Church of God members believed that such fundraising organizations were absolutely necessary. Not all members agreed. Some males

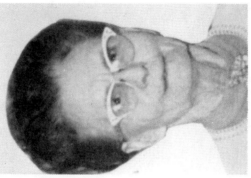

(Left): Alda B. Harrison, founder of the *Lighted Pathway*. *(Hal Bernard Dixon, Jr., Pentecostal Research Center, Cleveland, Tenn.)*

(Right): Mrs. S. J. Woods, founder of the Church of God Ladies' Willing Worker Band *(Hal Bernard Dixon, Jr., Pentecostal Research Center, Cleveland, Tenn.)*

argued that fundraising projects were demeaning to the work of God; what church members needed to do was to pray and have faith that God would supply all the church's financial needs. One churchman maintained that "if we won't belittle the work and resort to small, sorry methods of our own, God will give us large amounts as we have faith for."[42] For a few, faith was the only proper solution, but most members believed the scriptural admonition that "faith without works is dead." Faith and hard work proved to be the answer to the church's financial inadequacy. Despite criticism, the LWWB proved a valuable asset to the church. Within five or six years, congregations organized local chapters. Reports from these groups flooded the office of the *Evangel* during the 1930s, telling of their success in raising funds to remodel old buildings, construct new ones, pay debts, furnish parsonages, and supplement pastors' salaries, and in conducting countless other projects.[43]

The Ladies' Willing Worker Band was such a vital arm of the Church of God organization that the General Assembly in 1936 made it a part of the general church program. The church encouraged each congregation to establish a local chapter and elect a president, vice president, and secretary-treasurer. Although the officers were women, the local LWWB was placed under the direct supervision of the pastor, a male in most cases, an arrangement which did not seem to displease most women.[44]

In the post–World War II period, the Ladies' Willing Worker Band proved an important arena for women who wanted to be active in the ministry of the church but who consistently found their roles restricted. The women's organization gave females an opportunity to participate in a crucial area and to feel that their work was just as important to the church as that of males. As the Church of God continued to restrict the role of women, more and more seemed to find satisfaction in being "Willing Workers."

Mrs. Wood, the LWWB founder, reported that, besides the primary task of fundraising, women could "visit and pray for the sick, visit the hospitals, go and invite people to church, distribute literature, and many other things."[45]

In the decades of the 1950s and 1960s, the Church of God rapidly added new members, many of them from the middle class. During this period, the Ladies' Willing Worker Band became involved in nonreligious issues. The leaders of some local chapters encouraged ladies to become active in "PTA's and other worthy civic organizations where their influence could be effective for God, the church, and the community."[46] Such participation outside the spiritual realm reflects the influence of middle-class values and concerns, as well as the church's move into mainstream conservative evangelicalism.

In 1964, the women's organization had grown in numbers and influence to such an extent that the Church of God created a separate women's department.[47] The church appointed Dr. Ellen French, a former missionary and faculty member at Lee College, as the first executive secretary to coordinate the department's efforts. In 1966, LWWB started publishing its own magazine, *The Willing Worker*. At the meeting of the General Assembly in 1970, the church agreed to a name change, to reflect broader goals. The Ladies' Willing Worker Band would become the Ladies Auxiliary. At this meeting, Ladies Auxiliary leaders introduced numerous new groups to the organization, such as the Young Ladies Auxiliary.[48]

As the Ladies Auxiliary activities further broadened, the church changed the name of the organization in 1982 from Ladies Auxiliary to Department of Ladies Ministries.[49] This vital arm of the church continued to raise substantial amounts of money. By 1986, the organization was raising more than ten million dollars annually, although fundraising was only a part of its mission.[50]

Church of God women continued to discover opportunities for service outside the traditional realm of the "pulpit ministry," because fewer and fewer women took on that role. Since the early days of the church, the number of female ministers (that is, ones holding credentials) had consistently declined. In 1913, women had comprised about 30 percent of the ministers, but by 1987 that number had fallen to less than 3 percent.[51]

After World War II, the Church of God stressed more traditional roles for females. Articles in church publications informed women of their proper role as wives. Officers of the Department of Ladies Ministries reinforced this conservative attitude by en-

couraging females to accept and be content with such roles. Edna
Conn, president of the Ladies Auxiliary and wife of general overseer Charles W. Conn, wrote in 1961 that "the primary place of
women [sic] is by the side of her husband, as a wife and home-
maker and the mother of his children."[52] The church reminded
females that women were the weaker sex and must be dependent upon their husbands. Avis Swiger explained that it might
not "always be easy for you to keep your place . . . but keep it you
must!"[53]

Motherhood was another traditional role that the organization
emphasized. Church leaders extolled the virtues of the Christian mother. Some clergymen argued that the greatest roles
a woman could play were as wife and mother. "Regardless of
what else a woman may achieve," contended one churchman,
"she has not experienced God's best for her until she has filled
these two offices."[54] Church leaders also distinguished between
a woman who simply gave birth to a child and one who was a
"true" mother. One official maintained that "no embittered, sar-
donic, pants-wearing, cigarette-smoking, liquor-drinking, nasty-
tongued, club-loving, child-despising woman has any right to call
herself a 'mother' even though she may have brought children
into the world."[55]

Clergymen made declarations such as this in response to the
disruption of society during the 1960s, 1970s, and 1980s. The
Women's Rights Movement and the Equal Rights Amendment
threatened traditional social values, mores, and roles. Intellectuals, feminists, radical students, and liberal religious leaders
seemed to be undermining middle-class values and morals.

Many female church members were both wives and mothers
but also worked for pay. The Church of God taught that these
working mothers were ambassadors of Christ. Christian businesswomen witnessed to their fellow workers, ministered to the
needs of colleagues, and earned income which allowed them to
contribute to the work of the church. Businesswoman Barbara
Page pointed out that, in many small Church of God congregations where females greatly outnumbered males, it was the
contributions of females that kept the local church operating.[56]

The Church of God also encouraged women to be content

serving in nonpublic roles. Because the organization did not allow females to hold positions high in the hierarchy, women did not receive the recognition and credit they deserved. The church informed them that recognition was unimportant. What really mattered was that God took notice and kept an accurate record of their efforts. In 1963, Edna Conn noted that often a woman "must perform tedious tasks that will have their reckoning only in eternity."[57]

Not all churchwomen were willing to serve in such subordinate roles. Although the number of female ministers had decreased significantly by the 1980s, some women wanted equal access to opportunities available to men including ordination. Younger, better educated females felt "the call" to preach, and pursued the ministry as their vocation. The male-dominated administration severely restricted the rights and privileges of female ministers, and as women discovered these restrictions, some became resigned, others revolted, and some left the organization altogether. A few decided to fight for equal rights.

Emma Sue Webb is an excellent example of a woman who sought to change the church. Webb had been affiliated with the Church of God since childhood. In the early 1970s, she became a pastor. Soon she found that her ministry was limited, a circumstance that caused her much hardship and personal anguish. After entering graduate school in California in the late 1970s, she completed a master's thesis on "The Limitations On Women Ministers in the Church of God" in summer 1981. In this work she related her efforts to promote the idea of ordaining females, including writing a lengthy letter in 1977 to Church of God general overseer Cecil B. Knight. His response reiterated the usual reasons for the church's refusal to ordain females.[58]

The role of women in the Church of God has been both unique and paradoxical. Their access to the pulpit contrasted sharply with the usual Pentecostal policy of subordinating women, demonstrating that even biblical literalists choose scriptural passages selectively, to some degree tailoring theology to social reality. The church excluded women from leadership positions and restricted their roles by refusing to ordain females. Consequently, the number of female ministers declined significantly between 1913 and

1987. Church of God women, however, discovered other opportunities for service through the Department of Ladies Ministries, where they made outstanding contributions. As thousands of middle-class Americans joined the church after World War II, the organization adopted conservative mainstream values, including the notion that women should be content with their roles as wives and mothers.

CHAPTER 6

Turn the Other Cheek

When the flames of war engulfed Europe in summer 1914, Church of God loyalists believed that there was little possibility of a global war which would involve the United States. The moral climate of Progressivism, together with advances in popular democracy, social justice, and scientific achievement, fortified the belief that civilization had reached the point of abolishing war.

Even more important than Progressivism in sustaining the notion that war was unlikely was the nation's isolationist tradition. Although weakened by the Pan-Americanism and imperialism of the late nineteenth century, isolationism remained strong. Since the early days of the republic, America's leaders had believed that the United States had no stake in the quarrels of European nations. American isolationists remembered that George Washington had admonished, "The great rule of conduct for us in regard to foreign nations is, in extending our commercial relations to have with them as little political connection as possible."[1] Americans believed that their peace and security rested upon political and geographical isolation from the Old World. The proclamation of neutrality issued by President Woodrow Wilson expressed American public opinion as well as traditional policy.

The Church of God lauded Wilson's proclamation of 4 October 1914 as a day of national prayer for peace in Europe. General overseer A.J. Tomlinson wrote: "It is a great source of gratitude to us to read and know that the chief executive of our great nation has attributed such high honors to the father of our Lord

Jesus Christ by expressing himself thus."[2] Tomlinson encouraged members to pray for peace but, more importantly, to beg that God would save and fill fellow Americans with the Holy Spirit as they humbled themselves on this special day. This was the last word of praise given by the Church of God for any aspect of the war.

Until the 1916 presidential election, two ideologies split the country into opposing camps. The powerful peace movement, which the Church of God endorsed, supported mediation. The other group favored military preparedness as the best way of keeping the United States out of the conflict. The latter movement gained considerable strength from the submarine crisis with Germany in 1915 and from the disclosure of German plots against American security. Initially Wilson opposed a military buildup, but with the sinking of the *Lusitania*, he changed his views in favor of preparedness. When Wilson announced his new defense program on 4 November 1915, he created an immediate storm of opposition, particularly among rural southerners. Some Church of God members saw his plan as moving America another step closer to involvement in a war that did not concern their nation.[3]

In 1916, the Democratic party renominated Wilson and adopted the campaign slogan, "He kept us out of war." Although divided on the issues of neutrality and preparedness, the Republicans nominated Charles Evans Hughes, an associate justice of the Supreme Court and former governor of New York. The Republican campaign possessed many weaknesses, but its greatest was its association with huge defense spending advocates such as Teddy Roosevelt, who delivered bellicose speeches in favor of universal training and denounced Wilson as a weakling and a coward. Wilson won the election by only a slim margin of electoral votes.

While Church of God members seem to have been primarily Republicans who lived in traditional GOP strongholds, they also belonged to a religious organization which was strongly pacifist. Those members who planned to vote in the 1916 presidential race faced a dilemma. If they voted Republican, they would be aligning themselves with the party that was tainted by military preparedness and jingoism. To vote otherwise would be to desert the Republican party. Although the precise number of Church of God voters can not be ascertained, many of those who voted cast their ballots for Hughes, the Republican nominee, apparently in opposition to their religious ideology.[4] As pacifists, Church of God members theoretically should have voted for Wilson. There are a number of possible explanations for the pro-Hughes position taken by Pentecostals who supported him. They may have looked to the midwestern, noninterventionist wing of the Republican party as justification. The church also undoubtedly contained members who were not pacifists. Moreover, church members may have disagreed with some of Wilson's domestic policies, such as regulation of railroads. Members may have voted political tradition rather than religious ideology. Whatever their reasons for voting Republican, nearly all of the states in which church members resided supported Wilson in 1916.

Less than six months after the election, Congress adopted a joint resolution declaring war against Germany. The decision to enter the war drew criticism from clerical leaders within the Church of God, who voiced a variety of criticisms. Church of God leaders accused European diplomats of insensitivity and ineptitude because of their refusal to negotiate terms of peace in 1917. "Fond hopes of millions have been blasted," explained one church leader, "and it seems that those in authority [who] could have some control, care for none of these things. They seem to value human life as nothing."[5] Reflecting the Old Testament concept of collective guilt, according to which the entire population was responsible for the sins of an individual, Church of God adherents believed that the United States had become entangled in the war because of national sins. They believed that America, because its citizens had adopted hedonistic practices, had become a "proud" and "boastful" nation. Some churchmen compared the licentious conduct of Americans to that of ancient Romans and Greeks and reminded their countrymen of the consequences of such low morals. Some Pentecostal clerics believed that the only way to bring the nation back to the standards of Christian humility was for God to allow war to come upon the American people. Reflecting this opinion, A.J. Tomlinson hypothesized, "He [God] will have to bring about a state of humility that does not now exist, and how do we know but what this is to be accomplished by passing us over into the power of Satan for the destruction of our pride and haughtiness. 1 Corinthians 5:5."[6] The idea that war was a result of divine judgment had strong precedent in Christian theology.

Church of God clergymen also ascribed war to the forces of darkness. In Pentecostal thought, demons emanated from the pits of hell, causing war which dealt death and misery to mankind. In describing the expansion of the war, a concerned Church of God clergyman remarked, "It seems that the long demon-like claws are reaching out after new territory to drag other nations into the struggle."[7] The Church of God also attributed the consequences of war to demons. The editor of the *Evangel*, A.J. Tomlinson, wrote: "The awful war devil is still slaying his millions. His greed and thirst for blood is never satisfied. He is agitating war on every hand. He is dragging millions of souls into his cruel grasp."[8]

Churchmen also used vivid imagery to describe war. Employing descriptive symbolism was not new, nor was it unique to the Church of God. One of the most common Church of God symbols for the war was the great "iron hand." Fearful of American military involvement, Tomlinson warned that "the great iron hand seems to be slowly closing in on our own beloved land. In many places . . . our sons are dragged from the parental nest and are hurried away to the front. Some of our own church members have already had . . . their boys pulled away from them by the cruel monster."[9]

Church of God leaders characterized war as a "feeder of hell" which increased the population of the region of the damned. Young men were "snatched away from life so suddenly by satan's belching cannons and the devil's war artillery [that] they had no time to repent."[10] The thought of great masses dying without the saving grace of Jesus Christ was yet another argument against war.

The war motivated Church of God preachers to greater urgency in spreading the gospel. Churchmen believed that they lived in the "last days"; but the saints need not worry because "the Lord has been trying to prepare His children for this time." [11] Pentecostals were not to fret over the situation, for they were under divine orders and had an immense job to accomplish. As Tomlinson stated, "He [Christ] has one place for such as these [sanctified saints]. A place of rest and quietness, and at the same time they should be engaged in the most active service for Him." [12]

Apocalyptic rhetoric became more pronounced as the international crisis deepened. Wondering if World War I was the beginning of the apocalypse, Tomlinson wrote in 1916 that "people who know about it [the war] are almost breathlessly wondering if Washington's vision will yet be fulfilled. It is said that, in a vision, the 'father of our country' saw this country laid waste by the ravages of war—a later war than the civil war of the 'sixties.'" [13]

By the time the United States entered the war in 1917, some Church of God members no longer doubted that World War I was to initiate the apocalypse. C.A. Churchill, a prominent clergyman, confidently stated that "God's people are aware of the fact that this is the last great conflict." [14] Many Church of God people believed that they lived in the days when the rapture of the church would occur. In view of this belief, clergymen warned members "to live in constant expectancy of our Lord's return to redeem us from awful tribulations that it seems are almost ready to burst forth with all the hellish fury of his satanic majesty." [15] Such admonitions produced a strong sense of anxiety among the members, rendering them vigilant and making them feel that every facet or consequence of the war was another "sign of the times."

After America entered the war, church leaders looked for divine omens. Because of severe food shortages, government officials in England had no choice but to enforce a food rationing program. The government issued individuals food ration cards, and customers had to show their cards before they were allowed to make purchases. Many Church of God folk viewed such cards as indicative of the "mark of the beast." [16] In a reply to numerous queries from church members, Tomlinson explained, "I do not say this is the mark, but I do say that the spirit of the anti-christ is already working and it is becoming emboldened so as to march into our towns . . . commanding prices and placing a limit to the amount you purchase."[17] Church leaders also attributed the American government's powers of censorship to the Antichrist. One churchman complained that "we cannot communicate with our missionaries and friends across the sea without somebody opening the letters and reading the contents."[18]

Church of God members based most of their eschatological beliefs upon the idea that the Antichrist would possess great authority, and any person or government that exercised excessive powers was suspect. According to some clergymen, the entire war resulted from lust for power. As one confident church leader stated,

> The revelator [John, author of the Book of Revelation] tells us that this beast is given power to make war with the saints and overcome them. This war is already on. It is along about the time of the showing and exercising of great authority, and the overcoming of the saints that the mark of the beast will be placed on the foreheads or in the hands of the people.[19]

Churchmen advised members to refuse any such mark. To accept this identification meant allying with Satan and eternal damnation without any possibility of salvation. Summing up the hope of escaping such tribulation, another clergyman quoted a portion of a popular Church of God hymn:

> We may look for trouble
> And sorrows to come,
> But hold to God's strong arm;
> Till the battle's fought
> You'll be safe from all alarm.[20]

Because they believed that the "end time" was near, clergymen warned their parishioners not to get caught up in patriotic war fever. As it became more apparent that the United States would enter the war, general overseer Tomlinson wanted young men to know what their priorities should be. He left no room for doubt as to what the sect expected. "The war demon may try to persuade you that the first duty is to the stars and stripes," stated Tomlinson, "but this is a delusion."[21] With the sinking of four unarmed merchant vessels on 18 March 1917, the war fever spread even into the Great Plains and West, areas that previously had been strongly antiinterventionist. Church of God leaders, however, remained firm in their pacifist stand. On 31 March 1917, just two days before President Wilson called for war against Germany, church officials again warned against the excitement of war. Christians should remain calm and not allow misplaced enthusiasm to sway them: "If war is declared public speakers will soon be infesting our country to enthuse the war spirit into our young men to induce them to volunteer to fight for their country."[22]

It might appear to the casual observer that the Church of God spread a message of doom and despair instead of deliverance. Although there was an element of fatalism in their theology, most members apparently felt that they lived in the most exciting time in history, for this was the age in which they would be carried away to eternal bliss with their saviour. This rescue was viewed as the pinnacle of their otherworldly faith, and they wanted others to share in the rewards. The war was as much an opportunity for spreading the gospel as a warning of an impending Judgment Day.

Long before America entered World War I, Church of God ministers felt that, as members of Christ's church, their place was not on European battlegrounds but "on OUR battlefield winning precious lost souls for our Lord."[23] The battle of evangelism was far more important in the minds of these Pentecostals than any corporeal warfare. Tomlinson remarked, "We cannot afford to idle away our moments by taking an active hand in the world war."[24]

Pacifist sentiment was widespread in America, making it necessary for the government actively to promote public support for the war. To this end, on 14 April 1917, President Wilson signed a decree establishing the Committee on Public Information, with George Creel as chairman. The Creel Committee succeeded in selling the war to Americans, but at the price of fostering a spirit of conformity and intolerance. Its propaganda converted an existing fear of spies, saboteurs, and pro-German sympathizers into a hysterical hatred of all persons and organizations critical of American participation in the conflict. Patriots identified all dissenters with the enemy and pinned the badge of disloyalty on all who espoused unorthodox opinions. Vigilantes, including members of the American Protective League and the National Security League, were responsible for much of the hysteria and intolerance. They infringed upon civil liberties by using force to insure conformity. The passage of the Espionage Act of 1917 and the Sedition Act of 1918 codified these fears. Both laws provided stiff penalties for persons who obstructed draft recruitment. The Sedition Act further restricted free speech. The U.S. Justice Department conducted thousands of investigations and made numerous arrests for seditious utterances.[25]

After the United States officially entered the war in April 1917, the method of raising a large army provoked heated debate. Many Americans associated conscription with the draft laws of the Civil War, which had contained discriminatory provisions that enabled the rich and privileged to escape military service. Worse than that, some associated conscription with oppressive European governments. In the political controversy that erupted, Wilson favored conscription laws. After tumultuous debate, Congress passed the Selective Service Act on 18 May 1917. This act required all men between the ages of twenty-one and thirty to register for military service at local draft boards. Registrants were placed in one of five categories and called according to lottery numbers that were assigned to them.[26]

Many anticonscription groups, including the Church of God, vehemently opposed the draft. The question immediately arose as to whether or not church members should obey the law and register. If they did not comply, the consequence was imprisonment for up to one year, followed by forced registration in some branch of the military.[27] General overseer Tomlinson encouraged all male members between the ages of twenty-one and thirty to register on the date specified by the government. The chief executive of the Church of God declared, "We must obey the laws of our country so long as they do not conflict with the laws of God . . . but when the laws of our country are made to oppose the laws of the Bible we have to obey God and submit to the penalty."[28] On 2 June 1917, the Church of God gave precise instructions to its male members. While registering on June 5 as the law demanded, young men were encouraged to file for exemption "on the grounds that the church of which they are members objects to its members going to war."[29] Church officials further reminded prospective registrants that they could not take up arms and fight. Tomlinson advised these men, if drafted, to "plead for a place in the hospitals, relief corps, as chaplains or anything else besides taking a gun and going on the battlefield to fight."[30] About a month later, the sect published in the *Evangel* a long list of specific instructions for its men to follow in order to obtain an exemption. Leaders advised that anyone who did not understand the procedure for filing for exemption should obtain the assistance of a friend or lawyer who could help him. The Church of God expected its men to comply with its pacifist doctrine. To insure complicity, the organization warned:

> If any of our members should in any way advocate war, or try to persuade any of these registrants to go on to war, or urge or enthuse them into a desire to fight, such members will be considered disloyal to the Church and alas to the Christ of the Bible, and a continuance of the same may lead to the necessary action [expulsion] under our laws and principles.[31]

At its Thirteenth General Assembly, which was held 1–6 November 1917 at Harriman, Tennessee, the Church of God officially added to its list of teachings a statement that the church was "against members going to war."[32] More than five hundred delegates were in attendance, and the teaching passed by a "unanimous" vote. Pacificism later caused serious problems that had not been anticipated by church leaders.

The Church of God was successful in getting many of its men exempted from combat service. Because of this success, other Pentecostals who were friends of the sect but who were not members appealed to the church for help in obtaining draft deferments, but it refused assistance. One irritated clerical leader wrote sarcastically, "Pentecostal people ought to have seen something of the value of the great Church of God a long time ago. For years we have been heralding the message far and wide and trying to show those with whom we come in contact that the Church of God is a means of protection for God's children."[33]

For some church members, merely being exempted from military service was not enough. Many argued that they were forced by the government to aid the war effort by indirect means, such as the purchase at high cost of food and clothing, railroad tickets, postage stamps, revenue stamps, and war bonds. As one clergyman complained,

> It makes scarcely any difference what one engages in now, he is helping in the war more or less in some way. But we say we cannot kill; this is true, yet indirectly we are lending our assistance in the very thing our conscience condemns. We are helping to pull the triggers that fire the guns that take the lives of our fellow men. We do not want to do this but it is forced upon us.[34]

The government certainly did not single out the Church of God by forcing members to help pay the costs of war, but church members believed that they were being persecuted. This conclusion caused them to contemplate stronger resistance. Some considered not serving in the military under any circumstances. Tomlinson, who wielded considerable influence over Church of God people and policy, wrote,

> I could not take a gun and fire it at my fellow men even at the command of a military officer. I could submit to the penalty inflicted upon me for refusing, but I cannot kill. I doubt if I could take the obligation to become a soldier in the first place. I do not say that others should do so.[35]

Even though Tomlinson did not advise others to take this evasive course of action, the mere fact that the top church official, a man who was admired for his leadership and spiritual experience, gave such testimony served as a model. Perhaps Dave Allen, a member of the Church of God in northern Alabama, took Tomlinson's example literally. Within a few weeks of the publication of Tomlinson's article in the *Evangel*, Allen was brutally murdered, apparently by two law officers, for refusing to register for the draft. According to the testimony of Allen's wife, the two officers came to her home and asked for Dave Allen. Although her husband hid in his bedroom, one of the men asked Allen to come out and to hold his hands over his head. He did as he was instructed. The officers then handcuffed him and, for no apparent reason, beat him with their pistols until he was almost unconscious. After this brutal beating, the two law officers shot Allen twice in the chest, mortally wounding him.[36] J.B. Ellis, Alabama state overseer and author of the *Evangel* article that reported the incident, cautioned, "While we do not endorse the way he proceeded to evade war, yet we feel that from his viewpoint he might be classed among the martyrs. I am looking for the time to come when many of us will have to seal our testimony with our blood."[37]

Most followed the ideas of Tomlinson, although some Church of God clergymen apparently did not object to the military draft or resist supporting the war effort. These were few in number, however, and did not hold the highest positions or the most influence.[38]

Church of God leaders did not believe that the war was a righteous cause. Unlike other churches that acted patriotically once America entered the conflict, the Church of God remained immovable in its pacifism. Church leaders based their arguments on increasingly well-reasoned scriptural and ideological grounds. According to many churchmen, Jesus never favored war; on the contrary, "if they [the enemy] smite you on one cheek turn the other also."[39] Others argued that Christ's kingdom was not of this world; they were merely sojourners in this present world. The true citizenship of the otherworldly Pentecostals was in heaven. "If we are of the world, so we can take part in the wars," Tomlinson reasoned, "then we are not of His kingdom. We cannot be of the world and of the Lord at the same time. We cannot serve God and Mammon."[40] Church of God members believed that the Christian's proper response to war was the love of Christ, and clergymen pointed out that Scripture clearly taught believers to love their enemies, not to fight them.

A literal interpretation of the Bible taught that it was better to suffer wrong than to do wrong. Clerics advised members who were uncertain of this principle to ask the question, "What would Jesus do?" Afterwards, the Holy Spirit would reveal that fighting was not the answer.[41]

Ideologically, some Church of God clergymen believed that it was immoral to fight under any circumstances, even in a struggle for human rights. Although this attitude does not appear to have been pervasive among church members, a few espoused this philosophy. Unlike most Americans, who felt that World War I was a battle for democracy and human rights, some Church of God leaders did not believe in it at all. Taking Jesus as his example, Tomlinson replied to the war proponents, "If Jesus fought because His rights were trampled upon, then we should do the same. But where do we see Him slay the multitudes because they were trampling upon His rights?"[42] Pacifist church members believed that they held a "divine calling." To participate in the war effort would be to compromise their calling, which was inconceivable. They expected God to fight their battles while they spread the gospel to a lost and dying world.[43]

Because of its strident opposition to the war, the Church of God came under scrutiny by the Federal Bureau of Investigation. The probe began when the U.S. Solicitor of the Post Office Department concluded that several issues of the *Evangel* were unmailable under the Espionage and Sedition Acts.[44] Solicitor W.H. Lamar notified the FBI about the matter, and the agency assigned special agent James T. Finlay to the case.[45]

Investigations of religious pacifists were a common occurrence during the period 1917–18. Holiness-Pentecostal sects occupied much time of Justice Department agents. Almost all of these groups bitterly opposed the war and did not hesitate to preach and publish their pacifist beliefs. Legal authorities arrested many Pentecostals throughout the country, including some Church of God clergymen. Because of their opposition to war, the patriotism and sincerity of Pentecostals became suspect. Many Americans fancied them as radicals and anarchists who wore the cloak of religion to conceal their true identity. This compounded the negative public stereotype already emerging because of ecstatic and emotional conduct among Pentecostals. Investigative reports contained derogatory remarks concerning "holy rollers." D.S. Vinn's FBI report vilified Pentecostals and even accused their religious meetings of fostering sexual indiscretions. He declared:

> The ignorant class and lawless element are its followers . . . numerous arrests have been made for disorderly actions at their meetings and as a matter of fact their meetings, running as they do well into the morning hours, are nothing more than whore houses and are responsible for numerous cases of young girls being wronged.[46]

At the request of U.S. Attorney W.T. Kennerly of Knoxville, Tennessee, the FBI sent agent F.S. Shipp to investigate certain members of the Church of God who were suspected of spreading disloyal propaganda. Shipp instructed J.L. Scott, pastor of the Church of God at Ridgedale, Tennessee, to report to the FBI office in Chattanooga for interrogation concerning "seditious references [in a sermon] delivered by him on June 26, 1918."[47] During the questioning, Scott informed the agent that he, like all Church of God ministers, received his "instructions and inspiration" from the organizational hierarchy which A.J. Tomlinson headed as general overseer. Agent Shipp then departed for Cleveland, Tennessee, to interview Tomlinson. During the interrogation, the top church official stated the sect's antiwar position, which the investigator considered unsatisfactory. Shipp asked if Church of God members would make good soldiers in combat service. Tomlinson replied that they would not, because such service was against the religious principles of the church. Shipp pressed the issue, asking if members who were taken into combat service would shoot into the air if they engaged in battle with Germans, rather than killing the enemy. Tomlinson stated that Church of God people would rather be killed than kill their fellowman. At the conclusion of the interview, the FBI agent confiscated various pamphlets, books, leaflets, and records. He also obtained the mailing list of all *Evangel* subscribers (approximately six thousand) and various issues of the publication which had been declared unmailable by the U.S. Justice Department. He sent this material to FBI headquarters in Washington, D.C. It was Shipp's opinion that "this will not stop issues of seditious copies of the *Evangel* going through the mails, for the reason that the two copies sent to Washington are sent out at the same time as those mailed to subscribers."[48] The agent also stated that as the "higher up" man in the organization, Tomlinson was responsible for the disloyal propaganda spread by Church of God clergymen; however, the FBI made no formal charges.

Tomlinson was fortunate compared to other Pentecostal ministers who were arrested, tried, and convicted under the Sedition Act.[49] During the war years, people who refused to purchase savings stamps or war bonds were suspected by many Americans of disloyalty. L.G. Rouse, a Church of God evangelist, encountered such prejudice while living in Anniston, Alabama. Shortly after he and his family arrived in the North Alabama town, he obtained employment in one of the local coal mines. On Monday, 23 June 1918, the fiery evangelist did not report for work because, according to him, he could no longer work without receiving the "baptism of the Holy Ghost." He spent the day in prayer until he received the Pentecostal blessing. When he returned to work the next day, fellow miners accused him of having been absent because he did not want to buy a war savings stamp. Those who sold the stamps asked Rouse to purchase a stamp, but he refused to do so. They proceeded to question him about the origins of the war. Rouse replied, "I said it was of the devil and from the very pits of hell."[50] A mob promptly threatened to knock every tooth out of his mouth. The superintendent arrived on the scene and fired the preacher on the spot. To Rouse's surprise, two unidentified government agents came to his home that same evening and arrested him without informing him of the charges. They placed him in the Anniston jail, where he remained for more than three months.[51]

While he was in jail, other inmates subjected Rouse to harassment and humiliation. The prisoners held a "kangaroo court" and tried him. The new inmate was fined one hundred dollars or twenty-five lashes for "breaking into jail." According to Rouse, inmates conducted these mock trials often. As part of his daily routine, the evangelist prayed aloud, infuriating the other inmates. Believing that Rouse was insane, especially when the Spirit came upon him and he spoke in tongues, the prisoners asked that the evangelist be moved to the basement of the jail. These were not the only injustices endured by the Church of God preacher. Late one evening, Rouse's wife came to the jail and informed him that city officials planned to take their children and place them in an orphanage. Although this never happened, it caused the Pentecostal preacher much anxiety.[52]

Three months after Rouse's arrest, authorities held a preliminary hearing and set bail at one thousand dollars. An anonymous person paid the bail, and Rouse was freed pending trial. On the day of the trial, the judge called his name and informed the preacher that he was free. He departed and never heard anything more concerning the matter.[53]

James B. Ellis, Church of God overseer for the state of Alabama, experienced similar persecution. He attended a meeting in his community that was held for the purpose of selling war bonds. Everyone but Ellis bought them. When the Methodist minister who conducted the meeting asked him to purchase a bond, Ellis stated that he did not desire to do so because he felt that it would aid the war. The Methodist clergyman declared that a man who would not buy war bonds "was a traitor to his country and lower down than a suck-egg hound."[54] After the humiliating episode, members of a local Vigilance Committee followed the Pentecostal overseer to Bradford Mines in northwestern Alabama, where Ellis conducted a revival. About 1 A.M. on the second night of the meeting, government agents placed him under arrest without informing him of charges. During his stay in jail, he experienced harassment very similar to that meted out to Rouse. Local officials neither permitted his correspondence to be mailed nor allowed him to receive any. However, when he was transported to the courthouse for a preliminary hearing, Ellis managed to mail a letter which he had written to the Church of God headquarters. At the hearing, Ellis discovered for the first time that he was charged with being a German spy and speaking against the government.[55]

After his release on bond, Ellis went to the Church of God headquarters in Cleveland, Tennessee. Upon hearing his problem, A.J. Tomlinson obtained a lawyer to defend him.[56] While he was out on bond, an unidentified man came and confessed to Ellis that members of the Vigilance Committee had gotten him and three other men to give false testimony that would lead to Ellis's conviction. When Ellis and his lawyer went to court, the United States attorney informed them that all charges had been dropped and that he was free.[57]

J.B. Ellis and L.G. Rouse were not the only Church of God preachers harassed because of pacifist views. There were many others that the government investigated. F.L. Ryder, a Church of God evangelist from Chattanooga, Tennessee, left the United States on 24 May 1917, headed for Argentina. As he and his wife sailed on a steamer toward their destination, they made stops in the Virgin Islands to preach revival meetings. On 1 August 1917, the couple arrived in Buenos Aires.[58] A brief time later Ryder received a letter from Tom M. Cain of Chattanooga, Tennessee, who was apparently a Church of God layman. In the correspondence, Cain asked Ryder for advice on the procedure for obtaining draft exemption. U.S. postal authorities intercepted Ryder's letter of response and turned it over to the FBI. In the correspondence, Ryder stated that he was glad that he had gotten out of the United States before the draft began. He advised Cain to obtain the assistance of A.J. Tomlinson in his efforts to avoid being drafted.[59] The chief of the FBI, J. Edgar Hoover, instructed agent James Finlay to obtain the draft status of all parties; if Ryder was a draft evader, Finlay should submit his findings to the U.S. attorney for indictment under the Selective Service Act.[60]

Following the armistice ending World War I on 11 November 1918, the FBI discontinued its investigation of suspected draft evaders, including F.L. Ryder. It is not known what motivated Ryder to leave the country. Perhaps he was a draft evader; then again, it may have been a coincidence that he departed from this country just eleven days before draft registration was to begin. Regardless of his motivations, Ryder did not return to the United States until 1923.[61]

Just prior to the end of the war, the Church of God showed signs of softening its pacifist position. Apparently some members began to reconcile their Christian beliefs with war and military service. Margaret Pake, a teacher from Osprey, Florida, wrote a letter to the editor of the *Evangel*, in which she proposed that "never in the world's history has there been such a grand opportunity for real work for souls as now. The camps, hospitals, trenches, are presenting 'fields white for harvest.' It seems that no real Christian man could be in any of these places for twenty-four hours and not get his call to real ministration such as Jesus described . . . to 'get out of this' [the military] would be his last thought."[62] This opinion suggests that at least some members viewed the war from an entirely different perspective than that of Church of God leaders.

With the end of World War I, Church of God members

breathed a sigh of relief. Church leaders were happy not only because the fighting was over, but also because the church and its members were relieved of enormous stress and anxiety. Unlike denominations and Pentecostal sects which changed their pacifist views to more patriotic beliefs, the Church of God remained a pacifist organization during the entire war. Several factors explain such consistency. Like many sects, the Church of God was often at odds with American culture. Most important, members were biblical literalists who chose to emphasize that the Scriptures taught them not to fight but, on the contrary, to "turn the other cheek." Although a few people did not believe this interpretation, they were a small minority and apparently did not possess enough power within the heirarchy to exert any influence on church doctrine or on the minds of members. A.J. Tomlinson, the general overseer, possessed both position and power and used them effectively to shape church policy. Although the Church of God remained pacifist, it did not emerge from the war years unscathed. The church and many of its members were subjected to investigations and both personal and public ridicule. Even though it weathered these storms, the reputation of the Church of God received wounds that healed slowly.

The teaching against members going to war remained in the 1919 and 1920 minutes of the church but in 1921 mysteriously disappeared.[63] The official *Minutes* of the General Assembly of that year offer no explanation as to the reason for the removal of the pacifist teaching. The minutes contain no discussion concerning the previous war or the church's pacifist position. One can only speculate, therefore, as to the reason for the disappearance of this rule. Because church membership had increased dramatically—almost doubling between 1917 and 1921—the composition and character of the church may have changed, producing a membership that did not share pacifist beliefs.[64] In any case, some members had already begun to reconcile their pacifism with the war; a minority even discovered some advantage for Church of God members in serving in the armed forces abroad.

The teaching also may have been removed due to pressure exerted upon the Church of God by mainline Protestant denominations. Perhaps desiring social acceptance and respectability, the delegates to the 1921 General Assembly may have felt that discarding the pacifist teaching might bring the Church of God more in line with mainline conservative evangelicalism.

Still another possibility is that general overseer A.J. Tomlinson became aware that many members simply did not share his rigid pacifism. Realizing the lack of unanimity on the subject, he decided it was best not to enforce an unpopular teaching.

The removal also could have been the result of a decline in the influence and control that Tomlinson wielded. From the 1921 assembly meeting until July 1923, Tomlinson's power and popularity steadily declined. On 26 July 1923, he was impeached, removed from office, and expelled from the Church of God. Disgruntled members may have expressed to the general overseer personally or by letter their wish to see pacifist teachings dropped altogether from the minutes without discussion or debate.

As a result of Tomlinson's expulsion in 1923, Flavius J. Lee became the sect's second general overseer, serving until his death in 1928. Under his leadership, the Church of God grew significantly. Membership continued to increase, and the organization shared in the country's economic growth.

Many European nations, however, did not enjoy the material benefits of the prosperous 1920s. Hard times and political instability produced serious conflicts between European neighbors. Problems in other parts of the world, such as Japanese imperialism in East Asia, also heightened tension in the world. Painful memories of the recent past flashed into the minds of all Americans. It appeared that another war could erupt, despite the fact that "the war to end all wars" had ended just a few years earlier.

The Church of God leadership responded to the world situation on 13 October 1928, at a meeting of the Elders' Council. This body voted to recommend to the General Assembly that the church add to its list of teachings a new rule in regard to war.[65] Remembering the consequences of its past ruling, the sect felt compelled to modify its position. With a change in wording, the church moved from opposing "members going to war" to "members going to war in combatant service." This marked a significant change in Church of God strategy. Although the church remained pacifist, the modification signaled the sect's tacit approval for its male members to serve in the military, as long as they did not participate in combat. Because the church had removed the teaching against members going to war in 1921, churchmen felt that they must adopt some ruling but decided on a more moderate one than the earlier version. Within two weeks of the Elders' Council meeting, the Twenty-third General Assembly met and rubber-stamped the recommendation of the elders.[66]

During the 1920s and 1930s, Americans lived in the shadow of postwar disillusionment, stemming largely from the suspicion that World War I had created far more problems than it had solved. The Church of God suffered from disillusionment as well. As one clergyman explained:

> The last war was fought to "make the world safe for democracy"—and it made the world safe for nothing whatever. We hope that the war makers next time will come right out in the open and say plainly that they are out for conquest and spoils and to find markets for their products. Then at least we will not be caught making countless sacrifices for some high ideal which is only going to be turned into a mockery.[67]

Democracy seemed to be on the defensive. The successful Bolshevik Revolution in Russia and failed socialist revolutions in Bavaria and Hungary were among the first tremors. Right-wing revolutions began with the Fascist dictatorship of Benito Mussolini in Italy. In 1933, a much more dominant and ruthless dictatorship arose, led by Adolph Hitler and his Nazi Party. Hitler shocked Americans and the rest of the world when he denounced the Versailles Treaty, reoccupied the Rhineland, rearmed Germany, and demanded territorial annexations. His maniacal racial ideas horrified the civilized world.

The rapid spread of both right and left-wing dictatorships caused the Church of God much consternation. Some clergymen saw Fascism and Communism as natural enemies, vying for world superiority even at the risk of annihilation. E.C. Clark, editor of the *Evangel*, was certain that "the clash in Europe will eventually come between Romanism and Communism."[68]

By the mid-1930s, isolationism revived in America. Although

most isolationists were not pacifists, a strong antiwar sentiment arose. Noninvolvement became the chief objective of American foreign policy. Beginning in 1935, Congress reinforced this sentiment by passing a series of neutrality laws. The Church of God was right in step with public opinion, for once, and shared the idea of nonentanglement. Contemplating the possibility of a future war, one churchman noted, "Nobody knows where the next war will start—but products and manpower are accumulating at so much faster a rate than they can be used up in a state of peace that it would take very little excuse to start the conflagration. Presumably this country will keep out of the mix-up."[69]

The antiwar sentiment continued to spread rapidly, and by 1935 many isolationist groups began openly to protest the actions of European dictators. The Church of God kept its constituents informed of isolationist activities through its publications. On 9 March 1935, *Evangel* subscribers, including many non–Church of God members, read about a student strike conducted on 12 April by Columbia University's antiwar committee. Mistakenly, the author of the article believed that Communist sympathizers orchestrated the proposed strike. He explained, "This is but another of those foreign plots of communistic propaganda designed to weaken America's fighting strength in the event another war might some time be necessary."[70] Such a comment represented a radical departure from the antiwar rhetoric of twenty years earlier.

By 1935, it was quite clear that Adolf Hitler was attempting to create a new and powerful German nation. It appeared that the achievement of this goal was not only possible but highly probable. A few Germans looked upon Hitler as a superman. The Church of God acknowledged that some German people might believe this, but as one churchman admonished, "When enlightened nations begin to talk superman, then we may know that we are becoming dizzy and that statesmen have lost their balance."[71]

Believing that peace efforts in Europe were eroding quickly, American politicians recognized the need to plan for military preparedness. In the first part of 1935, the U.S. Senate voted to appropriate $400 million to initiate such a plan. It also called for a small increase in the standing army to 165,000 troops. Many

Church of God members interpreted this development as a bad omen and believed "that war is inevitable not too far distant."[72]

There were also signs of war in East Asia. Japan had seized Korea, Manchuria, and parts of China by the late 1930s. Concerned about the Far Eastern threat to world peace, President Roosevelt delivered a speech at Chicago on 5 October 1937, in which, for the first time, he took issue with isolationist sentiment. He called on Americans to support the principles of collective security, but few in the Church of God listened. By late 1938, the Japanese extended their control over huge sections of eastern China. One Church of God cleric vigilantly noted that "the war in the East is spreading like 'wild fire,' but we pray that America will steer clear this time of the bloody struggle."[73]

Hopes for American noninvolvement in the crisis faded from the minds of many Church of God members. As in World War I, clergymen began to apply eschatological symbols to world affairs. With world tensions mounting, Church of God members believed that nations across the world were gearing up for one last global war which would precede the Great Tribulation and the second advent of Christ. S.W. Lattimer, editor of the *Evangel* and former general overseer, conjectured that "if this is the last conflict before the tribulation week begins, she [the United States] will certainly be involved."[74]

It seemed that his prophecy would come true, as the world plunged into war. In Europe, the Nazi war machine moved swiftly into one country after another, bringing much of the continent under Hitler's control. In September 1939, the most dreaded event occurred, the beginning of another world war.

Immediately Roosevelt, in a "fireside chat," issued a proclamation of neutrality to a radio audience of millions. With the outbreak of war in Europe, isolationist sentiment strengthened, becoming the pervasive mood of the nation. Most Americans remained hopeful that the president and the world's diplomats could find an acceptable path to peace. However, by the end of 1939, that ray of optimism had turned to pessimism. Noting the great sums of money spent on preparations to wage war, one Church of God spokesman commented on the irony of spending such sums for destruction. He stated, "Should men strive as hard to promote something that would bring about peace, should there be as extensive study, and should there be at our disposal the endless flow of money to study plans for peace and bring about peace as there is today for war, we have no doubt that peaceful ends could be realized."[75] The Church of God was confident that a diplomatic solution could be found, but it was losing confidence in men who talked about peace while continuing to spend enormous sums to prepare for war.

By summer 1940, the United States had made significant strides in military preparedness. Even with the fall of France, America was divided between isolationists wanting to remain neutral and interventionists favoring military preparedness and aid to the Allies. One Church of God minister mirrored his church's attitude about the unpopular war and the consequent United States preparedness policy: "The authorities are not to be condemned for this frenzied action. War threatens from the East and from the West. The ambitions and aspirations of the dictators know no stopping place. The subjugations of free peoples will continue."[76]

The church's position on conscription also gave evidence of this new attitude. After a lengthy and stormy debate, Congress passed the Selective Training and Service Act. Roosevelt signed this first peacetime military draft measure in September 1940. It called for registering all males between the ages of twenty-one and thirty-five. Speaking on behalf of the Church of God, E.L. Simmons, editor of the *Evangel* and member of the Supreme Council, demonstrated the extent of change within the church since 1917:

> These provisions [of the Selective Training and Service Act] at first glance, or some of them, might seem repulsive to those who do not wish to take up arms against their fellowman but on close reading this repulsive feeling should disappear and a certain consolation takes its place . . . our government still acknowledges the right of those who object to bearing arms and makes provision for conscientious objectors. We do not feel that men should dodge the draft . . . there can be no discouragement in conforming to the draft bill.[77]

The new draft law produced much discussion at the Bishop's Council meeting in September 1940. Instead of one or two leaders exercising their influence to the exclusion of others, as had happened when Tomlinson dominated policy in 1917, all members of the Council expressed their opinions freely. All agreed that the church should oppose its members going into combatant service. Everyone also agreed that it was the individual's duty to register for the draft. Disagreement arose, however, as to whether the church should publicly or privately advise its men concerning registration and military training. The council formed a committee composed of five councilors to draft a resolution and provide advice for the church. A short time later, the committee recommended that the resolution be published in the church's two principal publications, *Evangel* and *Lighted Pathway*. This suggestion caused spirited debate concerning the wisdom of placing such information in church publications. Some members of the council remembered painful experiences during World War I: having issues of the *Evangel* censored, members arrested, and the organization investigated by the FBI. The Church of God did not want that kind of publicity again. Many council members feared that printing information concerning the draft, placing it in the publications, or distributing it privately, would bring reprisal from the government and ridicule from the public. The Bishop's Council finally voted to print the portion of the Selective Service Act concerning conscientious objectors and allow the general overseer of the Church of God to make any comment that he deemed necessary.[78]

Apparently the general overseer, J. Herbert Walker, decided not to publish any statement at all. Together with his advisors, he must have determined that organizational silence, at least for the present, constituted the best policy. When the Thirty-Fifth General Assembly met in October, the delegates discussed neither the draft nor the war. Only one comment was recorded, and that was made by Walker in his annual general overseer's address. He exhorted members "to cling to the Bible, to the Church of God, to that which will stand when the world is on fire."[79] The church remained cautious, and the absence of discussion suggests that the church did not want to appear to be strictly a pacifist organization as it had in the past. Perhaps church leaders also did not consider issuing a statement because the United States was not militarily involved in the war at that time.

Events in Asia and President Roosevelt's program to aid the Allies would soon change the church's posture. After a heated debate, Congress passed the Lend-Lease Act in March 1941. Under the provisions of this act, the president could sell, transfer, lease, or lend war materiel to any country whose defense was vital to the defense of America. To ensure that these items reached Britain and its allies, Roosevelt extended the neutral shipping zone from Greenland to just off the coast of Iceland. He continued to strike against the Axis powers by ordering the U.S. Coast Guard to seize Axis vessels in U.S. ports, and ordered all Axis assets in American banks frozen. This course of action brought him much criticism from isolationist groups. By spring 1941, it was obvious to almost everyone that the United States was neutral in name only. The growing evidence of American participation worried Church of God leaders. E.L. Simmons wrote a carefully worded article which appeared in the 26 April 1941 issue of the *Evangel*. He stated that the Church of God was a pacifist organization and always had been, but he emphasized that the church was also loyal, patriotic, and law-abiding. Moreover, he reported to his readers about a conference, conducted under the auspices of the National Service Board for Religious Objectors in Washington, D.C.), that he had attended a few days earlier. Gen. Lewis B. Hershey, head of the Selective Service Board in Washington, D.C., had been one of the principal speakers. The high-ranking official had assured his audience that the government would respect the religious convictions of conscientious objectors. Simmons happily explained that, "according to General Hershey [conscientious objectors] will be absorbed by the medical corps. If a mistake was made [for those already drafted] in assignment or classification, the case may be reopened. . . . It is not too late for an appeal."[80]

In fall 1941, various speakers at the Thirty-Sixth General Assembly echoed Simmons' cooperative tone. R.P. Johnson, assistant general overseer, urged Church of God members to pull together and remain loyal to the country.[81] Another keynote speaker sounded even more patriotic. He emphatically informed his listeners:

> I think I know that there are no people in all the world, let alone the United States, more patriotic than the members of the Church of God. We have ever been a group of people that could pay tribute and allegiance to the Stars and Stripes, but that of devotion and patriotism has been kindled anew and more especially the last few years. We are now, as we have been, so devoted to that [pointing to a U.S. flag] that we can say, "Thank God for Old Glory and for everything for which it stands."[82]

The war expanded with the German invasion of Russia in June and an attack on U.S. ships by German submarines in fall 1941. The Japanese also contributed to the escalation of war by continued aggression in the Far East, culminating in the attack on Pearl Harbor and the U.S. declaration of war a day later.

Although some Church of God men enlisted in the armed forces, most who served in the conflict were draftees. Despite the ruling forbidding members to participate in combat, some Church of God males fought. Many were draftees who applied for conscientious objector status but were assigned to combat units anyway. As one young soldier, James G. Osborne, explained, "I am in the infantry and have been trying to get out of it, but haven't had any success. I don't believe in taking up arms against my fellow man."[83] For every case like Osborne's, there were other Church of God men who were successful in obtaining conscientious objector status. Just as General Hershey had promised, many objectors were placed in noncombat service, which pleased church leadership.

Once America entered the war, the homefront mobilized quickly. Demands for war goods made for economic recovery. The costs of the war from 1941 to 1945 were staggering. The government paid these enormous costs by taxation and by selling war bonds. The Church of God had opposed the sale of stamps and bonds during World War I. Upon refusal to buy these, many members had been arrested, thrown in jail, beaten up, and fired from their jobs. Such reprisals did not happen during World War II. The church's new position on war partly explains the lack of persecution, but, more importantly, the church called for loyalty and patriotism from its members. Reflecting this new image,

B.L. Hicks, a Church of God clergyman, encouraged members to "save every dime we possibly can and buy defense stamps and bonds."[84]

Conversely, the United States government viewed the church from a different perspective than during World War I. It did not object to the church's distributing the *Lighted Pathway* on military posts across the nation. It did not confiscate Church of God mail or censor publications. The *Lighted Pathway* instead was welcomed by chaplains and servicemen, and both Church of God members and nonmembers read it and other literature written and published by the Pentecostal organization.[85]

As the fortunes of war turned against the Allies in the spring and summer 1942, the Church of God, along with all Americans, prayed for divine intervention. During these trying times, the Supreme Council of the Church of God sent President Roosevelt a telegram assuring him of its "loyal and moral support and earnest prayers in this great crisis."[86] Church officials felt strongly that members should support the nation and its leaders. Encouraging the membership to be patriotic, loyal, and willing to sacrifice, one churchman reminded his fellow members, "This country of ours is worth fighting for."[87]

By this time it was apparent that the church was willing to support the nation in any way it possibly could, short of giving formal approval for Church of God males to serve in combat. At the meeting of the Bishops' Council in 1942, a Mr. Cassady presented the guidelines of the civil defense program, in which he was an officer. Cassady explained that while participation was on a voluntary basis, it was

> not [the] Government's intention to make the Church an agency of the Government nor to drag the Church into the war but does not expect the Church to wait on the sidelines without taking some hold, especially in rendering services to the Community, which is believed in the long run to be just as much or more of a contribution to the Nation's success than the manufacture of munitions.[88]

Council members responded by pledging their full cooperation. A motion was made to establish a War Time Committee for the purpose of coordinating a civil defense plan with the National Defense Organization.[89] The three top officials—general overseer J.H. Walker; R.P. Johnson, first assistant general overseer; and Earl P. Paulk, second assistant general overseer—comprised the newly formed committee. Showing their patriotism and desire to participate, the committee members attended a two-day conference in January 1943, conducted by the U.S. Office of Civilian Defense for the purpose of discussing national problems related to civilian participation in national defense. General overseer Walker reported that the Church of God could aid the government in numerous ways. To ensure widespread participation, he instructed ministers to "contact the local Civilian Defense Officers and offer assistance in any and every way possible."[90]

Church officials had informed Mr. Cassady at the 1942 Bishops' Council meeting that, although the church had a policy opposing combat service, church leaders had not attempted "to enforce the teaching or make it a test of fellowship."[91] A year later, at the 1943 meeting, the council provided more definitive signs that some clergymen wanted to adopt a new ruling or eliminate reference to conscientious objectors altogether. But a few council members felt that the existing ruling should be enforced. After a heated debate, the council decided to leave the policy as it was, ruling against members going into combat service, but not to enforce it or make it a test of membership.[92] Many Church of God members obviously felt torn. Because they were biblical literalists, they believed that the Scriptures taught them that it was wrong to fight; yet they were not willing to stand by and turn the nation over to the likes of Adolf Hitler. In his opening address to the Thirty-eighth General Assembly, general overseer Walker lamented,

> We didn't want this war, but when this [Old Glory] was torn down and trampled underfoot, when our nation was disrespected, and when our manhood was dishonored, there was nothing else to do but defend this flag and the principles and ideals for which it stands. But the scripture still reads, "Ye fight and war, yet ye have not because ye ask not." Uncle Sam, you need to go to the altar until you can pray through, and then you can expect results from our Father.[93]

By 1944, the once strongly pacifist Church of God appeared to be moving into the mainstream of conservative evangelicalism and American society. Supporting the war effort substantially aided the upward mobility of the church. Writing a lengthy article for an Independence Day celebration, James L. Slay, a respected church leader, discussed why America was fighting. Among these reasons was protection of basic freedoms that the U.S. Constitution guaranteed and, indeed, of the whole democratic way of life. In his article Slay emphasized that freedom of religion was one of the most important guarantees contained in the Bill of Rights. That he listed this particular freedom is not surprising, because he knew that this reminder would strike deep into the hearts and minds of his readers. After discussing constitutional freedoms, he asked his readers to "think of this and surely you'll say this is worth fighting for."[94]

As the government drafted more and more Church of God men into the military, many decided to serve in combat units. Others remained pacifists and registered as conscientious objectors, serving as noncombatants. Aaron Ball, son of Winston W. Ball, a Church of God minister from Springfield, Alabama, was drafted in late 1944. In January 1945, the Army sent the young man to a military training camp where he informed his superiors that "they could put him in the guard house, shoot him or whatever they wished but he was not going to take human life."[95]

With the increasing number of male members serving their country, the Church of God felt a need to minister to their "brethren in uniform." The organization appointed "service pastors" to visit Church of God soldiers on various military installations and conduct services for them. The church also became involved in helping to establish and operate Christian Service Centers. The first center was founded at Camp Barkley in Abilene, Texas. This was a cooperative effort with two other Pentecostal organizations, the Assemblies of God and the Pentecostal Holiness Church. Each agreed to pay one-third of the cost and provide adequate personnel to staff the center.[96] Unexpectedly, this project proved the beginning of a new and lasting field of ministry for the Church of God.

Church of God males served in all branches of the military at home and abroad. Like Raymond Sanders, a soldier who fought in three major campaigns in the South Pacific, many saw action in combat missions. Ed Moore became a gunner in the Army Air

Church of God soldiers during World War II.
(*Hal Bernard Dixon, Jr., Pentecostal Research Center, Cleveland, Tenn.*)

Corps and flew thirty-two missions.[97] In bloody fighting during 1944, some of those who gave their lives were Church of God members. Two men, Fred McNabb and Ottis Hewett, members of the North Cleveland, Tennessee, congregation, were killed in action, the former in Belgium and the latter in France.[98]

As the war ended, the Church of God officially proclaimed what individual members had been demonstrating; it adopted a new policy regarding members and their involvement in war. On 3 September 1945, just one day after World War II ended, delegates to the Church of God General Assembly deleted the rule opposing combat service during wartime. The Church of God adopted a new policy which stated:

> The Church of God believes that nations can and should settle their differences without going to war; however, in the event of war, if a member engages in combatant service, it will not affect his status with the church. In case a member is called into military service, who has conscientious objections to combatant service, the church will support him in his constitutional rights.[99]

During the Viet Nam War, when refusal to serve was widespread, the Church of God stuck to its policy of September 1945.

The Church of God had changed a great deal since the early days of World War I. Both the organization and many of its members had suffered public ridicule and other hardships because of its strict pacifism during the war. When World War II began, many clergy and laity realized that the church needed to change its policy; that change evolved during the course of the war. This shift resulted from multiple causes: the upward socio economic mobility of the church as a whole, the desire to be accepted and respected, changes in leadership, and alteration in the composition and character of church membership. Within one day following the end of the war, the Church of God issued a new ruling on war. The ruling allowed individual members to make their own decision as to whether to participate in combat. Since then, many Church of God males have served in the armed forces. During the Korean and Viet Nam wars, most of those men chose to serve in combat units.

CHAPTER 7

From Back Alleys to Uptown

American society experienced dramatic socioeconomic changes in the post–World War II period, and probably no region was more affected than the South. The extent of change could be seen in the economic transformation from one-crop agriculture to an industrial society; increase in per capita income; urbanization; racial turmoil and the Civil Rights movement; disruption of the solid Democratic South; and religious pluralism. Some scholars have argued that the South in recent years has become Americanized and has lost its regional distinctiveness. Others maintain that a dual process has occurred: the South has become Americanized, but at the same time America has become "southernized." In 1974, historian George Tindall wrote that "the South has been a seedbed of population and cultural styles for the rest of the country."[1] The South exported parts of its culture, including jazz and blues music, colloquialisms, southern dishes described as "soul food," stockcar racing, and "countrypolitan" music, to name just a few. Sociologists such as John Shelton Reed have acknowledged the transformation but insisted that, in some ways, southern subculture retains distinct characteristics.

In the years following World War II, the Church of God completed its transformation from an obscure radical sect to a church within mainstream conservative evangelicalism. Prior to World War II, the organization had been isolated from other Protestant churches. In the postwar years, the Church of God's sectarianism mellowed. It repudiated snake handling, causing the flight of practitioners to "independent" Pentecostal groups. As a consequence, the practice disappeared from Church of God ranks. The church changed from a pacifist organization to a much more militant one. Even the church's insistence on rigorous personal morality began to erode. Pentecostal worship became less emotional and less dependent on the supernatural. The spontaneity of worship which had characterized services before the war became less obvious in the years following 1945. "Hell fire and brimstone" sermons slowly began to disappear. As local congregations became more urban and middle-class, they demanded an increasingly professional clergy and a more sophisticated liturgy.

The causes of the Church of God's move into mainstream conservative evangelicalism are multiple and complex. Church members rose into middle-class status as a result of the economic boom of the war years. With this ascension, many members shed their lower-class prejudices and adopted middle-class values and social mores. A younger generation of denominational leaders arose in the postwar period. Many clergymen and some officials were second- and third-generation leaders. Younger Church of God ministers were better educated and were earning university or seminary degrees. A greater number of the laity also obtained a higher education.

These factors help to explain the division of the church into two camps. Traditionalists were typically older, less educated, and less willing to accept change. Progressives were generally younger, better educated, and more willing to experiment. Although both groups were conservative, orthodox believers, the progressives helped to bring about changes which resulted in the church's rise to middle-class respectability and its movement into mainstream conservative evangelicalism. The traditionalists, on the other hand, helped the Church of God maintain its distinction as a conservative, mainline Pentecostal organization.

No issue more clearly illustrates changes within the Church of God than the evolution in the training of the organization's young people. From the earliest years, leaders showed concern for the training of workers, although the sect did not establish a school for this purpose until 1918. Delegates at the Thirteenth General Assembly decided that the sect needed such a school "for the training of young men and women for efficient service."[2]

On 1 January 1918, the Bible Training School (BTS) in Cleveland, Tennessee, began with a small group of twelve eager students. The school experienced slow but steady growth during the 1920s. In the next decade, the Church of God continued to provide additional educational opportunities for its youth. In 1930, under the direction of J.H. Walker, the sect organized within the Bible Training School, a high school department which was accredited by the State of Tennessee eleven years later.[3]

The Church of God continued to emphasize training for Christian workers and established a second Bible school during the years of the Great Depression. With the permission of the 1934 General Assembly, Paul H. Walker, Church of God state overseer of the northwestern states, founded a school in that region. In 1935 the Northwest Bible School, in Minot, North Dakota, began its first academic year as a two-year institution.[4]

By the end of World War II, student enrollment in the Bible Training School had climbed to more than six hundred. Because of increased enrollment, the school needed more adequate space and facilities, so the Church of God bought the small campus of Murphy Collegiate Institute in Sevierville, Tennessee. The church also added new faculty members who had earned degrees from some of the South's finest colleges and universities. For example, Earl M. Tapley, who served as faculty member and dean of the school, held academic degrees from Vanderbilt University and Peabody College.[5]

In 1946 the Church of God had another opportunity for expansion, when it received an invitation from Bob Jones College in Cleveland, Tennessee, to purchase its entire campus because the college was going to be relocated. The General Council voted to buy it for $1.5 million.[6] The Bible Training School received not only a new campus but also a new name. In 1947, the church changed the name to Lee College, after Flavius J. Lee, the church's former general overseer.[7]

In 1949 the organization added yet another regional Bible school to its growing list of educational institutions. On 16 February 1949, the West Coast Bible School (presently called West Coast Christian College) began operation in Pasenda, California, under the supervision of J.H. Hughes, state overseer.[8] A few months later the school was moved to the present site at Fresno. This addition reflected not only an expansion of educational opportunities but, more importantly, the church's economic growth and the increase in number of members from the middle class who saw the necessity of education.

In the post–World War II period more and more Church of God leaders began to believe in the importance of an educated clergy. Because of this realization, some progressive ministers wanted the church to establish a minimum educational standard for future applicants for ministerial ordination.[9] The church, however, did not pass an educational requirement.

Despite the fact that many of the progressive churchmen saw the great benefits of higher education, some traditionalist ministers who had less education associated higher learning with spiritual compromise and lacked the enthusiasm for education that their fellow clergymen had. Because of their antiintellectual bias, some traditionalist pastors discouraged young members from obtaining a higher education. To combat such attitudes, during the late 1950s church publications carried numerous articles in support of higher education, written by Church of God members who had earned degrees from such major universities as Emory, Maryland, and Ohio State. One writer astutely observed that the church was divided into two camps, those who favored higher education and those who believed that it was not needed.[10] This division probably also reflected class tensions within the church.

Progressive church officials and Lee College faculty members attempted to relieve the anxieties of those parents who believed that a higher education might have some ill effect on their children's spiritual life. They did this by informing mothers and fathers who were contemplating sending their children to a church school that "every class begins with prayer or the reading of the Word. Prayer requests are taken, students' needs presented and after a most uplifting conversation with the Lord, the teaching of the lesson is presented."[11]

The Church of God's attempt to relieve such anxieties proved successful, and the educational institution continued to grow. In 1956, the church expanded the liberal arts program of Lee College, which had been a two-year institution since 1941. Church leaders made plans for the college to offer a four-year program leading to a Bachelor of Arts degree.[12] The strategy worked, and the decade of the 1960s ushered in a period of unprecedented growth for Lee College and the church's other schools. Under the administration of President Ray H. Hughes, student enrollments at Lee College swelled to 629 in the fall of 1963. They also increased significantly in the other church schools. One cause of the boost in enrollments was the fact that the United States government approved Lee College for student loans under the auspices of the National Defense Education Act.[13] This program provided financial aid to students who previous would not have been able to attend. The academic standing of the college also was enhanced in 1960 when it obtained conditional accreditation from the Southern Association of Colleges and Schools. The church continued to improve its facilities at Lee College by remodeling some of the older buildings and constructing new ones. As part of the expansion program, the administration hired more faculty members who brought fresh ideas about higher education to the institution.[14] Many of these professors transmitted their progressive views to students, justifying traditionalists' fears about a "liberal arts" education.

The social revolution of the 1960s caused most Church of God leaders much anxiety. The decline of traditional moral values among college students frightened most church members, just as it alarmed other mainstream conservative evangelicals. Many of the "baby-boom generation" students held beliefs different from those of their parents concerning such topics as premarital sex, birth control, the use of hallucinogenic drugs, abortion, and prayer in public schools, to name just a few. Church of God leaders assured parents that if their child attended Lee College or any of the other church schools, he or she would live and learn in a wholesome Christian environment. As for those young people who were contemplating going to a secular college, one churchman stated, "It is imperative that Church of God youth attend one of our colleges . . . the students need and must have the godly, Christ-centered influence of a Christian campus. Many Church of God youth are lost from the Church each year because those students do not go to a Church of God school."[15]

According to the Church of God, public educational institutions had discarded Christian values. To remedy this deficiency, the church devised its own plan to restore such values in education on the primary and secondary school levels by establishing private Christian day schools. Robert A. Cook, president of the National Association of Evangelicals, suggested that the establishment of such schools provided an opportunity to educate and produce a new generation of leaders who could help change society. "This means," warned Cook, "stop thinking of Christian education as a luxury, and realize that it is as important as your jugular vein!" [16] The Church of God played a significant role —if small in comparison to other Protestant churches—in the proliferation of private schools. During the Vietnam Era, evangelical and Pentecostal groups established an unprecedented number of schools throughout the country. In 1960, the nation contained approximately 1,400 Protestant schools. By 1980 that number had skyrocketed to 16,000. Many Church of God pastors and laymen in local congregations organized, built, and operated their own private schools. Establishing such schools was undertaken first by the churches with large memberships and adequate financial resources. Despite the enormous sums needed for such projects, Church of God members were not overwhelmed. They went about the necessary tasks with an air of confidence and divine mission, believing that God surely would provide.

Because of the growing number of such schools and concern for the overall educational programs of the organization, the General Assembly authorized the formation of a General Board of Education. This body was "to review objectives of educational institutions in relation to the doctrine, belief, and polity of the Church and to promote loyalty of Church of God constituents to its educational institutions." [17]

The increased interest in Christian day schools caused the church in 1976 to publish a statement of philosophy on that subject. The stated purpose of such schools was to provide quality education in a Christian atmosphere. Robert White, director of general education programs, explained, "Since the foundation of all knowledge is to know God and His truth, the Word of God will hold a prominent place in the Christian day school. The

infallibility of the Word of God will be held forth."[18] The clergyman further stated that biblical precepts concerning the origin,
nature, and destiny of man would be taught and prayer would
be held daily. The school would provide a wholesome climate
for learning and development, through the example of Christian teachers. All activities would direct the student toward good
social behavior. One can readily see in this philosophy a total
rejection of what many Church of God members perceived as
the ills of public education: teaching of evolution, breakdown of
morals, prohibition of prayer, and "secular humanist" educators.
Although no statistical data is available, the growth of private
schools must have been significant in the late 1970s and 1980s,
since church officials were concerned enough to prohibit local
congregations to found such schools without the permission of
the respective Church of God state overseers.[19]

Church leaders consistently emphasized the need for higher
education and for institutions to meet its goals. The Church of
God continued to upgrade its schools. The year 1967 marked
a historic occasion for Lee College. Enrollment passed the one
thousand mark for the first time. Such growth necessitated sub-
stantive changes in the college. In November 1967, Dr. J.H.
Walker, Jr., dean of the College of Liberal Arts and Education, announced that the administration had merged the separate school
divisions into one four-year college, and that it would do everything humanly possible to expedite the accreditation process. In
1969, the school reached this important latter goal.[20]

By the late 1960s, an increasing number of Church of God
ministers accepted the fact that American society was more sophisticated than in the years before World War II. To reach
educated middle- and upper-class people, it was essential that
church workers have a college education. The church had up-
graded its educational programs with this fact in mind, but what
emerged from those programs was what Martin Marty has called
a type of "intellectual antiintellectualism" among evangelicals.
By the 1970s, most churchmen accepted that the various church
schools and the emphasis on a college education had become
permanent fixtures of the organization. Church leaders had been
careful to encourage and safeguard the spiritual aspect of the stu-

dent's educational experience. They encouraged young ministers and laymen, if possible, to attend only Church of God schools.[21]

In the early 1970s, many church officials saw the need for a theological seminary to train young ministers properly. When churchmen began to discuss the feasibility of such an institution, most agreed that divinity students who went to non–Church of God seminaries were exposed to what they considered to be liberal theology, and that this exposure was sure to have an effect on young minds. One Church of God educator maintained, "It is impossible for a person in his formative years to go through an institution of liberal persuasion without being affected to some degree."[22] At the meeting of the General Assembly in August 1970, general overseer Charles Conn echoed this belief when he informed his audience of the urgency of a theological seminary. He warned that "we must go forward in Christ-centered education or be buried in Christ-denying or Christ-ignoring secular education."[23] The general overseer further declared that it was no longer a question of whether Church of God youth would attend college or not; they would. He concluded his address by asking whether the church would satisfy this need or whether Church of God students would have to attend other universities and seminaries. Heeding his advice, the General Assembly in 1971 approved a measure authorizing church officials to establish a seminary. Classes at the Graduate School of Christian Ministries (presently called the Graduate School of Theology) began on 1 September 1975.[24] By the mid-1980s, the seminary had obtained accreditation.

The founding of a graduate school of theology was only part of the church's effort to adopt and implement an invigorating higher education policy. In the 1970s, the church established other new programs, such as a continuing education program and Bible institutes for ministerial and lay enrichment. The former offered members who could not attend college on a full-time basis opportunities for educational advancement. In 1976, the church also established another two-year school in Charlotte, North Carolina. The East Coast Bible College opened in fall 1976 with 122 students.[25] Adding still another educational program in 1978, the Church of God initiated a Ministerial Internship Program. Its purpose was "to more adequately ensure the formation of proper ministerial training."[26] This "on-the-job training" provided all young ministers with an opportunity to serve an internship period under the supervision of an experienced clergyman. With their continuing emphasis upon education and the formation of programs to provide educational opportunities, church leaders helped to change this old-line Pentecostal organization into a mainstream, conservative evangelical church.

Other alterations, too, indicated the Church of God's move into middle-class Christianity. Respectability helped to remove old ecclesiastical barriers. Beginning in the late 1940s, the church exhibited a spirit of cooperation with fellow evangelical believers by joining such organizations as the National Association of Evangelicals, World Pentecostal Fellowship, and the North American Pentecostal Fellowship (PFNA). Interest in social concerns was yet another indication of changes taking place within the Church of God. In its early years, the church had showed little or no interest in social problems, but after the war the organization became increasingly involved in social issues. Debates about many issues demonstrated the tensions between traditionalists and progressives within the church: denominational cooperation with other evangelicals, opposition to the ecumenical movement, healing-charismatic revivals, concern with social issues, involvement in politics, and the Civil Rights Movement.

In 1942, evangelical leaders invited Church of God officials to join approximately 150 leaders from other denominations at a convention in St. Louis, Missouri. The purpose of the meeting was to form a cooperative association of evangelicals. This was an important step in breaking down barriers that had separated the Church of God from mainstream evangelical churches. The Church of God sent four official delegates to the St. Louis convention—E.C. Clark, E.L. Simmons, M.P. Cross, and J.H. Walker.[27] The delegates decided that an association was possible, so the organizers asked them to reassemble at a constitutional convention in Chicago on 25 April 1943. In summer 1942 the Bishop's Council responded to this invitation, not only approving the meeting but pledging its full support. This was a dramatic step in the church's new spirit of cooperation. Although some churchmen were hesitant about an alliance with non-Pentecostals, most clergymen were eager to participate with other evangelicals in the preservation of evangelicalism and looked to the future with great expectation.[28]

Some six hundred delegates, representing sixty-five denominations, gathered in Chicago for the convention. Among those in attendance were a number of Church of God officials: general overseer J.H. Walker, Earl P. Paulk, E.L. Simmons, M.P. Cross, and E.C. Clark. The twenty-two-member Board of Administration created by the new National Association of Evangelicals (NAE) included representatives from only two Pentecostal organizations, the Church of God and Assemblies of God. Church of God clergymen served on various NAE boards and committees throughout the post-World War II period. Ray H. Hughes, assistant general overseer, served as president of the organization in 1987. Church of God leaders cooperated with the association in other related areas. Beginning in 1946, church leaders voted to "cooperate with the National Sunday School Association in its endeavor to produce a new uniform lesson series."[29] During the next few years, departments within the Church of God joined NAE affiliate associations such as the Evangelical Foreign Missions Association, the Evangelical Press Association, and National Religious Broadcasters.

Earlier attempts to link Pentecostals had failed. The Church of God and Assemblies of God had considered a merger in 1926, but merger talks had collapsed because Church of God officials accused the Assemblies of God of being "very slack as concerning their government and teachings."[30] By the 1940s, Pentecostal bodies adopted a much more tolerant and even congenial attitude toward each other. Relations between the Church of God and the Pentecostal Holiness Church became so amiable that the two organizations explored the possibility of an amalgamation in 1946, although no merger occurred. At the meeting of the NAE in May 1948, delegates investigated another area of interdenominational cooperation. Delegates from eight Pentecostal organizations discussed forming a Pentecostal fellowship.[31]

By the mid-1940s, conditions were favorable for the formation of such a fellowship. American Pentecostal organizations had been encouraged by the formation of the World Pentecostal Fellowship in March 1947. Delegates from around the globe had met in Zurich, Switzerland, in May and organized the association. Representatives from thirty-two nations attended a second conference in May 1949, and delegates implemented plans for a permanent basis of fellowship and cooperation.[32] The Church of God had participated in triennial meetings since 1947. The purpose of the WPF was to promote cooperation and fellowship among Pentecostals worldwide.

A year after the creation of the fellowship, Pentecostal bodies in the United States and Canada made bold plans to organize a Pentecostal fellowship a little closer to home. Immediately after the NAE meeting, representatives from eight Pentecostal groups met in Chicago on 7 May 1948. They chose John C. Jernigan, general overseer of the Church of God, as temporary chairman.[33] Participants held a second convention in August to formulate a tentative constitution which would be presented to representatives at a constitutional convention in October 1948. A committee of four, including a Church of God clergyman, assistant general overseer H.L. Chesser, was selected to draft the new constitution.[34] At the meeting of the Church of God Bishops Council, Jernigan reported the action taken by the delegates in Chicago. David J. duPlessis, a prominent Pentecostal leader from South Africa, was present at the council meeting. He addressed the ministers on the subject of Pentecostal ecumenicity. Upon conclusion of his speech, the council voted to cooperate in every possible way with the Pentecostal Fellowship of North America in its endeavors.[35]

Some two hundred delegates, representing a dozen Pentecostal organizations, assembled in Des Moines, Iowa, in October 1948 for the eagerly awaited constitutional convention. The delegates elected former general overseer John C. Jernigan chairman of the new Pentecostal association. Two important objectives of the PFNA were to demonstrate the unity of all Spirit-filled believers and to help evangelize the world more effectively.[36]

Despite a desire for closer fellowship with Pentecostals, the Church of God vigorously opposed the ecumenical movement within mainstream Christianity, as expressed by the World Council of Churches, National Church of Christ, and the Vatican Ecumenical Council. The World Council of Churches, an organization of Protestant, Anglican, and Orthodox churches, was founded in 1948 in Amsterdam. Less than two years later, the National Council of Churches was established in the United States. The founding of the two multidenominational organizations prompted an immediate reaction from the Church of God. The Pentecostal church bitterly opposed the ecumenical efforts of both organizations. One of the main concerns seems to have been that members of the movement would be forced to conform. Consequently, the Church of God felt that if it participated, it would lose its right of religious self-determination and hence its doctrinal distinctiveness. One churchman went so far as to warn, "if unification of Protestant Churches becomes an actuality, we should have another revolution comparable to the one in the days of Martin Luther . . . or the one in Europe [Puritan Revolution] that caused the birth of this nation."[37] Another reason for the Church of God's opposition was fear that its basic mission would be altered. Some clergymen worried that the task of the church no longer would be the salvation of mankind but simply improving social conditions. The Church of God had made giant strides in the transition from an obscure sect to mainstream conservative evangelicalism, but most members were not willing to align themselves with what they considered liberal "social gospellers."

Still another ecumenical matter of concern to the Church of God was the possibility of a unification of Protestants and Roman Catholics. The Pentecostal organization still clung to a deep-seated anti-Catholicism, as did many conservative Protestant groups. Combining prophecy and prejudice, one Church of God pastor wrote, "If this union takes place, it will only be a step more to the union of the 'harlot' [World Church of Christ and National Church of Christ] with the 'mother of harlots'—Roman Catholicism. . . . Thus the great whore of Revelation 17 will come to full strength."[38]

In the 1950s, the ecumenical movement made still larger gains. In 1959 it received a tremendous boost, when Pope John XXIII announced the convening of the Ecumenical Council (Vatican II), to which bishops from all over the world were invited.

The Pontiff also invited Protestant and Orthodox organizations to send representatives.

The papal announcement disturbed Church of God clergymen. Some ministers, like George L. Britt, who was the church's leading spokesman on eschatology, speculated that in the "end time" the Catholic Pope would be the prophesied "false prophet" who would control a vast religious federation. Britt believed that Pope John's announcement was the initial organizing stage of such a worldwide religious federation. According to the Church of God, it should never be a part of any Protestant-Catholic union. Taking issue with proponents of ecumenism who argued that the purpose of the Ecumenical Council was to find the will of God by forming one church, Britt stated, "This is just the opposite motive of Pope John's ecumenical council. The motive of this council is to obtain conformity to the Roman Catholic system."[39]

The Second Vatican Council lasted from October 1962 to December 1965. Although the council achieved only limited progress toward the goal of Protestant-Catholic union, the body issued a Decree on Ecumenism. Formerly, the Catholic Church had expected Christian believers to return to Roman Catholicism. The decree admonished Catholics to take an active part in the work of ecumenism.

Shortly after this declaration, another event occurred which had special relevance to the Church of God and all other Pentecostal organizations. Dr. Frederick Donald Coggan, Anglican Archbishop of York, called for the inclusion of Pentecostal groups in ecumenical plans for church union.

These two events caused Church of God leaders to realize that the organization now would be forced to take an official stand on the issue of Protestant-Catholic union. Writing on behalf of the Church of God, assistant general overseer Ray H. Hughes announced that the church could not support such a union because it represented theological liberalism, lack of evangelical conviction, substitution of social action for evangelism, and the search for unity at the expense of biblical truth.[40] Despite this opposition to Protestant-Catholic union, Hughes enthusiastically encouraged Pentecostal organizations to lay aside their differences. If this were done, a unification of all Pentecostal groups could occur. Hughes' message also marked a significant transition in Church of God philosophy. The assistant general overseer explained:

> Let the salt penetrate the icy crust of our society! Pentecostal ministers must not be afraid to affiliate with ministerial alliances or local councils of churches. Civic organizations, social movements in the mainstream, and political groups and parties must be infiltrated by Pentecostal laymen immediately, or we are in danger of becoming a dead force instead of a "third force" of Christendom.[41]

In the pre–World War II years, the church tended to teach its members to "be separate" and to withdraw from society. By the 1960s, the Church of God had made an about-face by encouraging participation in worldly affairs. In providing such encouragement, the church took another giant step forward toward gaining ecclesiastical acceptance and respectability.

Although the major factors leading the Church of God into mainstream conservative evangelicalism involved changes within the organization, at least one important change occurred in American religious culture which won the church a sympathetic hearing. Healing and charismatic revivals swept America in the immediate post–World War II period. These awakenings sprang from old-line Pentecostal organizations such as the Church of God. The careers of several evangelists with magnetic personalities and the ability to mesmerize audiences blossomed during the healing revival, which lasted from 1947 to 1958. Evangelists from the ranks of old-line Pentecostal churches— men such as Oral Roberts, Gordon Lindsay, Jack Coe, T.L. Osborn, A.A. Allen, and T.L. Lowery—led the revival. The explosion of this Pentecostal revival, with its emphasis on divine healing, resulted from many causes. A new spirit of cooperation, evidenced by the founding of the PFNA and WPF, set the stage for better relations among Pentecostal organizations. Pentecostal churches, including the Church of God, contained a new generation of members who were proponents of progress and modernity. No longer did the Church of God constituency come exclusively from lower socioeconomic classes. As early as 1946, general overseer John C. Jernigan had observed that "there was a time when the Church of God was pushed into the back allies [sic] and the outskirts of town. But, we have disposed of most of our back-alley property and moved uptown."[42] The church was changing and attracting a more affluent membership. Affluence, cooperation, and hunger for "old-time Holy Ghost" revival created an environment ripe for renewal in the late 1940s. The Church of God directly benefitted from the healing revival, which added impetus to the resurgence of Pentecostalism in the United States and throughout the world.

Since its inception, the Church of God had believed in and practiced divine healing. Although church militancy on this teaching had diminished significantly by the late 1940s, most members still believed that God could intervene and heal the ill. The Church of God endorsed the central message of the healing revival—that God could heal the sick in response to prayers of the faithful. By the early 1950s, many of the healing evangelists were conducting campaigns across the nation and "unto the utter most parts of the earth." Thousands of anxious seekers gathered under huge gospel tents night after night, waiting with great expectancy and yearning for a move of the Spirit. Believers and unbelievers alike listened and watched almost hypnotically to every word and motion of the "Holy Ghost–anointed" men of God. The Church of God raised no objection to individuals who were blessed by God at such meetings.

The tactics employed by some of the healing revivalists, however, constituted a problem. During the Supreme Council meeting in spring 1953, Church of God leaders discussed what they perceived as irregularities. Some council members expressed indignation at the deviations. J.D. Bright moved that a committee draft a resolution on divine healing. But other members wanted a resolution that would chastise only the culprits who were guilty of irregularities. Offering a substitute motion, H.D. Williams condemned healing evangelists for proselytizing, slandering the Church of God, teaching candidates for the baptism of the Holy Ghost how to speak in tongues by repeating certain words or syllables, personally attempting to impart the gifts of the Spirit to individuals, and "commercializing on the healing ministry."[43] Williams and many other Church of God ministers believed that such evangelists exploited their supporters and employed disreputable methods which discredited sincere ministers and Pentecostalism in general.

Although Church of God leaders did not agree with some of the methods employed by the healing evangelists, they did recognize that the revivalists' success in converting scores of individuals constituted a golden opportunity for the church. General overseer Zeno C. Tharp urged:

> There are many things about some of these evangelistic campaigns that we cannot endorse, but we cannot afford to let it prejudice us against their converts, many of which would make good Church of God members. . . . I believe if we would organize our forces and get every convert from these campaigns that we could, we would find that many of them would make just as good members as those we have.[44]

Like the healing revival, the charismatic revival emerged from the old-line Pentecostal churches. The healing revival of 1947–58 gave birth to a charismatic revival, which began in 1958. More educated and respected Pentecostal leaders such as David J. duPlessis, who was a leader in the World Council of Churches, brought a more sophisticated charismatic message into public view. The affluence of the postwar period also contributed to the emergence of the revival. Popular evangelists such as Oral Roberts left their parent churches and launched independent evangelistic associations. Historian David Edwin Harrell notes that "their organizations were the only bridge that spanned the entire expanse of Pentecostalism."[45]

As the healing revival declined, many of the shrewdest and most enterprising evangelists looked for other opportunities. The massive healing campaigns greatly broadened the diffusion of the Pentecostal/charismatic message; consequently, thousands of Christians in the historic denominations became sympathetic to speaking in tongues. By the late 1950s and early 1960s, hundreds of these believers, searching for a deeper religious experience, had received the baptism of the Holy Spirit and spoken in tongues. Prior to the revival, Christians who experiencedglossolalic inspiration either voluntarily left or were forced out of their parent churches and sought fellowship with believers in old-line Pentecostal organizations. But by the early 1960s, those who received the glossolalic experience no longer felt required to leave their own churches. The outpouring of the Holy Spirit among believers in traditional churches initiated the movement called Neopentecostalism. Participants were referred to as charismatics or Neopentecostals. A similar phenomenon occurred among American Roman Catholics in 1967. Catholics identified this as a charismatic renewal or Catholic Pentecostalism. Although charismatics included individuals from many different churches who adhered to diverse theological and doctrinal persuasions, the Holy Spirit baptism and charismata, or "gifts of the Spirit," united them.[46]

There had been scattered forerunners of the charismatic revival prior to 1960, but an episode at Van Nuys, California, brought the revival to nationwide attention. On 3 April 1960, Father Dennis Bennett, rector of St. Mark's Episcopal Church, related to a public audience an experience of the Holy Spirit baptism and speaking in tongues which had befallen him the preceding fall. Approximately one hundred members of St. Mark's received the charismatic experience in the following months. Bennett's announcement caused an immediate public reaction. The press and news media publicized the episode. In spite of adverse reaction, mainly from old-line Pentecostals, the charismatic revival spread rapidly.[47]

The Church of God split into opposing schools of thought concerning the organization's relationship to the charismatic movement. The top of the church hierarchy, composed mostly of older traditionalists, seemed to favor caution, if not repudiation of the movement. But many among the rank and file endorsed the movement and promoted a genuine spirit of cooperation.

In some ways the charismatic revival promoted competition between two rivals, the old-line Pentecostals and the Neopentecostals. In the early stages of the movement, the Church of God viewed Neopentecostals as "Johnny-come-latelies" who were attempting to supplant old-line Pentecostal organizations such as the Church of God, as cornerstones of the entire Pentecostal-charismatic movement. The prospect of losing its preeminence worried Church of God leaders. In an editorial message, Charles W. Conn, editor-in-chief and public relations director, informed his readers that many believers outside the old-line ranks were receiving the Pentecostal experience and were relating their testimony to others across the nation. Members of traditional churches now placed great emphasis on this experience, which many had rejected in the past. With a note of jealous concern, Conn warned that "if our emphasis should decrease while the emphasis of others increases, then we will lose our distinction."[48] Some clergymen feared that unless the organization increased its emphasis on the Pentecostal experience, the Church of God would be swept from the leading edge of the wave of Pentecostalism to the backwaters of complacency and lethargy.

To retain its leadership role, the church decided that the organization should remain aloof from the charismatic explosion and its leadership. The old-line church tried to avoid any direct contact with the movement. By 1963, this was clearly the church's strategy. Oral Roberts invited the Church of God to share its spiritual heritage with other charismatic Christians at a seminar which was to be held on the campus of Oral Roberts University during the week of 25 April–1 May 1963. Church of God officials discussed the invitation at the meeting of the Supreme Council in March of that year but concluded, "It is advisable that we accept his invitations."[49] It did not take Church of God leaders long to find fault with the charismatic movement. In his opening address at the meeting of the Fiftieth General Assembly, general overseer Wade H. Horton acknowledged that thousands from the historic churches had had Pentecostal experiences. Horton, who was one of the leading critics of the charismatic revival, stated that the Church of God should guide these believers into "real" Pentecostal worship, suggesting that what the Neopentecostals were enjoying was less than genuine. The general overseer's main concern—one that most older members shared—was that Neopentecostals who received the baptism of the Holy Spirit did not live according to Holiness doctrine, with its emphasis on a puritanical code of morality. In short, they did not live holy lives. Excoriating these charismatics, Horton declared that they evidenced

> no outward change, thus demonstrating that no inward work of grace has been wrought in their hearts. Some practice speaking in tongues at will. They have been taught just to open their mouths and say what comes to their minds. But that is not the old-fashioned Pentecostal way.[50]

Clearly, the general overseer and church members of the older generation believed that modernism and worldliness had penetrated the charismatic movement.

Church of God clergymen and laymen who believed that true Pentecostal experience came in three distinct stages became very upset when it seemed to them that many of the Neopentecostals were bypassing sanctification, the second essential "work of grace." According to their theology, it was impossible to receive the spirit baptism without first being sanctified. Anyone claiming such an experience simply had not experienced the genuine scriptural baptism of the Holy Spirit.

With the rapid growth of the charismatic revival, the possible effect of such heretical beliefs on the organization disturbed some Church of God leaders. Apparently some members were not only sympathetic to the charismatic movement but also receptive to its doctrine. The concern of church leaders was expressed in many forms, one being a series of articles by M.G. McLuhan, published in the *Evangel*. The author reminded his readers that the church had not reached its present size and status by imitating others. He warned, "The main danger lurks in a form of non-Pentecostal conformity that is moving among us."[51]

Not all Church of God clergymen shared McLuhan's concerns. He represented the traditionalist element within the Church of God. Most traditionalists belonged to the older generation and came from the South, which was the center of the church's strength. Other clergymen represented a more progressive element. Instead of repudiating the charismatic movement, Arnold D. Thrash, pastor of a Church of God congregation in West Orange, New Jersey, promoted the idea of cooperation between his church and Neopentecostals. He related a story about an Episcopal priest who received the baptism of the Holy Spirit while attending the Church of God at West Orange. Apparently, the priest had heard about the charismatic renewal earlier, but it was Mrs. Thrash who introduced him to the old-line Pentecostal organization when she attended services at St. Mark's Episcopal Church. Reverend Thrash enthusiastically reported that he and members of his congregation had also attended a study group meeting at St. Anthony's Catholic Church in North Vale, New Jersey. The Church of God pastor and some of his members had spoken to the Catholic audience about the baptism of the Holy Spirit and related subjects. Thrash stated that the meeting lasted until almost midnight and that "everyone seemed convinced that God had brought us that way and that this was one of the best services they had ever attended."[52] By the early 1970s, the charismatic revival was gaining momentum, and in America it became almost fashionable to be a charismatic believer and to speak in tongues. At the height of this excitement, O.W. Polen, editor-in-chief of church publications, wrote an editorial in which he attempted to answer the question, "What Should Mainstream Pentecostals' Attitude Be?" Although he noted some doctrinal differences, he prudently stated that the Church of God should no longer remain aloof from charismatics. "One thing we Pentecostals must guard against," he instructed, "is having a 'stand-offish' attitude towards neo-Pentecostals and Catholic Pentecostals."[53]

The winds of change that had begun to blow left some Church of God officials unconvinced. Evidence indicates that a diversity of opinion existed concerning the charismatic revival. Some leaders believed that such diversity was dangerous and posed a threat to the church's doctrinal uniformity. Ray H. Hughes, the general overseer, was so concerned that he made this issue the central theme of his address ("A Call to Unity") to the General Assembly in late summer 1972. Accusing some charismatics of departing from biblical standards, he bitterly labeled them imposters. Returning to the old theme of prerequisites for Holy Spirit baptism, Hughes insisted that "as fish cannot live out of the water, the baptism of Holy Ghost cannot exist without holiness [sanctified life]. Holiness is a prerequisite for the reception of the Baptism and for the maintenance of the Baptism."[54]

Continuing his fight against the infiltration of Neopentecostal doctrine into the Church of God, Hughes less than a month later wrote a three-part series in the *Evangel* on Neopentecostalism versus old-line Pentecostalism. Quoting from a unidentified magazine article, the general overseer reported that many Neopentecostals felt no obligation to adhere to Holiness taboos against use of tobacco and alcohol and against attending movies. But what troubled him most was the effect that this type of personal conviction was having upon the belief system of the Church of God. More progressive church members were beginning to hold convictions similar to those of Neopentecostals. Recognizing this difference of opinion concerning theological matters, Hughes lamented:

> Some have begun to rationalize that possibly certain traditional holiness restrictions are not as binding as they had thought. This attitude has caused a breakdown of conviction or a tolerance which makes allowances for a life pattern contrary to the Scriptures.[55]

The Church of God continued to be divided concerning charismatics throughout the later years of revival. Changes in leadership had little effect in healing this division, since traditionalists managed to maintain control of the church hierarchy. For example, Wade H. Horton was elected general overseer for a second time and served from 1974 to 1976. Upon leaving office in 1976, he delivered a sermon in which he castigated Pentecostals, including Church of God members, who identified with what he called pseudo-Pentecostals. The retiring general overseer explained that it was impossible "to try to be Pentecostal and yet appear to be like other people [charismatics]."[56] He urged his listeners to obey the teachings and doctrine of the Church of God. The clergy also received a stern warning that "no preacher's got a right to preach anything contrary to what the ordained ministers [General Council] decide in the General Assembly."[57]

Though the organization's position changed slightly during the 1980s, the Church of God continued to pursue a policy of cautious cooperation with its charismatic rivals, hoping to influence the other side while avoiding being influenced by it. As late as 9 July 1987, general overseer Raymond E. Crowley wrote an open letter to all Church of God clergymen regarding participation in a meeting of the North American Conference on the Holy Spirit and World Evangelism. He stated:

> There will be present those with whom we do not agree. Our participation is in no wise to be considered a blanket approval of all that will take place, nor is it an endorsement of all the participants. We do feel, however, that we should have a presence in the conference to represent the classical Pentecostal position. . . . We feel that this will give us an

ideal opportunity to learn more of what is taking place in the charismatic renewal movement and, hopefully, will provide us with an opportunity to have a positive impact on it.[58]

Despite criticism and caution by the traditionalist leadership of the Church of God, the charismatic revival had an impact upon the organization. It promoted a healthy spirit of competition between the two, increasing the growth of both. The Church of God feared that it might lose its place on the cutting edge of Pentecostalism. As a result, the old-line church increased its evangelistic effort and encouraged believers to receive the Pentecostal blessing. Membership had increased every year since the beginning of the organization, so several factors contributed to growth. When the revival began in 1958, the Church of God had 155,541 members in the United States. By 1974, membership had increased to 324,553, doubling during the sixteen-year period.[59] By 1986, church membership had reached 542,608 in the United States. Total membership, including foreign missions, was 1,652,089.[60] The increase in property values for the same period also reflected growth. In 1958, property value amounted to $53,997,661 in the United States. In 1974, that figure had increased to $284,932,999.[61] By 1986, the Church of God was a billion-dollar institution.[62]

The charismatic movement helped to widen social acceptance of the Pentecostal message. Many of the Neopentecostals came from more affluent middle and upper classes. Had it not been for the charismatic revival, it probably would have taken much longer for old-line denominations such as the Church of God to break into the higher stratum of American society. By the 1960s and 1970s, people from all socioeconomic classes had discovered Pentecostalism. A much wider sector of American society had accepted the Church of God and the egalitarian appeal of the pentecostal message. Pentecostalism had become "respectable." By the mid-1970s, the Pentecostal message of the Church of God had moved into mainstream conservative evangelicalism, and the church had become one of the fastest-growing Protestant organizations in America.

To some extent, the charismatic movement aided in breaking

down longstanding ecclesiastical barriers. Since World War II, the Church of God slowly had moved toward bettering relations with other Protestant denominations, beginning with its membership in the NAE, PFNA, and WFC. By the 1960s and 1970s, the Church of God not only showed signs of religious tolerance but exhibited a remarkable degree of cooperation with charismatics within the historic churches. This was especially true among more progressive Church of God clergymen and laymen.

With the influx of new members during the decades following World War II, the Church of God developed other pronounced characteristics of mainstream conservative evangelicalism. This metamorphosis began in the years immediately after the war and developed slowly but continuously after that.

The church's reaction to the secularization of American society during the Vietnam War era testifies to this remarkable transition. As we have noted, the United States experienced profound political and social changes during these tumultuous times. In the minds of some churchmen, liberal religious leaders were responsible for the erosion of traditional values and mores. As one Church of God official put it, "Modernism with its leadership of liberals and ultra-liberals is making rapid inroads into the minds and masses of the church-going people of our day."[63] The rise of neoorthodoxy and situational ethics, or the New Morality, produced a "crisis" mentality among church leaders, who were troubled by such complex moral and social issues as abortion, gay rights, the Equal Rights Amendment, pornography, prayer in public schools, civil disobedience, and civil rights.

The crisis mentality surrounding issues such as these motivated many church members to embrace political activism. During the 1970s and 1980s, the Church of God increased its involvement in issues ranging from abortion to international terrorism. Church leaders proposed various solutions for the nation's problems. They instructed members to pray for divine intervention. Included in such prayers was a request that God-fearing Christian leaders be elected who could find proper solutions to society's ills.

Prior to World War II, the Church of God had not encouraged its members to vote, but by 1960 this apolitical position had been abandoned. In that year the organization passed a resolution urging members to register and vote on national, state, and local issues.[64] There were many reasons why the church took this action. In 1960, there was a strong possibility that a Catholic candidate could be elected to the presidency. The mere chance of such an occurrence frightened many Protestants. Like their fellow believers, many Church of God members believed that if a Catholic were elected president, Protestants would lose their religious freedom and there would be a union of church and state. One clergyman warned that "a Catholic president would either share these views and work as hard as he could toward bringing them to pass, or he would be under constant pressure from his church to do so."[65]

In spring 1960, thousands of letters flooded Church of God headquarters in Cleveland, Tennessee. Members asked for advice on how they should vote in the upcoming presidential election. The general overseer, James A. Cross, answered these requests in an open letter in the *Evangel*. Although he did not openly instruct members to vote against John F. Kennedy, Cross admonished, "If we Protestants sit idly by and fail to exercise our constitutional right to express ourselves at the polls, let no-one complain if a Catholic is elected to the presidency. Let us be prepared, however, to accept the consequences which will follow."[66]

By late summer it was apparent that the Catholic nominee of the Democratic Party was running an effective campaign and had an excellent chance of winning the election in November. The Church of God reacted by passing a resolution reaffirming its belief in the separation of church and state.[67]

Other social issues motivated Church of God members to become political activists. Progressive Church of God leaders not only encouraged participation but also chastised members who seemed apathetic. R. Hollis Gause, professor of religion at Lee College, noted that the church had considered political and civic duties too corrupt for involvement by Holiness people in the past. "This is not a spiritual attitude," remarked Gause, "it is one form of accepting second best."[68]

Faculty members at Lee College proved indispensable in helping the church change from an apolitical to a politicized organization. Professor Terrell McBrayer and others with similar convictions were instrumental in nudging the church forward during this transition period. In summer 1966, McBrayer wrote,

> The Christian is not isolated by his church membership from other humanity or freed from his obligation in community affairs. The Christian is called upon to identify himself with the problems of society. The Christian should be involved on the frontiers of government and in all the corporate processes of our society.[69]

One month later, at the General Assembly, officials decreed that the church "go on record as heartily supporting any and all bipartisan legislation that seeks to maintain the Christian principles that have made our nation great and influential."[70]

This became the clarion call for Church of God members for the next twenty years. Those who were activists advised their fellow members on why and for whom they should vote. Roy Jussell, a Church of God political enthusiast, maintained that members should be informed on the issues of the day and be familiar with their political representatives and where they stood on issues. Jussell declared, "May it not be said of Christian voters that they were lax in informing themselves on issues and candidates."[71]

In 1968, the Church of God took another step toward involvement. It instructed members to vote only for those persons who were dedicated to the Christian principles upon which America had been founded. With the election of Richard Nixon, Church of God members thought that they had found a leader who would initiate "a new era of moral and spiritual restoration." The Watergate scandal and subsequent revelations of corruption in the Nixon administration dispelled these high hopes. Far from disillusioning members concerning political activism, this revelation caused them to become even more active in social and political affairs. In an article that appeared in the November 1973 issue of *Lighted Pathway*, Belinda Roope, a young female church member, wrote that young people not only should take advantage of the lower voting age but also should become involved in day-to-day politics. Concluding her message, Roope stated, "This article in essence is a plea for more Christian youth involvement in politics."[72]

Like other conservative religious organizations, such as the Moral Majority, the Church of God's plea for political involvement evolved into a religious crusade during the 1970s and 1980s. Because of its campaign against the forces of "secular humanism," church leaders charged members to evaluate political representatives and to hold them accountable for the moral content of their decisions and activities. According to the Church of God, if politicians were not acceptable, members should vote them out of office.[73] In 1984 the church passed a resolution encouraging members to vote, but added a call for "its members, and especially its ministers, to consider carefully the guiding principles of Scripture in deciding social, civil, political, and religious issues."[74] A church that had shunned politics in its early history did almost everything but command members to become activists in political and civic affairs. Many members heeded the command. During the 1970s and 1980s, Church of God members voted, held public office, and served as political representatives mostly on a local or regional level.

The Church of God also was divided on such issues as civil rights. Church members, especially those in the South, seemed to agree about blacks and their role in society. Most Church of God members, like many white southerners, were racially prejudiced. Both young and old exhibited prejudice toward blacks. A sociology class at Lee College, under the supervision of professor George Brazell, conducted a survey pertaining to white student relationships with blacks and Orientals. Some 450 students participated. Charles Beach, a student in the class who later became a church educator, wrote a term paper entitled "Jim Crow or Jesus Christ." The paper dealt with one of the questions to which students had responded: "Would you permit yourself to be given a blood transfusion from a Negro?" Of the 450 students, 60.7% said no, 31.8% said only if it meant life or death, and only 7.5% stated that they would consent without any reservation. An overwhelming majority, 92.5%, expressed fears that such a transfusion might cause a change in the color in their skin or transmit other "undesirable" characteristics of the Negro to them. Beach concluded that the findings of the survey proved that most students' views on race were the result of nothing more than a deep-seated prejudice. Moreover, Beach believed that most of the students surveyed "would rather see the Negro under the binding law of 'Jim Crow' than the saving law of Jesus Christ."[75]

Like most southerners, Church of God members viewed the black man and his role in society through paternalistic eyes. They accepted discrimination and segregation of the races as a way of life—one that they believed had worked rather well. Many Church of God clergymen believed that the races should remain segregated in order to retain racial purity. They argued that God had created different races and commanded that they remain separate. Presenting the same arguments that their fellow white southerners used, Church of God ministers argued that blacks were descendants of Ham, the accursed son of Noah. Clergymen encouraged all blacks to be content with segregation and with their place in society. A few adamant preachers claimed that no organization, law officer, American president, or Supreme Court would ever remake society. Disclaiming any racial prejudice, T.L. Lowery, a prominent Church of God evangelist who later held the office of assistant general overseer, warned: "When man tries to overstep the purposes of God and break down the barrier between the races, he only brings trouble, discord, confusion, malice, and murder."[76]

To support the segregationist viewpoint, the *Evangel* in 1949 published part of an article entitled "A Negro's Viewpoint on Civil Rights." The story contained excerpts from an article written by Lee Davis, a black publisher of the New Jersey *Telegram*. After an extensive tour of the South, Davis had concluded that segregation was the best thing for all parties concerned, and he stated that it had been the economic salvation of blacks in the South. According to Davis, the paternalistic attitude of southern whites was a natural psychological reaction to and aftermath of the Civil War and Reconstruction. "It is not hatred for the Negro," maintained Davis, "the South just doesn't believe that the Negro has grown up."[77] Support for segregation from middle-class black leaders reinforced paternalism among southern whites.

Convinced that most blacks were satisfied with the *status quo,* Church of God clergymen, like most white Americans in the

1940s, believed that agitation for civil rights did not come from blacks but from "outside agitators" and unscrupulous politicians. In January 1949, J.D. Bright, editor of church publications, suspected that President Truman and the Americans for Democratic Action (ADA) were playing "cheap politics" with the civil rights issue. Reflecting a typical southern attitude, Bright warned:

> The South is the only section of the country that is capable of dealing with this particular race question, and if outsiders will keep their noses out of our business down here, we, the white and colored people, will solve this problem to the satisfaction of the South, and that by all means should be satisfactory to everybody concerned.[78]

The paternalistic bias that was so pervasive in the early Church of God slowly began to fade in the 1950s as a result of multiple complex factors: confrontations between civil rights advocates and segregationists in the South; within the Church of God, a struggle for equal rights by its black members, and pressure from white progressives who wanted the church to integrate.

As blacks struggled for their rights in the South, black Church of God members too, while avoiding violence, fought for equal rights in the white male–dominated church. Although the Church of God had begun as an interracial religious sect, separation of white and black congregations began about 1912, when Edmund S. Barr, the sect's first ordained black minister, accepted an appointment as state overseer of black churches in Florida. Two years later, however, the organization replaced Barr with a white overseer, Sam C. Perry. In the period 1912–22, black Church of God members increasingly pushed for equal rights. They wanted their own General Assembly and leaders. At first, white members were more than happy to acquiesce in the black churches' to have a black overseer. The Church of God General Assembly in 1922 officially approved separation of the black and white churches, and all-white male Elders' Council appointed a black clergyman, Thomas F. Richardson, as overseer of the black church.[79]

Continuing the struggle, black clergymen requested permission to convene their own annual assembly. The organization granted this request, but with the restriction that the white general overseer be allowed to attend. This was done to keep the black church under the supervision of the white-dominated government of the Church of God. There were some black members, however, who were unhappy with the organization's segregation policy. Apparently, black members residing in some northern states objected and wanted to attend the white General Assembly instead. F.J. Lee, the general overseer, granted this request.[80]

From 1922 to 1958, black churches remained under the supervision of a black overseer. In 1951, church officials considered replacing the black overseer with a white clergyman. Revealing their paternalism, members of the all-white Supreme Council felt that black churches "might make progress working under the supervision of the white overseers."[81] The council, however, did not make the change. During the late 1940s and early 1950s, many black clergymen and laymen believed that their needs were not receiving proper attention from the white leadership. They felt isolated, subjugated to an all-white leadership, and almost betrayed by their white brethren.[82]

To help overcome this feeling of powerlessness, five of the leading black ministers presented a resolution to the Supreme Council which pointed out that blacks had been denied the right to have their overseer sit in meetings of the council and asked that this policy be overturned. The white council argued that the black overseer never had had this right. The council then voted to allow the black members this privilege but *without* voting rights.[83] Apparently council members believed that this concession would please most blacks. Just three days later, however, the council received a letter from the black overseer, George A. Wallace, stating that he would not be able to attend the next council meeting.[84] This may have been a silent protest against the council's decision not to allow the black overseer voting privileges.

Relations between the black churches and the rest of the Church of God remained friendly until 1958. In that year the organization amended the rule concerning the selection of the black overseer. From this point on, blacks were not allowed to have an overseer of their own race. J.T. Roberts, a white clergyman, was appointed as overseer of the black church for an indefinte period.[85] The Supreme Council had suggested the change at its March 1958 meeting because "the colored work of the Church of God is making such slow progress."[86] On the morning of May 13, during the meeting of the black General Assembly, the general overseer of the Church of God, Houston R. Morehead, informed his black audience that the Supreme Council had decided to appoint Roberts as their new overseer. According to church historian Charles Conn, the announcement was greeted "with some question and considerable optimism."[87] The optimism must have been expressed only by the white leadership, because an emotional storm of controversy immediately engulfed the black audience. One by one, black members protested the decision. Tempers flared to the point that Morehead decided to call the session to a close. During the afternoon meeting, black members continued to express their opposition to the appointment. But, as the minutes of the assembly attest, "Howbeit, the appointment remained unchanged."[88] Obviously many blacks were unhappy with the decision; nevertheless, most decided to remain in the organization. However, relations between the two groups became strained.

In spite of significant growth, from three thousand black members in 1958 to about seven thousand in 1963, relations between blacks and whites in the Church of God remained tense during the early 1960s.[89] Racial tensions also increased in the South during the same period, but by the mid-1960s, blacks had made significant progress in their struggle for equal rights. This battle forced major changes in society. The Church of God also felt the effect of the fierce struggle and slowly made important changes that affected the black church. To maintain racial harmony, the General Assembly in August 1964 adopted a human rights resolution, stating that "no American should, because of his race, or religion, be deprived of his right to worship, vote, rest, eat, sleep, be educated, live, and work on the same basis as other citizens."[90] The Church of God, however, continued to feel increased pressure from within and outside the organization.

Despite the 1964 passage of a human rights resolution, the Church of God was still unwilling to integrate. However, the struggle for equal rights within the black church gained momentum. In June 1965, J.T. Roberts inexplicably resigned as overseer of the black church, but the Executive Council, despite opposition from black members, still decided to appoint another white minister to this post. At the meeting of the black assembly, the Church of God general overseer, Wade Horton, announced the council's appointment of David L. Lemons, a white clergyman, as the black overseer. Angry protests immediately erupted from the audience. Black ministers stood and voiced adamant opposition to the council's decision. In 1958 they had acquiesced in the decision of white church officials for the sake of maintaining harmony within the organization, but they had informed general overseer Morehead then that, when the time came for Roberts to be replaced, black members wanted a black overseer. One of the former black overseers, George A. Wallace, pleaded, "If our General Overseer and the Executives love us they will not leave this white man here."[91]

Another black leader, H.A. Hawes, national youth and Sunday school director, argued that the black church could have gained more members if it had had a black overseer. He cited a case in Baltimore, Maryland, in which an entire congregation refused to join the black Church of God because it had a white overseer.[92] Responding to these protests, general overseer Horton nevertheless indignantly remarked, "I have traveled over many countries but never before had I had my word challenged from the pulpit as to whether I spoke the truth."[93] Regardless of opposition, the appointment went unchanged.

Once again, racial tension mounted in the Church of God, and it remained quite high during the following months. By summer 1966, however, much to the delight of blacks and progressive whites who wanted the church to integrate, the organization showed signs of changing its segregation policy. As early as 1962, some professors at Lee College wanted to see the school admit black students. In 1963, Supreme Council members discussed the possibility but decided against the open admission policy. Supporters of integration had wanted the policy recommended to the General Assembly, but council members had refused to do so. At the council meeting of July 1966, J.T. Roberts, former overseer of the black church, presented a long resolution con-

H. G. Poitier, black leader in the Church of God.
(Hal Bernard Dixon, Jr., Pentecostal Research Center, Cleveland, Tenn.)

cerning black members. He called for the church to integrate. "The Negro is fully aware of his rights," declared Roberts. "We are an intelligent group and cannot fool ourselves any longer."[94] Based upon numerous recommendations similar to this one and reacting to other pressures, the council finally decided to recommend integration to the General Assembly for final disposition. In the following month, the assembly voted to integrate the organization. The Church of God subsequently reorganized, removing all references to "colored" ministers, churches, or members from the official *Minutes* and other records.[95]

The integration of the Church of God helped to relieve long-standing tensions. There continued to be some problems concerning black-white relations, but, during the next two decades, the church took steps to find functional solutions. During this period, both black and white clergymen expressed the need for patience and cooperation. In 1974, John D. Nichols, director of evangelism and home missions, invited black students at Lee College to meet with him and other church leaders. The purpose of the meeting was to give the students an opportunity to express their feelings about the organization and its responsibility to the black membership. The students made some rather enlightening suggestions. These included: more black students and faculty members in all Church of God colleges, appointment of more black ministers on all levels of administration, and a more aggressive evangelism of blacks.[96]

As black Church of God membership grew in the 1970s and 1980s, blacks continued to push for equality and for greater representation in the church hierarchy. Many requested the church to appoint more blacks to higher offices, including standing boards and committees. The Church of God appointed a few blacks to lower-level positions, but it did not have a black representative on the powerful Council of Twelve until 1986. At that time the church increased the size of this body from twelve to eighteen members, and the ordained ministers (General Council) elected two black clergymen to serve on this body.[97] At present, blacks account for approximately 4 percent of total church membership in the United States. Although no statistics on black members outside the country are available, the number

A storefront Church of God in an unidentified city.
(*Hal Bernard Dixon, Jr., Pentecostal Research Center, Cleveland, Tenn.*)

is much higher. As blacks living in America and those abroad continue to join the church, they should play a more salient role, and the number of blacks who hold positions in the upper ranks of the administration likely will increase.

By the 1980s, the Church of God not only had moved into mainstream conservative evangelicalism, but also it indirectly had become involved in the Civil Rights struggle. It was one of the few southern-based denominations that integrated during the 1960s. In the post-World War II period, most southern churches were segregated. Some retained black congregations as satellite organizations under the control of paternalistic whites. The liberal racial thought that emerged from the Church of God during the Civil Rights movement was associated with the growing sophistication of the organization. The church now had younger, better-educated members who followed middle-class values and social mores. The question of racial equality produced internal divisions along class lines and between progressives and traditionalists. The integration of the Church of God in 1965 resulted from three forces: the struggle between civil rights advocates and segregationists outside the church, a struggle for equality by black members within the church, and pressure from middle-class progressives who supported integration of the church.

In the years before World War II, to many Americans, the Church of God, despite substantial growth, seemed an obscure religious sect composed of sincere but fanatical believers. Still others who were more critical viewed the church as composed of tongue-speaking lunatics. In the postwar years, the church adopted many changes that moved it into mainstream conservative evangelicalism. Beginning with its membership in the National Association of Evangelicals, the Church of God aligned itself with other evangelical Christians, effectively breaking down longstanding ecclesiastical barriers. From that time on, the church ran a new and steady course of denominational cooperation and growing social involvement.

Epilogue

The Church of God was founded as part of a larger "come-outism" movement which erupted in America in the latter part of the nineteenth century. The movement included religious and political wings. During this period the South experienced profound changes which resulted in an extensive disruption of society. Some ordinary people who held orthodox beliefs left their churches because they identified the historic denominations with the middle-class aspirations of the New South. These class-conscious "come-outers" felt alienated, isolated from sources of power, and surrounded by an unfriendly culture. As a result of this crisis, many former Baptists and Methodists seceded from parent denominations and formed religious sects in an attempt to recover primitive Christianity.

Pentecostals sprang from an older "come-out" phenomenon, the Holiness movement which had arisen in the 1870s. They emerged from the more radical and extreme fringe of the Holiness movement. Pentecostalism won wide support from poor, rural southerners, especially subsistence farmers, tenants, sharecroppers, coal miners, and mill workers. The Church of God and other Pentecostal churches, such as the Pentecostal Holiness Church, Assemblies of God, and the Church of God in Christ, found its early converts and flourished among this humble group during the first few decades of the twentieth century. The Pentecostal message gave believers, who lived in a chaotic and rapidly changing world, a sense of direction and meaning in their lives.

It offered them escape from their suffering and hope for a better life, if not in this world then surely thereafter.

Pentecostal doctrine was radically fundamentalist. No aspect of the sect better demonstrated this characteristic than its austere, puritanical code of personal morality. Members abstained from alcohol, tobacco, secret societies, labor unions, carnivals, dancing, movies, chewing gum, soft drinks, public swimming, jewelry, cosmetics, certain styles of dress, and most sports. The Church of God taught that, after conversion, a believer should seek the blessing of sanctification or the "second work of grace." This cleansing experience placed an individual in a position to seek a third work in the spiritual progression: the baptism of the Holy Ghost, which was accompanied by speaking in tongues. Glossolalia became the primary trademark of all Pentecostals.

No single characteristic of the Church of God was more salient than its insistence on a literal interpretation of Scripture, a fact which led to eccentric practices among its early constituency. Snake handling was the most bizarre practice which developed among Church of God folk. In 1910, George W. Hensley, a former Baptist, initiated the practice near the community of Grasshopper Valley, Tennessee. Two years later he joined the Church of God. The ritual spread to many congregations, with some clergymen and laymen practicing it and others denying its validity. Although the practice originated in southern Appalachia, Church of God members from Florida to Ohio handled poisonous reptiles. In 1928, amid growing public criticism of the practice, the Church of God repudiated the custom after some snake handling members died as a result of bites. More zealous members continued to handle serpents, but the practice apparently declined by the end of the 1930s.

Pacifism was another sectarian trait of the Church of God. Church leaders bitterly denounced the decision of the United States to enter World War I. Evangelism was far more important in the minds of Church of God members than any corporeal warfare. The church protested America's participation in the war effort by opposing conscription. Church officials instructed young males to file for exemption while registering for the draft. If drafted, they were to seek only noncombatant duty. The Church of God warned draft-age men that the church believed that it was wrong to take up arms against their fellow man. Because of this strong pacifist position, the Federal Bureau of Investigation conducted an official inquiry concerning the Church of God, its overseer A.J. Tomlinson, and numerous clergymen. Federal investigators confiscated records, censored publications and correspondence, and arrested churchmen who were suspected of draft evasion, obstructing the war effort, or having pro-German sympathies. It was not until after World War II that the Church of God shed its pacifist beliefs and became a more militant organization.

Unlike most mainstream churches, the Church of God afforded women the opportunity for active service within most of its departments. Leaders realized that female workers, who constituted a majority of the membership, could be a valuable asset in the organization's growth and so had to be utilized. Because of this realization and the subsequent decision by the leadership to encourage female participation, women played a variety of roles in the early Church of God. They served as evangelists, pastors, missionaries, secretaries and treasurers of local congregations, instructors in church schools, supervisors of orphanages, musicians, and Sunday school teachers. The first clergy was all male, but because evangelism was an urgent goal, the Church of God allowed female members who felt "the call" to preach the gospel. Most Protestant denominations banned women from preaching. Although Church of God leaders were biblical literalists, they proved capable of accommodating theology to social reality.

From its beginning to World War II, the Church of God was an obscure religious sect. Since that time the church has moved rapidly into mainstream conservative evangelicalism. This ascent has not come without a struggle. Forces within the Church of God and outside it have contributed to the organization's rise.

The charismatic revival which began in 1958 also contributed to the old-line Pentecostal church's ascent into middle-class Protestantism. Prior to the Neopentecostal movement, members of historic Protestant denominations believed that the Holy Spirit baptism, speaking in tongues, and other "gifts of the Spirit" were either heretical beliefs or, at best, doctrinal aberrations.

The charismatic revival erupted among upper- and middle-class members of traditional churches. Their acceptance of the Pentecostal message made the entire Pentecostal movement more respectable. The ministry of the Church of God was widely accepted as a result. The old-line Pentecostal organization also obtained many of its new members during the charismatic revival.

Upward social mobility, strongly linked to the economic effects of World War II, has marked the Church of God and its constituency in recent decades. As a result of this upward mobility and enhanced respectability, the church has attracted many new members from upper socioeconomic classes during the past forty years. The addition of these better-educated, more affluent members, who possessed greater social awareness, motivated the Church of God to become deeply involved in social issues. By the 1980s, the organization was identified with the "religious right." The Church of God, along with others of the right wing, became active in the struggle against so-called "secular humanism." This activity took many forms, including protests and boycotts. Church of God members supported "Christian" legislation and voted for political representatives who supported such laws. Members also contributed votes to remove politicians who did not support their preferred policies. This social and political involvement is illustrative of the church's march into mainstream conservative evangelicalism.

Americanization has transformed both region and church. The South has changed from a distinctly separate region to one less distinguishable from the nation. The Church of God has changed from an obscure religious sect to a mainstream conservative evangelical denomination. Constant social pressures caused the organization to modify its doctrine and teachings in response to social realities. As a result, the Church of God gained respectability and moved into the middle class. Beginning in the 1940s, progressive members joined the church and served in leadership roles. These progressives greatly facilitated the church's move into mainstream conservative evangelicalism.

Simultaneous with the Americanization of the Church of God, a concomitant "Pentecostalization" of America occurred. The tumultuous events of the Vietnam War era disrupted society and

The new Church of God General Offices in Cleveland, Tennessee
(*Hal Bernard Dixon, Jr., Pentecostal Research Center, Cleveland, Tenn.*)

resulted in profound social changes. Conservative and middle-class values and habits came under attack by intellectuals, radical students, and liberal religious leaders. Traditional notions of morality gave way to "the New Morality" and situational ethics. Many believed that alternative lifestyles such as those of homosexuals or "swinging singles" threatened to replace the traditional family unit. Such threats deeply disturbed millions of Americans. Some of these troubled middle-class residents discovered the Church of God during that traumatic and chaotic period.

Through the years, the denomination has remained a rock of conservatism, of traditional values and morals. Thousands of middle-class Americans have joined the church since 1960. Their acceptance of Pentecostalism, their Pentecostal experiences, and their affiliation with the Church of God have given them a sense of direction amid chaos, a measure of control over their lives, and, perhaps most important, a conviction that they understand the meaning of personal and historical events.

Notes

Abbreviations

COG	Church of God
NA	National Archives, Washington, D.C.
PH	Publishing House
PRC	Hal Bernard Dixon, Jr., Pentecostal Research Center, Lee College, Cleveland, Tenn.
USGPO	United States Government Printing Office, Washington, D.C.
WGS	William G. Squires Library, Lee College, Cleveland, Tenn.

Chapter 1

1. L. Howard Juillerat, ed., *Book of Minutes, 1–13, 1906–1917* (Cleveland, Tenn.: COG PH, 1922), p. 8.

2. Daniel M. Robison, "Tennessee Politics and the Agrarian Revolt, 1886–1896," *Mississippi Valley Historical Review* 20 (Dec. 1933): 367.

3. Roger L. Hart, *Redeemers, Bourbons, and Populists* (Baton Rouge: Louisiana State Univ. Press, 1975), p. 145.

4. Ibid.

5. Robison, "Tennessee Politics," 379.

6. A.J. Tomlinson, *Answering the Call of God* (Cleveland, Tenn.: White Wing PH, n.d.), p. 4.

7. Homer A. Tomlinson, *The Shout of a King* (Queens Village, N.Y.: COG, USA Headquarters, 1968), p. 16.

8. A.J. Tomlinson, *Answering the Call*, p. 9.

9. Ibid., p. 10.

10. Sister [Nettie] Bryant, interview by an anonymous person, 8 Feb. 1954, Typescript, Document 8A, files of PRC, p. 1.

11. Names and places of residence of the early Church of God members were collected by the author from extant sources.

12. Charles W. Conn, *Like a Mighty Army* (Cleveland, Tenn.: Pathway Press, 1977), p. 71.

13. June Glover Marshall, *A Biographical Sketch of Richard G. Spurling, Jr.* (Cleveland, Tenn.: Pathway Press, 1974), p. 18.

14. A.J. Tomlinson, *Answering the Call*, p. 8.

15. James A. Muncey, "My Life and Work," n.p., n.d., p. 32, PRC. Also see Mrs. L. Howard Juillerat, comp., *Gems of Religious Truth* (Cleveland, Tenn.: COG Evangel Press, 1919), p. 1; and Charles W. Conn, *Like A Mighty Army*, p. 105.

16. U.S. Dept. of Commerce, Bureau of the Census, *Eleventh Census of the United States, 1890: Reports on the Statistics of Agriculture in the U.S.* (Washington, D.C.: USGPO, 1896), p. ccxxxvi.

17. James Spurling (grandson of Richard G. Spurling, Jr.), interview by Mickey Crews, Turtletown, Tenn., 25 Sept. 1982. The 640 acres of land were purchased at 25 cents per acre under the preemption clause of the Homestead Act.

18. Marshall, *Biographical Sketch of Richard G. Spurling, Jr.*, pp. 17–18.

19. Ibid.

20. Hunter D. Farish, *The Circuit Rider Dismounts: A Social History of Southern Methodism, 1865–1900* (Richmond, Va.: Dietz Press, 1938), pp. 100–101.

21. Farish, *Circuit Rider Dismounts*, pp. 73–74. For a study of Landmarkism, see W. Morgan Patterson, "The Influence of Landmarkism Among Baptists," *Baptist History and Heritage* 11 (Jan. 1976): 43–54.

22. Farish, *Circuit Rider Dismounts*, p. 104.

23. Bruce Palmer, *Man Over Money: The Southern Populist Critique of American Capitalism* (Chapel Hill: Univ. of North Carolina Press, 1980), p. 207.

24. Richard G. Spurling, Jr., *The Lost Link* (Turtletown [Cleveland], Tenn.: COG PH, 1920), p. 26.

25. L. Howard Juillerat, *Book of Minutes*, pp. 7–9. Also see Charles W. Conn, *Like A Mighty Army*, pp. 5–9.

26. L. Howard Juillerat, *Book of Minutes*, p. 10.

27. Ibid., p. 11.

28. Ibid., pp. 12–13.

29. M.S. Lemons, "History of the Church of God," unpublished manuscript, PRC.

30. Spurling, *Lost Link*, p. 24.

31. Ibid., p. 30.

32. Bruce Palmer, *Man Over Money*, p. 4.

33. Bruce Palmer, "The Rhetoric of Southern Populists: Metaphor and Imagery in the Language of Reform" (Ph.D. diss., Yale Univ., 1972), p. 334.

34. Mrs. F.J. Lee, *Life Sketches and Sermons of F.J. Lee* (Cleveland, Tenn.: COG PH, 1929), p. 197.

35. Richard Hofstadter, *The Age of Reform: From Bryan to FDR* (New York: Knopf, 1955), p. 24.

36. COG 1st General Assembly (1906), *Minutes*, p. 1. Also see Sister Nettie Bryant interview, 8 Feb. 1954.

37. Bruce Palmer, *Man Over Money*, p. 127.

38. See Bruce Palmer, "Law and Government," *Man Over Money*, ch. 4; Norman Pollack, "The Farmer and Working Class Discontent," *The Populist Response to Industrial America: Midwestern Populist Thought*, ch. 3 (Cambridge, Mass.: Harvard Univ. Press, 1962); and Walter K. Nugent, *The Tolerant Populists: Kansas Populism and Nativism* (Chicago: Univ. of Chicago Press, 1963), pp. 103–105.

39. Lemons, "History of the Church of God," p. 11. Also see W.F. Bryant, interview by Geneva Carroll, 1949, typescript, Document 27A, files of PRC. Nora Jones (daughter of W.F. Bryant), interview by Mickey Crews, Cleveland, Tenn., 8 July 1982.

40. L. Howard Juillerat, *Book of Minutes*, pp. 8–9.

41. Carolyn Dirksen, "Let Your Women Keep Silent," unpublished manuscript, PRC, p. 1. Julian Robinson, director of the Department of Records, COG, Cleveland, Tenn., interview by Mickey Crews, 1 Nov. 1982.

42. A.J. Tomlinson, "Journal of Happenings," unpublished diary, 4 June 1912, PRC.

Chapter 2

1. See organizational chart.

2. Mrs. L. Howard Juillerat, *Gems of Religious Truth*, pp. 12–13.

3. Ibid., p. 14.

4. COG 17th General Assembly, *Minutes*, p. 14.

5. Ibid., pp. 18–19.

6. Ibid., p. 22.

7. Charles W. Conn, *Like A Mighty Army*, p. 94.

8. COG 17th General Assembly, *Minutes*, pp. 35–36.

9. COG 6th General Assembly, *Minutes*, p. 12. Also see E.L. Simmons, *History of the Church of God* (Cleveland, Tenn.: COG PH, 1938), p. 24.

10. Ibid., pp. 45–47.

11. COG 9th General Assembly, *Minutes*, p. 11.

12. COG 6th General Assembly, *Minutes*, p. 242.

13. Ibid.

14. COG 15th General Assembly, *Minutes*, p. 19. Also see A.J. Tomlinson, "Journal," 2 Sept. 1921. Also see a one-page document entitled "Notes," n.d., A.J. Tomlinson Personal Correspondence, PRC.

15. L.G. Rouse, "Modern Miracles," n.p., n.d., pp. 103–104; M.P. Cross, "In The Good (?) Ole Days," n.p., n.d., pp. 27–28.

16. COG 16th General Assembly, *Minutes*, pp. 52–53.

17. Ibid., pp. 35–36.

18. Ibid., pp. 59 and 65. Also see Daniel J. Preston, *The Era of A.J. Tomlinson* (Cleveland, Tenn.: White Wing PH, 1974), pp. 122–23.

19. E.L. Simmons, *History of the Church of God*, p. 37–38.

20. Perry E. Gillum, *Historical Annual Addresses* (Cleveland, Tenn.: White Wing PH, 1970), pp. 188, 197, 204.

21. Ibid., pp. 199–200. Also see "Notes," A.J. Tomlinson Correspondence.

22. COG 19th General Assembly, *Minutes*, pp. 48–51.

23. Ibid.

24. A.J. Tomlinson, "Journal," 2 Sept. 1921.

25. COG 17th General Assembly, *Minutes*, p. 58.

26. COG Elders' Council, "Report of Investigation," 12–21 June 1923, p. 1.

27. Lee H. Battle Audit Company, "Audit Report: Church of God, Cleveland, Tenn., December 1, 1922." This is a 23-page document in the files of the PRC.

28. Ibid. Also see A.J. Tomlinson to E.J. Boehmer, 23 Apr. 1923, A.J. Tomlinson Correspondence.

29. COG Elders' Council, "Report of Investigation," pp. 8–13.

30. A.J. Tomlinson, "Journal," 21 May 1923. The information cited occurred following the Elders' Council meeting on 21 June. Tomlinson includes information regarding this meeting and his reaction to it, but he does not date the information. It is presented with the last entry, that of 21 May. Also see F.J. Lee to A.J. Tomlinson et al., 26 July 1923, F.J. Lee Correspondence.

31. A.J. Lawson, "A Declaration" (Cleveland, Tenn.: COG Bureau of Information, n.d.), p. 1.

32. COG Elders' Council, *Minutes*, 26 July 1923, pp. 188–89.

33. "The Call Council of the Church of God Held at Chattanooga, Tennessee, August 8, 1923," an unpublished document, n.d., pp. 22–23, PRC.

34. A.J. Tomlinson, "Journal," 2 Sept. 1923.

35. COG Supreme Council, *Minutes*, 26 July 1923, p. 188; also see COG 18th General Assembly, *Minutes*, p. 7.

36. Charles W. Conn, *Like A Mighty Army*, pp. 186–87.

37. A.J. Tomlinson to F.J. Lee, 12 July 1923, A.J. Tomlinson Correspondence.

38. Tennessee, Bradley County, Chancery Court, *Church of God v. A.J. Tomlinson et al.*, File Number 1891.

39. Tennessee, Bradley County, Chancery Court, *Minutes Book No. 17*, pp. 132 and 143.

40. Tennessee, State Supreme Court, *Records for Bradley County*, 1925, p. 70.

41. Tennessee, State Supreme Court, *Volume of Supreme Court Opinions*, 1927, p. 70.

42. Tennessee, Bradley County, Chancery Court, *Minutes Book No. 18*, p. 185.

43. Tennessee, Bradley County, Chancery Court, *Church of God v. Tomlinson Church of God*, No. 1891, 1 May 1952, pp. 18–20.

44. COG 21st General Assembly, *Minutes*, p. 31.

45. Ibid., pp. 32–34.

46. Ibid., p. 32.

47. COG 23rd General Assembly, *Minutes*, p. 50.

48. COG 25th General Assembly, *Minutes*, pp. 22–23. The term *Bishop* was chosen because ordained clergymen were called bishops, and the Bishops' Council was composed of all ordained clergymen.

49. Mrs. S.J. Wood, "History of the LWWB," *Evangel*, 2 Mar. 1940, p. 7.

50. COG 31st General Assembly, *Minutes*, p. 35.

51. COG 59th General Assembly, *Minutes*, p. 42.

52. COG 36th General Assembly, *Minutes*, p. 18.

53. COG Supreme Council, *Minutes*, Aug. 1944, pp. 18–19; COG 39th General Assembly, *Minutes*, pp. 22–23; COG Supreme Council, *Minutes*, Aug. 1945, p. 37; COG 40th General Assembly, *Minutes*, p. 26.

54. Frank W. Lemons, "Divisions in the Church," an unpublished manuscript, n.d., p. 24.

55. Paul H. Walker, *Paths of a Pioneer* (Cleveland, Tenn.: Pathway Press, 1971), p. 248.

56. Frank W. Lemons, "Divisions in the Church," p. 26.

57. Paul H. Walker, *Paths of a Pioneer*, p. 248.

58. Frank W. Lemons, "Divisions in the Church," p. 28.

59. COG 39th General Assembly, *Minutes*, p. 23.

60. COG 61st General Assembly, *Minutes*, pp. 79–102.

61. COG 50th General Assembly, *Minutes*, p. 27.

62. COG 51st General Assembly, *Minutes*, p. 53.

Chapter 3

1. M.S. Lemons, "History of the Church of God," p. 7; Nora Jones interview, 8 July 1982; D.B. Smith, interview by Mickey Crews, Auburn, Ala., 31 Oct. 1982.

2. Robert M. Anderson, in his study, *Vision of the Disinherited: The Making of American Pentecostalism* (New York: Oxford Univ. Press, 1979), argues that Pentecostals were lacking in verbal skills because they demeaned education and inculcated rigid taboos against social and cultural activities that might have ameliorated their verbal ineptitude. Bryan R. Wilson, the British sociologist of religion, in his work *Religious Sects: A Sociological Study* (London: Weidenfeld and Nicolson, 1970), holds similar views. Numerous studies have been made of psychological aspects of Pentecostal religion. Most of these are unsympathetic and describe Pentecostals as social deviants. Some of these are: George B. Cutten's *Speaking with Tongues: Historically and Psychologically Considered* (New Haven, Conn.: Yale Univ. Press, 1927); Anton T. Boisen's *Religion in Crisis and Custom* (New York: Harper, 1945); *Religion, Altered States of Consciousness and Social Change* (Columbus: Ohio State Univ. Press, 1973), edited by Erika

Bourguignon; and Donald Metz's *Speaking in Tongues: An Analysis* (Kansas City, Mo.: Nazarene PH, 1964).

3. Mrs. F.J. Lee, *Sketches and Sermons*, p. 197.

4. Abbie Brown, "Church Amusement," *Evangel*, 7 Aug. 1915, p. 4.

5. Ibid.

6. Ibid.

7. Mrs. F.J. Lee, *Sketches and Sermons*, p. 259.

8. F.J. Lee, Jr., interview by Mickey Crews, Cleveland, Tenn., 3 Sept. 1982. D.B. Smith interview, 31 Oct. 1982. Nora Jones interview, 8 July 1982. J.R. Kinser, interview by Mickey Crews, Cleveland, Tenn., 1 Sept. 1982. Milton Tomlinson, son of A.J. Tomlinson and general overseer of the Church of God of Prophecy, interview by Mickey Crews, Cleveland, Tenn., 1 Sept. 1982.

9. John C. Jernigan, "From the Gambling Den to the Pulpit," n.p., 1939, pp. 36–39.

10. Ibid.

11. D.B. Smith interview 31 Oct. 1982; J.R. Kinser interview, 1 Sept. 1982; Milton Tomlinson interview, 1 Sept. 1982.

12. James A. Cross, "From Jerusalem to the Uttermost," COG 48th General Assembly, *Minutes*, p. 15.

13. Wade H. Horton, "Pentecostal Flames," COG 51st General Assembly, *Minutes*, p. 15.

14. James A. Cross, "Answers From the Word," *Evangel*, 30 Dec. 1968, p. 11.

15. M.S. Lemons, "History of the Church of God," p. 7; D.B. Smith interview, 31 Oct. 1982; J.R. Kinser interview, Tenn. 1 Sept. 1982; Nora Jones interview, 8 July 1982.

16. COG 28th General Assembly, *Minutes*, p. 42.

17. COG Council of Twelve, *Minutes*, 20 Aug. 1941, p. 39.

18. "Editorials," *Evangel*, 6 Dec. 1947, p. 2.

19. COG Executive Council, *Minutes*, May 1970, p. 64.

20. COG 61st General Assembly, *Minutes*, "Church of God Teachings," p. 7.

21. COG General Council, *Minutes*, 13 Aug. 1952, p. 19.

22. J.C. Vore, "Is Television a Church Robber?", *Evangel*, 6 Feb. 1954, pp. 6–7.

23. Alda B. Harrison, "What About Television?", *Lighted Pathway*, June 1956, p. 11.

24. Avis Swiger, "Youth Wants to Know," *Lighted Pathway*, May 1958, p. 1.

25. Earl P. Paulk, Jr., "Church of God Makes Television Debut," *Evangel*, 6 Feb. 1954, p. 11.

26. Ray H. Hughes, "Perspectives," *Evangel*, 13 Aug. 1973, p. 2.

27. COG 55th General Assembly, *Minutes*, p. 51.

28. COG Executive Council, *Minutes*, May 1976, p. A–25.

29. "Television Protest Gains Wide Support," *Evangel*, 23 May 1977, p. 18.

30. COG 57th General Assembly, *Minutes*, p. 45.

31. COG Executive Council, *Minutes*, May 1982, p. A–6.

32. COG Executive Council, *Minutes*, Jan. 1984, p. 14.

33. Pat Watters, *Coca-Cola: An Illustrated History* (Garden City, N.Y.: Doubleday, 1978), pp. 5, 41, 43.

34. Mrs. F.J. Lee, *Sketches and Sermons*, p. 191; C.C. Aikens to F.J. Lee, 16 Sept. 1926, F.J. Lee Personal Correspondence, PRC.

35. Mrs. F.J. Lee, *Sketches and Sermons*, p. 191.

36. Ibid.

37. COG 30th General Assembly, *Minutes*, p. 36.

38. A.J. Tomlinson, "Some Bible Teaching and Counsel," *Evangel*, 27 Jan. 1917, p. 1.

39. COG 6th General Assembly, *Minutes*, pp. 45–47.

40. M.P. Cross, "In the Good (?) Ole Days," p. 22.

41. J.B. Ellis, "An Appeal," *Evangel*, 23 Feb. 1935, p. 5.

42. COG Supreme Council, *Minutes*, 12 Aug. 1942, p. 14.

43. COG 37th General Assembly, *Minutes*, p. 22.

44. "Editorials," *Evangel*, 18 Oct. 1947, p. 4.

45. Ibid., pp. 4–5.

46. Paul H. Walker, "The Bible, The Christian and the Liquor Traffic," *Evangel*, 9 Feb. 1952, p. 9.

47. COG 47th General Assembly, *Minutes*, p. 44.

48. Mrs. Howard L. Juillerat, *Gems of Religious Truth*, p. 69.

49. Ibid., pp. 71–72.

50. Ibid., p. 72.

51. A.J. Tomlinson, "Some Bible Teaching," p. 1.

52. Mrs. Howard L. Juillerat, *Gems of Religious Truth*, p. 73.

53. COG 1st General Assembly, *Minutes*, p. 16.

54. Charles W. Conn, *Like A Mighty Army*, p. 66.

55. Mrs. Howard L. Juillerat, *Gems of Religious Truth*, p. 74.

56. William Shakespeare, *Othello*, Act 2, Scene 1.

57. A.J. Tomlinson, "Some Bible Teaching," p. 1.

58. Ibid.

59. Ibid.

60. Mrs. Howard L. Juillerat, *Gems of Religious Truth*, pp. 69–70.

61. Ibid., p. 69.

62. Ibid., pp. 69–71.

63. COG 11th General Assembly, *Minutes*, p. 21.

64. E.J. Boehmer to A.J. Tomlinson, 12 Jan. 1923, A.J. Tomlinson Correspondence.

65. COG 28th General Assembly, *Minutes*, p. 43.

66. William J. Krutza, "You Ask Me Why I Don't Smoke," *Lighted Pathway*, May 1964, p. 7.

67. Charles W. Conn, "The Spectre of Tobacco," *Evangel*, 14 May 1962, p. 3.

68. Cecil E. Burridge, "Should Christians Smoke?", *Lighted Pathway*, June 1969, p. 22.

69. Ibid.

70. Ethel Lee, "Adornment," *Evangel*, 5 Apr. 1919, p. 4.

71. Mrs. F.J. Lee, *Sketches and Sermons*, p. 196.

72. Mattie Lemons, "An Exhortation," *Evangel*, 8 Aug. 1914, p. 5.

73. Mrs. F.J. Lee, *Sketches and Sermons*, p. 37.

74. Ethel Lee, "Adornment," p. 4.

75. Zeno C. Tharp, "Were Made to Wander," *Evangel*, 10 Aug. 1929, p. 1.

76. Mrs. F.J. Lee, *Sketches and Sermons*, p. 35.

77. Ibid.

78. L.G. Rouse, "Marvelous Miracles and Incidents in My Life," n.p., n.d., p. 18.

79. Ibid., pp. 18–19.

80. COG Elders' Council, *Minutes*, 13 Oct. 1928, p. 140.

81. Myrtle Whitehead, "A Separate People," *Evangel*, 8 Aug. 1931, p. 1.

82. COG 28th General Assembly, *Minutes*, p. 43.

83. COG Supreme Council, *Minutes*, Sept. 1934, p. 6.

84. COG Supreme Council, *Minutes*, Sept. 1940, p. 7.

85. COG Bishops' Council, *Minutes*, Sept. 1940, pp. 430–31.

86. COG 35th General Assembly, *Minutes*, p. 31.

87. Earl P. Paulk, "Be Not Conformed To This World," *Evangel*, 28 Apr. 1958, p. 9.

88. Hazel Brewer, "A Beautiful Woman," *Evangel*, 25 June 1962, p. 4.

89. James A. Cross, "Answers From the Word," *Evangel*, 29 July 1963, p. 7.

90. "Statement on Modest Apparel from the Executive Council," *Evangel*, 17 June 1968, p. 4.

91. Walter and Mamie Alice Barwick, "Are You What You Wear?", *Lighted Pathway*, June 1974, p. 19.

92. Mattie Lemons, "Exhortation," p. 5.

93. COG 11th General Assembly, *Minutes*, p. 3.

94. Mattie Lemons, "Exhortation," p. 5.

95. Ibid.

96. A.J. Tomlinson, "Some Bible Teaching," p. 1.

97. COG 25th General Assembly, *Minutes*, p. 22.

98. COG 31st General Assembly, *Minutes*, p. 34.

99. COG Supreme Council, *Minutes*, Aug. 1942, p. 7.

100. COG Supreme Council, *Minutes*, Aug. 1945, p. 35.

101. COG 47th General Assembly, *Minutes*, p. 31.

102. COG 56th General Assembly, *Minutes*, pp. 55–56.

103. D.B. Smith interview, 31 Oct. 1982; Nora Jones interview, 8 July 1982; Milton Tomlinson interview, 1 Sept. 1982.

104. COG 3rd General Assembly, *Minutes*, p. 28.

105. Ibid.

106. COG 8th General Assembly, *Minutes*, p. 68.

107. COG 11th General Assembly, *Minutes*, p. 20.

108. Ibid.

109. "Religion and the World," *Evangel*, 17 July 1943, p. 4.

110. Dr. Oswald J. Smith, "How to Choose a Life-Partner," *Lighted Pathway*, June 1967, pp. 14–15.

111. Arthur H. Townsend, "Watch That Yoke," *Evangel*, 15 Sept. 1969, p. 11.

112. COG 3rd General Assembly, *Minutes*, p. 28.

113. COG 11th General Assembly, *Minutes*, p. 33.

114. COG 10th General Assembly, *Minutes*, p. 29.

115. Ibid.

116. Ibid.; see also COG 11th General Assembly, *Minutes*, p. 19.

117. Mrs. F.J. Lee, *Sketches and Sermons*, p. 235. Quoted from *Collier's Encyclopedia*. Lee was obviously influenced by the anti-Bolshevik article.

118. Mrs. F.J. Lee, *Sketches and Sermons*, p. 236.

119. Ibid., p. 242.

120. COG 23rd General Assembly, *Minutes*, p. 32.

121. COG 29th General Assembly, *Minutes*, p. 49.

122. Tracy Ingram, "The Christian and the Labor Union," *Evangel*, 8 Sept. 1975, pp. 8–9. Also see COG 61st General Assembly, *Minutes*, "Supplement to the Minutes," p. 8.

Chapter 4

1. Mary Howell, "The Church of God," *Evangel*, 20 Jan. 1917, p. 4.

2. COG 2nd General Assembly, *Minutes*, 1907, p. 25.

3. F. J. Lee, Jr., interview, 3 Sept. 1982.

4. David Edwin Harrell, Jr., *All Things Are Possible* (Bloomington: Indiana Univ. Press, 1975), pp. 85–86.

5. Nora Jones interview, 8 July 1982.

6. Mrs. F.J. Lee, *Sketches and Sermons*, pp. 15–16; S.J. Heath, "Life and Writings of S.J. Heath," n.p., n.d., p. 11.

7. A.J. Tomlinson, "Marvelous Healings," *Evangel*, 21 May 1914, p. 1.

8. Mrs. F.J. Lee, *Sketches and Sermons*, p. 284.

9. Ibid., p. 16.

10. Ibid., pp. 17–18.

11. H.L. Trim to the editor, *Evangel*, 20 Jan. 1915, p. 2.

12. Virginia, Wythe County Circuit Court, *Commonwealth* v. *Walter Barney, Wythville, Va.*, *Common Law Order Book 3*, p. 359.

13. A.J. Tomlinson, "Some More About Brother Barney," *Evangel*, 15 May 1915, p. 4.

14. A.J. Tomlinson, "Editor's Note," *Evangel*, 29 May 1915, p. 2.

15. Florida, State Supreme Court, *James Bradley* v. *State of Florida*, "Report of Decision," 134p., located at Florida State Supreme Court Library, Tallahassee, Fla., pp. 29, 34, 40, 52.

16. Ibid., p. 4.

17. Florida, State Supreme Court, *James Bradley* v. *State of Florida*, "Report of Decision," p. 2.

18. A.J. Tomlinson, "The Gospel of Jesus and Laws of This Country," *Evangel*, 15 May 1915, p. 1.

19. Ibid.

20. A.J. Tomlinson, "Journal," 26 Feb. 1917.

21. *Minutes*, 14th General Assembly (1920), p. 43. The Church of God's antimedical position was reflected in other areas. Children who had not received vaccinations were prohibited from attending public school by officials of local boards of education. See A.J. Tomlinson, "Journal," 26 Mar. 1914.

22. A.J. Tomlinson, "Victory For The Church," *Evangel*, 15 May 1920, p. 1.

23. Rebecca Dixon, "Healed of Diphtheria," *Evangel*, 6 Aug. 1927, p. 4.

24. C.W. Cole, "Not Afraid To Trust God," *Evangel*, 22 Dec. 1928, p. 2.

25. B.L. Hicks, "A Few Words From Brother B.L. Hicks," *Evangel*, 31 May 1930, p. 1.

26. B.L. Hicks, "Walter Barney Behind Bars for the Word of God and the Testimony of Jesus Christ," *Evangel*, 23 Jan. 1915, p. 2.

27. Celia Mahan, "Tho' He Slay Me Yet Will I Trust Him," *Evangel*, 8 Jan. 1927, p. 3.

28. J.B. Ellis, *Blazing the Gospel Trail* (Cleveland, Tenn.: COG PH, 1941), p. 107.

29. COG 24th General Assembly, *Minutes*, p. 35.

30. Sam Holcomb, "Divine Healing," *Evangel*, 6 May 1944, p. 14.

31. Ibid.

32. Sgt. Glenn Eason, "Why Preach and Practice Divine Healing Today?", *Evangel*, 3 July 1943, p. 10.

33. Ibid.

34. Merle H. Greene, "Divine Healing," *Evangel*, 12 Oct. 1946, p. 15.

35. W.E. Johnson, "What I Believe About Divine Healing," *Evangel*, 10 July 1954, p. 3.

36. J.E. DeVore, "We Believe in Divine Healing," *Evangel*, 4 Dec. 1954, p. 3.

37. COG General Council, *Minutes*, 21 Aug. 1942, p. 42.

38. Charles W. Conn, "Divine Healing and the Church of God," *Evangel*, 25 Feb. 1956, p. 4.

39. Wade H. Horton, "We Believe Divine Healing," *Evangel*, 25 June 1962, p. 6.

40. Louis H. Cross, "These Signs Shall Follow," *Evangel*, 27 Aug. 1962, p. 6.

41. Dale V. Moffet, "Full-Time Christian, Part-Time Physician," *Evangel*, 24 Aug. 1970, p. 5.

42. Joseph Bayly, "Prayer and Terminal Illness," *Evangel*, 14 Sept. 1970, pp. 4–5.

43. Donald B. Gibson, "As They Lay Dying," *Evangel*, 14 Sept. 1970, p. 7.

44. Weston LaBarre, *They Shall Take Up Serpents: Psychology of Southern Snake-Handling Cults* (Minneapolis: Univ. of Minnesota Press, 1962), p. 11. Nora Jones interview, 8 July 1982. Mrs. Jones, who was a member in the early church and was acquainted with Hensley, confirmed that he started this practice while a minister in the Church of God.

45. Homer Tomlinson, *Shout Of A King*, p. 42.

46. Steven M. Kane, "Snake Handlers of Southern Appalachia," Ph.D. diss., Princeton Univ., 1979, pp. 36–37.

47. J.B. Ellis, *Blazing the Gospel Trail*, p. 46.

48. Ibid., pp. 46–47.

49. Kane, "Snake Handlers of Southern Appalachia," p. 38.

50. Nora Jones (daughter of W.F. Bryant) interview, 8 July 1982.

51. Kane, "Snake Handlers of Southern Appalachia," pp. 45–46.

52. L.G. Rouse, "Marvelous Miracles," p. 23.

53. Ibid., pp. 28–29.

54. Ibid., p. 30.

55. Bessie E. Walker, "Signs Will Follow Believers," *Evangel*, 3 Sept. 1927, p. 3.

56. "Christianity, Men And Methods," *Pentecostal Holiness Advocate*, 10 Jan. 1918, p. 2, and 17 Jan. 1918, p. 4. Quoted in Kane, "Snake Handlers of Southern Appalachia," p. 54.

57. [A.J. Tomlinson], "Manifestations of the Spirit," *Faithful Standard*, Sept., 1922, p. 12.

58. D.G. Phillips, "Christian Perfection," *Evangel*, 16 July 1927, p. 4.

59. P.F. Barnewall, "The Bible Proven As Divinely Inspired," *Evangel*, 1 Sept. 1928, p. 2.

60. S.J. Heath, "Signs Following Believers," *Evangel*, 28 July 1928, p. 3.

61. COG 23rd General Assembly, *Minutes*, p. 42.

62. W.C. Mize, "Serpent Handled," *Evangel*, 17 Apr. 1928, p. 4.

63. Mrs. Frank Dasher, "Serpents Handled," *Evangel*, 18 Oct. 1930, p. 4.

64. Ibid.

65. E.C. Clark, "An Exposition of Mark 16:18," *Evangel*, 8 Sept. 1934, p. 5.

66. E.L. Simmons, "Religion and Snakes," *Evangel*, 1 June 1940, p. 4.

67. Rev. B.A. Hall to F.J. Lee, 2 July 1926, F.J. Lee Correspondence.

68. Ibid.

69. Jennie Crawford to F.J. Lee, 30 Dec. 1926, F.J. Lee Correspondence.

Chapter 5

1. Nora Jones interview, 8 July 1982; F.J. Lee, Jr., interview, 3 Sept. 1982; James Spurling interview, 25 Sept. 1982; Milton Tomlinson interview, 1 Sept. 1982. Also see Mrs. F.J. Lee, *Sketches and Sermons*, p. 358.

2. Dirksen, "Let Your Women Keep Silent," p. 4.

3. COG 2nd General Assembly, *Minutes*, p. 22. Quoted in Dirksen, "Let Your Women Keep Silent," p. 7.

4. Ibid.

5. COG 4th General Assembly, *Minutes*, p. 33.

6. J.W. Buckalew, *Incidents in the Life of J.W. Buckalew* (Cleveland, Tenn.: COG PH, 1920), p. 33.

7. "A Pattern of Service," unpublished manuscript by an anonymous student at Lee College, Cleveland, Tenn., 1979, p. 5, PRC files.

8. Ibid., p. 7.

9. Ibid., pp. 7–8. With the establishment of a Negro church in the Bahama Islands, the Church of God became one of the few racially integrated denominations in the South. In 1912, the denomination founded three black congregations in Florida—at Jacksonville, Miami, and Coconut Grove. In 1913, a black congregation was established in Betsytown, Tenn., but within a few years disbanded. By 1920, there were a total of 25 black congregations in the Church of God. These were: 12 in the Bahama Islands, 9 in Florida, 1 in Georgia, 2 in North Carolina, and 1 in Virginia. The work among blacks prospered for a short time but later stagnated, probably because of pervasive southern customs and white racist attitudes.

10. COG 8th General Assembly, *Minutes*, p. 130.

11. Dirksen, "Let Your Women Keep Silent," p. 9.

12. Ibid., pp. 15–16. Dirksen states that Charles W. Conn maintains that women were mainly responsible for the church's evangelistic impulse.

13. Charles W. Conn, *Where the Saints Have Trod* (Cleveland, Tenn.: Pathway Press, 1959), p. 15.

14. Walter Hollenweger, *The Pentecostals* (Minneapolis: Augsburg PH, 1972), p. 487.

15. Charles W. Conn, *Where Saints Have Trod*, pp. 15–16.

16. Ibid., pp. 17–19.

17. Ibid., pp. 19–20.

18. Dirksen, "Let Your Women Keep Silent," p. 6.

19. Ibid. Also see COG 7th General Assembly, *Minutes*, p. 13; A.J. Tomlinson, "A New One Started," *Evangel*, 25 Apr. 1914, p. 2. It appears that Dirksen based her evidence on an interview with Charles W. Conn, for her footnote contains only the opinions of Conn.

20. Nora Jones interview, 8 July 1982; D.B. Smith interview, 1 Nov. 1982.

21. A.J. Tomlinson, "A New One Started." p. 2.

22. Ibid.

23. Ibid., p. 3.

24. Ibid., p. 2.

25. Charles W. Conn, in *Like A Mighty Army*, describes such fanatical teachings as "holy dynamite," "holy lyddite," and "holy oxidite," saying that they almost destroyed the Christian Union. The disruption was such that the church was reorganized in 1902 with only 20 members. The author of these teachings was Edward Irwin, a leader of the "Fire Baptized" movement. See Vincent Synan, *The Holiness-Pentecostal Movement in the U.S.* (Grand Rapids, Mich.: Eerdmans, 1975), p. 82.

26. A.J. Tomlinson, "Great Campaign in New York City," *Evangel*, 12 July 1919, p. 1.

27. COG 21st General Assembly, *Minutes*, p. 32.

28. COG 14th General Assembly (1920), *Minutes*, p. 54. A survey of the names of all clerks listed in the minutes of the 1920 General Assembly reveals that at least one-third were females.

29. A.J. Tomlinson, "A New One Started," p. 3.

30. Charles W. Conn, *Like A Mighty Army*, pp. 105–6.

31. COG 13th General Assembly, *Minutes*, p. 292.

32. Charles W. Conn, *Where Saints Have Trod*, pp. 15–16.

33. W.F. Bryant interview by Geneva Carroll, 1949, p. 2.

34. Church of God, "Pictorial Review of the Church of God Orphanage, 1940, 20th Anniversary," n.p., n.d., p. 3.

35. Dirksen, "Let Your Women Keep Silent," p. 24.

36. A.J. Tomlinson, "What Shall We Do?", *Evangel*, 16 Sept. 1916, p. 1.

37. Charles W. Conn, *Like a Mighty Army*, p. 149.

38. V. Elaine Stewart, "A Look at the Life of Alda B. Harrison," unpublished manuscript by a Lee College student, 30 Jan. 1986, pp. 1–2. PRC files.

39. Ibid., p. 5.

40. Mrs. Bertie Harrison, "Woman's Work in the Church," *Evangel*, 8 Dec. 1928, pp. 1–3.

41. Mrs. S.J. Wood, "History of the LWWB," 1940, p. 7.

42. "Raising Money for the Lord's Work," *Evangel*, 1 Nov. 1930, p. 3.

43. Mrs. W.G. Webb, "Faith Without Works Is Dead," *Evangel*, 17 Jan. 1931, p. 4.

44. COG 31st General Assembly, *Minutes*, p. 35.

45. Mrs. S.J. Wood, "Origin and Progress of the LWWB," *Evangel*, 5 Dec. 1949, p. 9.

46. COG 45th General Assembly, *Minutes*, p. 36.

47. COG 50th General Assembly, *Minutes*, p. 63.

48. COG 53rd General Assembly, *Minutes*, p. 43.

49. COG 59th General Assembly, *Minutes*, p. 44.

50. Dorothy Jennings, executive secretary, COG Department of Ladies Ministries, interview by Mickey Crews, Cleveland, Tenn., 25 May 1987.

51. These figures were determined by comparing the number of females holding credentials in 1913 and 1987. The figures for 1913 were found in the *Minutes* of the General Assembly for that year. The numbers for 1987 were gathered from Georgia West, COG Business and Records Department, interview by Mickey Crews, Cleveland, Tenn., 29 May 1987.

52. Edna Conn, "So God Made A Woman," *Evangel*, 14 Jan. 1963, p. 16.

53. Avis Swiger, "Glorifying God," *Evangel*, 2 Sept. 1963, p. 7.

54. Charles W. Conn, "Mothers and God," *Evangel*, 7 May 1949, p. 2.

55. Charles W. Conn, "Some Are Mothers," *Evangel*, 8 May 1961, p. 3.

56. Barbara Moore Page, "Christian Women In The Business World," *Evangel*, 9 Dec. 1963, p. 11.

57. Charles W. Conn, "So God Made A Woman," *Evangel*, 14 Jan. 1963, p. 16.

58. Emma Sue Webb, "The Limitations on Women Ministers in the Church of God," M.A. thesis, California Graduate School of Theology, 1981, pp. iv–v and 86–88.

Chapter 6

1. Robert A. Divine, ed., *American Foreign Policy* (New York: New American Library, 1960), p. 37.

2. A.J. Tomlinson, "President of United States Calls The People To Prayer," *Evangel*, 26 Sept. 1914, p. 2.

3. Milton Tomlinson interview, 1 Sept. 1982.

4. James Spurling interview, 25 Sept. 1982. Spurling stated that his grandfather, Richard G. Spurling, Jr., who was one of the Church of God founders and an early leader, voted the Republican ticket in every election until his death in 1935. The only exception was when his grandfather voted for a personal friend who ran as a Democratic candidate in a local sheriff's race. James Spurling also stated that intense loyalty to the GOP was common among early Church of God people who lived in the Appalachian region.

5. A.J. Tomlinson, "The Awful World War," *Evangel*, 24 Feb. 1917, p. 1.

6. A.J. Tomlinson, "The Awful War Seems Near," *Evangel*, 31 Mar. 1917, p. 1. In Church of God thought, Christians who committed grave sins were turned over to Satan so that the "flesh" might be destroyed but the "spirit" saved.

7. A.J. Tomlinson, "While the Wars Rage," *Evangel*, 8 July 1916, p. 1.

8. A.J. Tomlinson, "The Awful World War," p. 1.

9. A.J. Tomlinson, "While the Wars Rage," p. 1.

10. A.J. Tomlinson, "The Awful World War," p. 1.

11. A.J. Tomlinson, "Questions and Problems Cause Much Perplexity and Anxiety," *Evangel*, 11 Dec. 1915, p. 1.

12. Ibid.

13. A.J. Tomlinson, "While the Wars Rage," p. 1. Apparently this reference was to Washington's Farewell Address; however, this was not what the president said. Washington only advised that American should not entangle itself politically in the affairs of Europe.

14. C.A. Churchill, "Beginning of Sorrows," *Evangel*, 6 July 1918, p. 4.

15. A.J. Tomlinson, "The Awful War Seems Near," p. 1. Interviews with surviving members of the early Church of God support this view. "The rapture" is a term that denotes the second coming of Christ. This coming is seen as imminent, and many believe that Christ will not come down to earth, but will remain in the upper air. Those who die in the Lord are to be raised from the dead, the living saints are to be transfigured, and together they are to be caught up to meet the Lord in the air.

16. The "mark of the beast," designated by the number 666, was to be placed on the forehead or in the palm of those who would become allies of the antichrist. Receipt of this mark signified sale of one's soul to eternal hell. Without this symbol, an individual could not buy or sell. The person would become an enemy of the antichrist forces and would be hunted down and killed.

17. A.J. Tomlinson, "The Mark of the Beast," *Evangel*, 9 Feb. 1918, p. 1.

18. Ibid.

19. Ibid.

20. C.A. Churchill, "Beginning of Sorrows," p. 4.

21. A.J. Tomlinson, "The Awful World War," p. 1.

22. A.J. Tomlinson, "The Awful War Seems Near," p. 1.

23. A.J. Tomlinson, "While the Wars Rage," p. 1.

24. A.J. Tomlinson, "The Awful War Seems Near," p. 1.

25. H.C. Peterson and Gilbert C. Fite, *Opponents of War, 1917–1918* (Seattle: Univ. of Washington Press, 1957), p. 215.

26. Ibid., pp. 21–23.

27. *United States Statutes at Large*, vol. 40 (Washington, D.C.: USGPO, 1919), statute 1, ch. 15, sec. 5, p. 80.

28. A.J. Tomlinson, "The War Draft," *Evangel*, 2 June 1917, p. 2.

29. Ibid. This became the official position of the Church of God from 1917 to 1928. From 1928 to 1945, the denomination objected to its members' going to war in combatant service. Since 1945, the church has left this decision up to the individual. See *Minutes*, COG 40th, General Assembly, 1946, p. 31. Also see Charles W. Conn, *Like A Mighty Army*, p. 150. Although World War I had a profound impact upon the denomination, Conn ignores it in his study.

30. A.J. Tomlinson, "The War Draft," p. 2.

31. "War Notice," *Evangel*, 4 Aug. 1917, p. 3.

32. COG 13th General Assembly, *Minutes*, 1917, p. 65.

33. A.J. Tomlinson, "Days of Perplexity," *Evangel*, 26 Jan. 1918, p. 1.

34. Ibid.

35. Ibid.

36. J.B. Ellis, "The Murder of Brother Dave Allen," *Evangel*, 27 Apr. 1918, p. 4.

37. Ibid.

38. In interviews with members of the families of Richard G. Spurling, Jr., and William F. Bryant, all confirmed that neither of these two leaders had any objections to church members supporting the war effort.

39. A.J. Tomlinson, "The Awful World War," p. 1.

40. Ibid.

41. A.J. Tomlinson, "The Awful War Seems Near," p. 1.

42. A.J. Tomlinson, "The Awful World War," p. 1.

43. Ibid.

44. W.H. Lamar, Washington, D.C., to Postmaster, Cleveland, Tenn., 6 and 9 Aug. 1918; Document #06262854, U.S. Department of Justice, FBI, "Investigative Files of the Old Germans from the Years 1914–18 Inclusive," Civil Archives Division, NA. Hereafter cited as "Investigative Files."

45. Chief of FBI to James T. Finlay, Chattanooga, Tenn., 21 Aug. 1918, Civil Archives, NA.

46. D.S. Vinn, "Holiness or Holy Rollers," an FBI investigative report, Emory, Texas, 30 Aug. 1918, Document #121580, U.S. Department of Justice, FBI, "Investigative Files," Civil Archives, NA.

47. F.S. Shipp, "Members Holy Roller Church-Spreading Disloyal Propaganda," 6-page FBI investigative report, Chattanooga, Tenn., 30 Aug. 1918, p. 1, Civil Archives, NA.

48. Ibid., p. 5. Shipp was correct; it did not stop issues containing antiwar rhetoric from being mailed to subscribers. The *Evangel* inculcated and reinforced Church of God doctrine. It appears to have been successful.

49. Ibid., pp. 5–6; For information on persecutions and convictions of Pentecostals, see H.C. Peterson and Fite, *Opponents of War*.

50. L.G. Rouse, "Marvelous Miracles," p. 12.

51. Ibid.

52. Ibid., pp. 13–16.

53. Ibid., pp. 17–18.

54. J.B. Ellis, *Blazing the Gospel Trail*, pp. 81–82.

55. Ibid., pp. 80–81.

56. "J.B. Ellis Free," *Evangel*, 28 Sept. 1918, p. 2.

57. J.B. Ellis, *Blazing the Gospel Trail*, pp. 81–82.

58. Charles W. Conn, *Where Saints Have Trod*, pp. 17–19.

59. U.S. Postal Censorship Report, Document #203958, U.S. Department of Justice, FBI, "Investigative Files," NA; F.L. Ryder, Buenos Aires, Argentina, to Tom M. Cain, Alton Park, Chattanooga, Tenn., 21 May 1918, Index #41762, NA.

60. Chief of FBI to James Finlay, Chattanooga, Tenn., 31 Mar. 1918, NA.

61. COG 18th General Assembly, *Minutes*, p. 43.

62. Margaret Richie Pake, "Osprey, Fla.," *Evangel*, 9 Nov. 1918, p. 3.

63. COG 16th General Assembly, *Minutes*, p. 72.

64. Ibid., p. 60.

65. COG Elders' Council, *Minutes*, 13 Oct. 1928, p. 139.

66. COG 23rd General Assembly, *Minutes*, pp. 24–25.

67. E.C. Clark, "War Clouds," *Evangel*, 4 Nov. 1933, p. 9.

68. E.C. Clark, "The Growth of Fascism and Communism," *Evangel*, 3 June 1933, p. 5.

69. E.C. Clark, "War Clouds," p. 9.

70. "Student's War Strike," *Evangel*, 9 Mar. 1935, p. 1.

71. "Germans Think Hitler Superman," *Evangel*, 18 May 1935, p. 4.

72. "Senate Votes Increase in Army," *Evangel*, 16 Mar. 1935, p. 12.

73. "War," *Evangel*, 14 Mar. 1938, p. 4.

74. S.W. Lattimer, "World Wide Conflicts," *Evangel*, 23 Sept. 1939, p. 4.

75. E.L. Simmons, "Preparations," *Evangel*, 16 Dec. 1939, p. 4.

76. "Leaves From the Fig Tree," *Evangel*, 27 July 1940, p. 8.

77. E.L. Simmons, "The Draft Bill," *Evangel*, 27 July 1940, p. 8.

78. COG Bishops' Council, *Minutes*, 27 Sept. 1940, p. 21.

79. COG 35th General Assembly, *Minutes*, p. 26.

80. E.L. Simmons, "Our Government and War," *Evangel*, 26 Apr. 1941, p. 4.

81. R.P. Johnson, "Our Part in the Present Emergency," COG 36th General Assembly, *Minutes*, p. 19.

82. E.L. Simmons, "A Tribute to Old Glory," COG 36th General Assembly, *Minutes*, p. 7.

83. "In the Army," *Evangel*, 24 Jan. 1942, p. 11.

84. B.L. Hicks, "A Word of Warning," *Evangel*, 7 Mar. 1942, p. 5.

85. "The *Lighted Pathway* Joins in U.S. Service," *Evangel*, 14 Mar. 1942, p. 8.

86. COG Supreme Council, *Minutes*, 21 Aug. 1942, p. 18.

87. "Christian Responsibility in the War Effort," *Evangel*, 14 Nov. 1943, p. 6.

88. COG Bishops' Council, *Minutes*, 21 Aug. 1942, pp. 28–29.

89. Ibid., p. 388.

90. J.H. Walker, "Civil Defense," *Evangel*, 13 Feb. 1943, pp. 2, 11.

91. COG Bishops' Council, *Minutes*, 21 Aug. 1942, p. 29.

92. COG Bishops' Council, *Minutes*, 15 Aug. 1943, p. 14.

93. J.H. Walker, "The Supreme Need in this Crisis," COG 38th General Assembly, *Minutes*, p. 16.

94. James L. Slay, "Is This Worth Fighting For?", *Evangel*, 1 July 1944, pp. 6, 14.

95. Manning Thornton, "W.W. Ball: A Warrior of Faith," unpublished paper by a student at the COG School of Theology, Cleveland, Tenn., Jan. 1986, pp. 2, 29.

96. COG Supreme Council, *Minutes*, 8 Aug. 1944, p. 14.

97. Charles W. Conn, *Cradle of Pentecost* (Cleveland, Tenn.: Pathway Press, 1985), pp. 123–24.

98. "H. Ottis Hewett, Publishing House Employee Killed in Action," *Evangel*, 25 Nov. 1944, p. 2.

99. COG 40th General Assembly, *Minutes*, p. 31.

Chapter 7

1. George B. Tindall, "Beyond the Mainstream: The Ethnic Southerners," *Journal of Southern History* 40 (Feb. 1974):9.

2. COG 13th General Assembly, *Minutes*, p. 10.

3. Charles W. Conn, *Like A Mighty Army*, p. 150; E.L. Simmons, *History of the Church of God*, p. 98.

4. E.L. Simmons, *History of the Church of God*, p. 98.

5. Charles W. Conn, *Like A Mighty Army*, p. 263.

6. COG Supreme Council, *Minutes*, 13 Aug. 1946, pp. 60–61.

7. Ibid., p. 12.

8. E.L. Simmons, *History of the Church of God*, p. 106.

9. Manuel Campbell to the COG Council of Twelve, Jan. 1948, in Civil Archives, NA. COG Supreme Council, *Minutes*, 15 Mar. 1948.

10. Edward Shoupe, "Higher Education for Pentecostal?", *Evangel*, 5 Nov. 1956, p. 14.

11. June Becker, "The Spiritual Aspect of the Classroom," *Lighted Pathway*, Jan. 1958, p. 1.

12. R.L. Platt, "Lee College Expands," *Lighted Pathway*, July 1956, p. 15. Also see Charles W. Conn, *Like A Mighty Army*, pp. 310–11.

13. "Lee College Approved for National Defense Education Act," *Evangel*, 9 Jan. 1961, p. 11.

14. Charles W. Conn, *Like A Mighty Army*, p. 311.

15. Clyne W. Buxton, "Education Plus Christ," *Lighted Pathway*, June 1964, p. 8.

16. Robert A. Cook, "What If the Supreme Court Says No?", *Evangel*, 27 May 1963, p. 19.

17. COG 52nd General Assembly, *Minutes*, p. 4.

18. Robert White, "The Christian Day School: Why Are Christian Day Schools Needed?", *Evangel*, 23 Feb. 1976, p. 8.

19. COG 57th General Assembly, *Minutes*, p. 38.

20. J.H. Walker, Jr., "Lee: A Four-Year Liberal Arts College," *Lighted Pathway*, Nov. 1967, p. 6.

21. T.L. Lowery, "The Man God Calls To Preach: Should He Go To College," *Evangel*, 9 Feb. 1976, pp. 18–19.

22. R. Hollis Gause, "A Theological Seminary for the Church of God," *Evangel*, 17 Mar. 1969, p. 5.

23. COG 53rd General Assembly, *Minutes*, p. 26.

24. Ibid.

25. "Graduate School of Christian Ministries," *Evangel*, 10 Feb. 1975, p. 2.

26. Charles W. Conn, *Like A Mighty Army*, pp. 384–85.

27. *Evangelical Action* (Boston: United Action Press, 1942), pp. 92–100.

28. COG Bishops' Council, *Minutes*, 21 Aug. 1942, p. 16. Also see COG 37th General Assembly, *Minutes*, p. 36.

29. COG Supreme Council, *Minutes*, 13 Aug. 1946, p. 7.

30. A.C. Brawner to F.J. Lee, 25 Jan. 1926, F.J. Lee Correspondence.

31. COG Supreme Council, *Minutes*, 26 Feb. 1946, p. 56.

32. William Menzies, "The Assemblies of God, 1941–1967: The Consolidation of a Revival Movement," Ph.D. diss., Univ. of Iowa, 1967, pp. 82–83.

33. COG Supreme Council, *Minutes*, 19 May 1948, p. 5. See also *Minutes of the Conference of Pentecostal Leaders*, Chicago, Ill., 7 May 1948.

34. Menzies, "Assemblies of God," p. 84.

35. COG Bishops' Council, *Minutes*, 24 Aug. 1948, p. 34.

36. Charles W. Conn, *Like A Mighty Army*, p. 274.

37. Earl J. Gilbert, "Why I'm Against Protestant Church Unification," *Evangel*, 11 Mar. 1950, p. 11.

38. Ibid., p. 15.

39. George L. Britt, "Is Unity Always Good?", *Evangel*, 7 June 1960, pp. 10–11.

40. Ray H. Hughes, "Pentecostalism and Ecumenism," *Evangel*, 16 Jan. 1967, p. 15.

41. Ray H. Hughes, "Pentecostal View of the Ecumenical Movement," *Evangel*, 31 Oct. 1966, p. 9.

42. John C. Jernigan, "Annual Address of the General Overseer," COG 41st General Assembly, *Minutes*, p. 17.

43. COG Supreme Council, *Minutes*, 5 March 1953, pp. 23–24.

44. Zeno C. Tharp, "Annual Address of the General Overseer," COG 46th General Assembly, *Minutes*, p. 12.

45. David E. Harrell, Jr., *All Things Are Possible*, pp. 4–5.

46. Ibid., pp. 3–7. Nine "gifts of the Spirit" are listed in 1 Cor. 12:8–10. These are the word of wisdom, the word of knowledge, faith, gifts of healing, working of miracles, prophecy, discerning of spirits, diverse kinds of tongues, and interpretation of tongues.

47. John L. Sherrill, *They Speak With Other Tongues* (New York: McGraw-Hill, 1964), p. 64.

48. Charles W. Conn, "Let Us Hold Our Distinctives," *Evangel*, 27 Nov. 1961, p. 3.

49. COG Supreme Council, *Minutes*, 8 Mar. 1963, pp. 76–78.

50. Wade H. Horton, "For Such a Time," COG 50th General Assembly, *Minutes*, p. 15.

51. M.G. McLuhan, "The Bulwark of Pentecostal Uniqueness," *Evangel*, 7 Apr. 1969, p. 13.

52. Arnold Delane Thrash, "An Episcopal Priest Discovers the Holy Ghost Baptism," *Evangel*, 25 May 1970, pp. 12–13.

53. O.W. Polen, "What Should Mainline Pentecostals' Attitude Be?", *Evangel*, 14 Aug. 1972, p. 31.

54. Ray H. Hughes, "A Call to Unity," COG 54th General Assembly, *Minutes*, pp. 19–20.

55. Ray H. Hughes, "Perspective," *Evangel*, 11 Sept. 1972, p. 2.

56. Wade H. Horton, "Where the Spirit of the Lord Is There is Liberty," COG 56th General Assembly, *Minutes*, p. 26.

57. Wade H. Horton, "Where the Spirit of the Lord Is, There is Liberty," sermon delivered at 56th General Assembly and recorded on audio tape, now owned by Mickey Crews.

58. An open letter from Raymond E. Crowley, general overseer, to all Church of God ministers, 9 July 1987, R.E. Crowley Correspondence, COG General Headquarters, Cleveland, Tenn.

59. COG 55th General Assembly, *Minutes*, preface.

60. COG 61st General Assembly, *Minutes*, preface.

61. COG 55th General Assembly, *Minutes*, preface.

62. COG 61st General Assembly, *Minutes*, preface.

63. Wade H. Horton, "Pentecostal Flames," COG 51st General Assembly, *Minutes*, p. 12.

64. COG 48th General Assembly, *Minutes*, pp. 54–55.

65. "A Roman Catholic President?", *Evangel*, 16 May 1960, p. 5.

66. James A. Cross, "How Shall the Christian Vote in the Presidential Election?", *Evangel*, 16 May 1960, p. 9.

67. COG 48th General Assembly, *Minutes*, p. 25.

68. R.H. Gause, "The Beginning of Spiritual Decay," *Evangel*, 23 Apr. 1962, p. 9.

69. Terrell McBrayer, "Proper Role of Christians in Politics," *Evangel*, 4 July 1966, p. 7.

70. COG 51st General Assembly, *Minutes*, p. 65.

71. Roy Bernard Jussell, "Christian in a Voting Booth," *Lighted Pathway*, Oct. 1966, p. 14.

72. Belinda Roope, "Me, Watergate, and Freedom," *Lighted Pathway*, Nov. 1973, p. 8.

73. Kohatha Culpepper, "Prayer Intercessors for America," (Cleveland, Tenn: COG Department of Ladies Ministries, 1984), p. 3.

74. COG 60th General Assembly, *Minutes*, p. 57.

75. Charles R. Beach, "Jim Crow or Jesus Christ," unpublished manuscript, 8 Jan. 1947, preface and pp. 1, 6, PRC.

76. T.L. Lowery, *America's No. 1 Problem: Segregation*, 3d ed., (Cleveland, Tenn.: T.L. Lowery Evangelistic Association, n.d.)

77. [J.D. Bright], "A Negro's Viewpoint on Civil Rights," *Evangel*, 8 Jan. 1949, p. 13.

78. Ibid.

79. COG 17th General Assembly, *Minutes*, p. 49.

80. T.W. Hamilton to F.J. Lee, 9 Dec. 1926, and L.C. Hill to F.J. Lee, 16 Nov. 1926, both in F.J. Lee Correspondence.

81. COG Supreme Council, *Minutes*, Apr. 1951, p. 21.

82. COG 44th General Assembly, *Minutes*, p. 18.

83. COG Supreme Council, *Minutes*, 28 July 1952, pp. 1–2.

84. COG Supreme Council, *Minutes*, 31 July 1952, p. 19.

85. COG 48th General Assembly, *Minutes*, p. 34.

86. COG Supreme Council, *Minutes*, 6 Mar. 1958, p. 28.

87. Charles W. Conn, *Like A Mighty Army*, p. 311.

88. COG 34th Annual Assembly of the Colored Churches, *Minutes*, pp. 55–56.

89. COG Supreme Council, *Minutes*, 13 Aug. 1963, p. 27.

90. COG 50th General Assembly, *Minutes*, p. 67.

91. COG 39th Annual Assembly of the Colored Churches, *Minutes*, p. 22.

92. Ibid., p. 24.

93. Ibid., p. 27.

94. COG Executive Council, *Minutes*, p. 45.

95. Ibid., p. 67.

96. John D. Nichols, "Ministry Among Blacks," *Evangel*, 25 Mar. 1974, p. 8.

97. COG 61st General Assembly, *Minutes*, pp. 29, 79.

Bibliography

A. A Note on Historical Works

In a standard scholarly work, one expects to find either a bibliographical essay or a list of entries. This bibliography, however, begins with a short essay on the historical studies that examine the Pentecostal movement. The longer list of entries which follows contains works related specifically to the Church of God, Cleveland, Tennessee.

Numerous historical works have dealth with the Pentecostal movement. A few of these are surveys which trace the movement as a worldwide phenomenon. A starting point for any serious research on the topic should be Walter J. Hollenweger's comprehensive study, *The Pentecostals: The Charismatic Movement in the Church*. This English translation is a shortened version of a multivolume Zurich dissertation, "Handbuch der Pfingstbeuegung," written by the former executive of the World Council of Churches. Hollenweger is the son of a Pentecostal minister and himself served as pastor of a Pentecostal congregation. His background provided him with insight to analyze and interpret the Pentecostal movement.

Pentecostalism, written by John Nichol, presents an overview of the development and growth of the movement on a global scale. His work, which began as a Boston University dissertation, discusses various denominations and places them in categories according to size of membership.

Another significant work is Nils Bloch-Hoell's *The Pentecostal Movement: Its Origin, Development, and Distinctive Character*. This English translation of the Norwegian study, *Pinsebevegelsen*, is a work which examines the Pentecostal movement as an international phenomenon. Although it is generally excellent, the part dealing with the American wing of Pentecostalism, except for a discussion of the Pentecostal revival which erupted in 1906 at the Azusa Street Mission in Los Angeles, California, is rather superficial. The extensive bibliography contains notes useful to any researcher. It also includes references to numerous non-English titles which do not appear in most works on Pentecostalism.

A number of excellent anthologies deal with old-line Pentecostals and Neopentecostals. *Aspects of Pentecostal-Charismatic Origins,* edited by the Pentecostal scholar Vinson Synan, and *Gifts of the Spirit in the Body of Christ: Perspectives on the Charismatic Movement,* edited by J. Elmo Agrimson, are books written mostly by Pentecostal writers that point out strengths and shortcomings of Pentecostalism.

There are different ways to classify Pentecostal groups. Bibliographer Watson E. Mills (in his *Charismatic Religion in Modern Research: A Bibliography*) places them into three main groups. He lumps all of the old-line Pentecostals into one group, the Neopentecostals into a separate group, and the "Jesus Movement," which arose outside mainstream Christianity in the late 1960s and 1970s, into a third. Bibliographers William Faupel and Everett L. Moore chose another means of classification. In his study "The American Pentecostal Movement: A Bibliographical Essay," Faupel followed the pattern Moore had established previously. In Moore's 1954 master's thesis, "Handbook of Pentecostal Denominations in the United States," he had grouped the old-line denominations into three separate categories according to theology: Holiness (Wesleyan Perfectionism), Keswick, and those which espouse the concept of "Jesus Only." Faupel made a significant contribution by distinguishing further among black Pentecostals, the Latter Rain movement, the salvationist-healing movement, the charismatic movement, Catholic Pentecostals, and the "Jesus Movement." The preeminent bibliographer of the Pentecostal movement is Charles E. Jones. Without a doubt, he has written the most exhaustive work on the subject. He classifies more than four hundred Pentecostal groups in his two-volume study, *A Guide to the Study of the Pentecostal Movement.*

Within these various categories one finds an enormous range of works. Most have been written by participants in the Pentecostal movement. Klaude Kendrick's *The Promise Fulfilled: A History of the Modern Pentecostal Movement* is a good survey of the origins of the old-line Pentecostal churches. Kendrick was probably the first to categorize various denominations according to the major issues that he feels helped to form them. Kendrick contends that doctrine, race, government, and strong personalities were determining factors in the rise of some old-line Pentecostal churches. In a revised University of Georgia dissertation, Vinson Synan, an educator and executive in the Pentecostal Holiness Church, argues that the Pentecostal movement sprang from the Wesleyan Perfectionist theological tradition. He correctly maintains that Pentecostalism emerged from division in the ranks of the nineteenth-century Holiness movement. This radical wing initiated the modern Pentecostal movement.

In 1979, Robert M. Anderson published perhaps the best historical analysis yet written, *Vision of the Disinherited: The Making of American Pentecostalism,* the author contends that Pentecostals came primarily from the lower socioeconomic classes. Pentecostal religion provided these powerless members of American society with a sense of control over their own lives. It also gave them a conviction of personal worth and meaning.

Numerous histories of the major Pentecostal denominations have been written since the 1970s. Vinson Synan's excellent study, *That Old Time Religion: A History of the Pentecostal Holiness Church*, was published in 1973. This scholarly work supplanted a much older institutional study, Joseph E. Campbell's *The Pentecostal Church, 1898–1948: Its History and Background*, which was published by the denomination.

One of the oldest and largest of the old-line groups in the Holiness tradition is the Church of God of Cleveland, Tennessee. Church of God leaders have written two denominational histories. The first was E.L. Simmons's *History of the Church of God*, a short summary published in 1938. The second, *Like A Mighty Army*, was written by Charles W. Conn, published in 1955, and revised in 1977.

By far the largest old-line Pentecostal denomination is the Assemblies of God. Numerous studies have been written about this group. Three of the most popular are: *With Signs Following, In The Last Days: A History of the Assemblies of God*, and *Suddenly From Heaven: A History of the Assembly of God*. William W. Menzies has written an excellent work, a revised University of Iowa dissertation, *Anointed to Serve: The Story of the Assemblies of God*. Church historian Menzies focuses on a period of approximately twenty-five years, from the 1940s to the mid-1960s. He maintains that the denomination experienced two major shifts after World War II. After a long period of isolation from other Protestant churches, the organization moved toward interdenominational cooperation with other evangelical organizations. The denomination also experienced a centralization of government and growth of denominational bureaucracy.

There are few good books on the origin and history of the "Jesus Only" or "Oneness" groups. The movement began in 1916, when G.T. Haywood, a black minister, helped to form the Pentecostal Assemblies of the World. Although the organization was interracial at first, in 1924 a group of white clergymen withdrew and organized their own church. In 1945, the two groups again merged. The merger produced the United Pentecostal Church, the largest of the Jesus Only groups. One of the first works to deal with these groups, Fred J. Foster's *Think It Not Strange, A History of the Oneness Movement*, was published in the 1960s. In 1970 Arthur L. Clanton wrote a history of the United Pentecostal Church entitled, *United We Stand*, published by the Pentecostal Publishing House in Hazelwood, Missouri. Other authors, such as Synan and Menzies, discuss the subject in a chapter of their works.

In 1948, a healing revival erupted. Scores of Pentecostal evangelists preached divine healing and divine deliverance under huge gospel tents scattered across the nation. The most successful and best-known campaigner was Oral Roberts, who began his ministry in the Pentecostal Holiness Church in Oklahoma. A number of recent scholarly and popular works discuss this revival era. One of the most favorable books about the famous evangelist is *Oral: The Warm, Intimate, Unauthorized Portrait of a Man of God*, by Wayne A. Robinson. The most critical work published to date is the study by Jerry Sholes, *Give Me That Prime-Time Religion*. Two of the best scholarly studies on Roberts are *All Things Possible: The Healing Charismatic Revivals in Modern America* by David Edwin Harrell, Jr., and Richard Quebedeaux's *The New Charismatics*. By far the best and most comprehensive biography of the charismatic leader was written by Harrell: *Oral Roberts: An American Life* (1985).

The charismatic revival emerged from the healing revival. People within mainline denominations, called Neopentecostals, began displaying behaviors associated with baptism of the Holy Spirit and other "spiritual gifts." Michael Harper examined the development of the charismatic revival in his book, *As At the Beginning: The Twentieth-Century Pentecostal Revival* (1965). An earlier work, *They Speak With Other Tongues*, was written by John L. Sherrill, a noncharismatic who himself became deeply involved in the movement before he completed his study. A number of articles document the growth of the charismatic movement. One of the first and most important was "Outbursts of Tongues: The New Penetration," by Frank Farrell, published in *Christianity Today* in 1963. In a 1981 article in the charismatic journal *Pneuma*, Peter Hocken examined the relationship of old-line Pentecostals to Neopentecostals within traditional mainline denominations.

Thousands of Catholics also received the Spirit baptism and became participants in the Charismatic Renewal. There are few good studies of Catholic Pentecostalism. Three are *Perspectives on Charismatic Renewal* and *The Pentecostal Movement in the Catholic Church*, by Edward D. O'Connor, and *The Catholic Pentecostal Movement*, by John G. Melton. The Catholic Pentecostal movement began in 1967 with lay faculty members at Duquesne University in Pittsburgh, Pennsylvania. During the "Duquesne Weekend," some thirty persons received the baptism of the Holy Spirit. Interest among Catholics spread rapidly.

Several books regarding the Catholic Charismatic Renewal have been written by Catholic and non-Catholic authors. Kevin and Dorothy Ranaghan's *Catholic Pentecostals*, among the first to appear, traces the development of the Catholic Pentecostal movement. Kilian McDonnell's *Charismatic Renewal and The Churches* provides a sociological analysis of Catholic Pentecostalism and shows how various denominations responded to the movement. Many works try to analyze Pentecostalism in the context of Roman Catholic theology and tradition. Some of these are: *The Pentecostal Movement in the Catholic Church* and *Perspectives on Charismatic Renewal* by Edward D. O'Connor; *Pentecostalism: A Theological Viewpoint* and *Experiencing God: A Theology of Human Experience*, by Donald L. Gelpi; and *The Pentecostal Experience: A New Direction for American Catholics* and *Baptism of the Spirit: Three Essays on the Pentecostal Experience*, by Massynglerle Ford. Ford also contributed an essay, "The Catholic Charismatic Gifts in Worship," in *The Charismatic Movement* edited by Michael Hamilton.

The Jesus Movement which originated in the late 1960s remained outside mainstream Christianity. Only a few accounts exist to introduce readers to the movement. Ronald M. Enroth and his coauthors narrate the growth and development of the movement in *The Jesus Movement*. Another such work is Robert S. Ellswood, Jr.'s *One Way: The Jesus Movement and Its Meaning*. Scholars such as William S. Cannon have attempted to assess the significance of the Jesus Movement in the light of traditional evangelical theology.

Black awareness, which emerged in the 1960s and 1970s, created a keen interest in the origin and development of the Pentecostal movement among blacks. Walter J. Hollenweger charts that course in an article, "A Black Pentecostal Concept: A Forgotten Chapter of Black History," which appeared in 1969 in *Concept*. Another article that makes a significant contribution to the understanding of black Pentecostalism is James S. Tinney's "Black Origins of the Pentecostal Movement," published in *Christianity Today* (1971). The definitive work to date on black Pentecostalism is *Black Pentecostalism: Southern Religion in an Urban World*, by Arthur E. Paris.

No adequate systematic theology of Pentecostalism has been written. Most of the early Pentecostal clergymen relied heavily upon their predecessors from the Holiness movement. Although he does not come from the ranks of Pentecostalism, Frederick D. Bruner has produced the best theological treatise on Pentecostal religion: *A Theology of the Holy Spirit: The Pentecostal Experience and the new Testament Witness*. Bruner divides his book into two parts. The first deals with the Pentecostal interpretation of the doctrine of the Holy Spirit. The latter examines biblical evidence for the interpretation. A few other books have been written on the subject in recent years. Two of these are *A Charismatic Theology* by Heribert Muhlen and *Charisms and Charismatic Renewal: A Biblical and Theological Study* by Frances A. Sullivan.

In spite of the numerous works which have been written in the last twenty-five years or so, more sophisticated analytical studies, especially by professional historians, are needed.

B. Primary Material

I. PENTECOSTAL COLLECTIONS

Hal Bernard Dixon, Jr. Pentecostal Research Center. Located in Cleveland, Tennessee.

William G. Squires Library. Located on the campus of Lee College, Cleveland, Tennessee.

Archives of the Church of God. Located at the General Headquarters in Cleveland, Tennessee.

Pathway Press Archives. Located in Cleveland, Tennessee.

Archives of Church of God World Missions. Located in Cleveland, Tennessee.

Holy Spirit Research Center. Located on the campus of Oral Roberts University, Tulsa, Oklahoma.

Archives of the Pentecostal Holiness Church. Located in Franklin Springs, Georgia.

Archives of the Assemblies of God. Located in Springfield, Missouri.

2. AUTOBIOGRAPHIES, BIOGRAPHIES, AND MEMOIRS

"A Pattern of Service." Paper by an unnamed student, Lee College, Cleveland, Tenn., 1979. WGS, PRC.

Batts, Albert H. "Here a little; there a little." N.p., n.d. WGS, PRC.

Bava, John. *My Life Story and the Beginning of the Gorman Church of God*. Davis, West Virginia: Privately published, n.d.

Buckalew, J.W. *Incidents in the Life of J.W. Buckalew*. Cleveland, Tenn.: COG PH, 1920.

Bulaga, Peter. *Prison to Paradise*. Edited by Thomas R. Nickel. Hartford, Conn.: Great Commission International, 1973.

Clark, E.C. *Marvelous Healings God Wrought Among Us*. Cleveland, Tenn.: COG PH, 1946.

Cowart, Rufus Newitt. "Work and Ministry Wrought of God Through R.N. Cowart." N.p., n.d. WGS, PRC.

Cross, M.P. "In the Good (?) Ole Days." N.p., n.d. WGS, PRC.

Daffe, Jerald J. "The Church of God in the Dakotas During the Depression of the 1930s." N.p., 1973. WGS, PRC.

Duggar, Lillian, ed. *A.J. Tomlinson: Former General Overseer of the Church of God*. Cleveland, Tenn.: White Wing PH, 1964.

Ellis, James Benton. *Blazing the Gospel Trail*. Cleveland, Tenn.: COG PH, 1941.

Grant, Earle J. *My Experience With God*. Dexter, Mass.: Candor Press, 1970.

Hand, Marcus V. *I Saw a Vision: A Biography of Missionary Lovell Cary*. Cleveland, Tenn.: Pathway Press, 1980.

Hand, Marcus V. *Reaching People: A Biography of Missionary Bill Watson*. Cleveland, Tenn.: Pathway Press, 1979.

"Happy as a Lark." Paper by an unnamed student, Lee College, Cleveland, Tenn., 1979. PRC.

Harrison, Alda. *Mountain Peaks of Experience*. Cleveland, Tenn.: COG PH, n.d.

Heath, S.J. "Life and Writings of S. J. Heath." N.p., n.d. WGS, PRC.

Jernigan, John C. "From the Gambling Den to the Pulpit." Rev. ed. N.p., 1939.

Lauster, Bobbie. *Herman Lauster: One Man and God*. Cleveland, Tenn.: Pathway Press, 1967.

Lee, Mrs. Flavius J. *Life Sketches and Sermons of F.J. Lee*. Cleveland, Tenn.: COG PH, 1929.

Lemons, David L. *Bread Upon Waters: The Life Story of the Preacher and Prophet, R.P. Johnson*. Cleveland, Tenn.: Pathway Press, 1986.

Marshall, June Glover. *A Biographical Sketch of Richard G. Spurling, Jr.* Cleveland, Tenn.: Pathway Press, 1974.

McWhorter, Fred. "It Happened in Georgia." N.p., n.d. PRC.

Miller, Amanda. *Surrendered to God*. Cleveland, Tenn.: COG PH, 1967.

Monsees, Casey F. *At Last I Am Free*. Atlanta: Broadwell Press, 1956.

Muncey, James A. "My Life and Works." N.p., n.d. PRC.

Newman, Emma. "Some High Points in My Life." N.p., n.d. PRC.

Rexrode, R.L. "Testimony." N.p., n.d. PRC.

Rouse, L.G. "Marvelous Miracles and Incidents in My Life." N.p., n.d. PRC.

Scarborough, Peggy. *J.H. Ingram: Missionary Dean*. Cleveland, Tenn.: Pathway Press, 1966.

Spurling, Pinckney. "The Life of Rev. R.G. Spurling, Jr." N.p., n.d. Xerox copy in Crews' possession.

Sustar, Bob R. *Yet Will I Serve Him*. Cleveland, Tenn.: Pathway Press, 1976.

Thornton, Manning. "W.W. Ball: A Warrior of Faith." N.p., n.d. PRC.

Tomlinson, A.J. *Answering the Call of God*. Cleveland, Tenn.: White Wing PH, n.d.

Tomlinson, Ambrose Jessup. *A.J. Tomlinson: God's Anointed, Prophet of Wisdom*. Cleveland, Tenn.: White Wing PH, 1970.

Walker, Paul H. *Paths of a Pioneer*. Cleveland, Tenn.: Pathway Press, 1971.

Walker, R.R. *My Testimony*. Cleveland, Tenn.: COG PH, 1942.

3. DIARIES, CORRESPONDENCE, MINUTES, AND SERMONS

Campbell, Manuel F. *One Minute Please: One-Minute Sermons*. Cleveland, Tenn.: Pathway Press, n.d.

Church of God. Colored Work. *Minutes*. Vols. 3–39. 1927–65. Cleveland: COG PH, 1927–65.

Church of God. Council of Twelve (Elders' Council). *Minutes*. 1916–82. PRC.

Church of God. Executive Council (Supreme Council). *Minutes*. 1916–84. PRC.

Church of God. General Assembly. *Minutes of the General Assembly of the Church of God*. Vols. 1–61. Cleveland, Tenn.: COG PH, 1906–86.

Church of God. General Council (Bishops' Council). *Minutes*. 1936–82. PRC.

Creshaw, G.E. "Three Sermons." N.p., n.d. PRC.

Cross, James A. *The Glorious Gospel.* Cleveland, Tenn.: COG PH, 1956.
Crowley, Raymond E. Personal Correspondence. COG Headquarters, Cleveland, Tenn.
Free, J.D., ed. "Campmeeting Sermons." N.p., n.d. PRC.
Hand, Marcus V., comp. *A Potpourri of Pentecostal Preaching.* Atlanta, Ga.: Lee College Alumni Association, 1971.
Hinkley, Emmett B. "The Unseen Worlds." N.p., n.d. PRC.
Horton, Wade H. *Evangel Sermons.* Cleveland, Tenn.: Pathway Press, 1977.
Horton, Wade H. *Pentecost Yesterday and Today.* Cleveland, Tenn.: Pathway Press, 1964.
Hughes, Ray H. *Religion on Fire.* Cleveland, Tenn.: Pathway Press, 1956.
Jernigan, John C. *Doctrinal Sermon Outlines.* Cleveland, Tenn.: COG PH, n.d.
Lattimer, S.W. Personal Correspondence. PRC.
Lane, G.W. *But His Man.* Cleveland, Tenn.: Pathway Press, 1960.
Lane, G.W. *The Voice of Calvary.* Cleveland, Tenn.: Pathway Press, 1958.
Lee, Flavius J. Diary. WGS, PRC.
Lee, Flavius J. Personal Correspondence. PRC.
Lemons, Frank W. *Perennial Pentecost.* Cleveland, Tenn.: Pathway Press, 1958.
Lowery, Thomas L. *The Next World Dictator.* Cleveland, Tenn.: Lowery Publications, 1966.
Milligan, Joseph L. *The Blushing Bride and Other Sermons.* Cleveland, Tenn.: Pathway Press, 1968.
Padgett, Carl. Diaries. 1907–65. PRC.
Paulk, Earl P. *Earnest Pastoral Pleas.* N.p.: Privately published, 1941.
Pettyjohn, Glenn C. "Hearthrobs from Calvary." N.p., n.d. PRC.
Tharp, Zeno C. *Inspirational Short Sermons.* Cleveland, Tenn.: COG PH, 1956.
Timmerman, Floyd J. "Life's Greatest Discovery." N.p., n.d. WGS, PRC.
Timmerman, Floyd J. *The Pathway of Promise.* Cleveland, Tenn.: Pathway Press, 1968.
Tomlinson, Halcy Olive. *Our Sister Halcy.* Cleveland, Tenn.: White Wing PH, 1974.
Tomlinson, A.J. *Diary.* Edited by Homer Tomlinson. 3 vols. New York: Ryder Press, 1949.
Tomlinson, A.J. "Journal of Happenings." 5 vols., 1901–23. WGS, PRC.
Tomlinson, A.J. Personal Correspondence. PRC.

4. PERIODICALS

Church of God Evangel. Vols. 1–77, Cleveland, Tenn.: COG PH, 1910–86.
Lighted Pathway. Vols. 1–58, Cleveland, Tenn.: COG PH, 1929–86.
Pentecostal Holiness Advocate. [Franklin Springs, Ga.] 1918.

Samson's Foxes. 1902. PRC.
The Faithful Standard. 1922–23. PRC.
The Way. 1904. PRC.

5. NEWSPAPERS

Bradley County Journal. 1909–10.
Cleveland Daily Banner. 1912–45.
Cleveland Herald. 1914–32.

6. GOVERNMENT DOCUMENTS

Florida. State Supreme Court. *James Bradley* v. *State of Florida*. A 134-page report located at the Florida State Supreme Court Library in Tallahassee, Florida.

United States Statutes at Large. Volume 40. Statute 1.

U.S. Department of Commerce. Bureau of the Census. *Census of Religious Bodies, 1916*. Vols. 1–2. Washington, D.C.: USGPO, 1919.

U.S. Department of Commerce. Bureau of the Census. *Census of Religious Bodies, 1926*. Vols. 1–2. Washington, D.C.: USGPO, 1929.

U.S. Department of Commerce. Bureau of the Census. *Fourteenth Census of the United States, 1920: Population*. Vols. 1 and 3. Washington, D.C.: USGPO, 1921.

U.S. Department of Commerce. Bureau of the Census. *Statistical Atlas of the United States*. Washington, D.C.: USGPO, 1925.

U.S. Department of Justice. Federal Bureau of Investigation. "Investigative Files of the Old Germans From the Year 1914 to 1918 Inclusive." Documents #06262854, #203958, #121580, Civil Archives Division, NA.

Virginia. Wythe County. Circuit Court. *Commonwealth* v. *Walter Barney*. Common Law Order Book. A one-page report located at the Wythe County Courthouse, Wytheville, Virginia.

7. INTERVIEWS

Bryant, W.F. Interview by Geneva Carroll, 1949. Typescript, PRC files.

Bryant, W.F., and Lemons, M.S. Interview by C.L. Chesser, 17 March 1954. Typescript, document 27A, PRC files.

Bryant, Mrs. W.F. Interview by unnamed person, 8 Feb. 1954. Typescript, document 8A, PRC files.

Conn, Charles W. COG state overseer, Virginia. Interview by Mickey Crews, 19 Oct. 1982, Roanoke, Va.

Denson, Whitt. Interview by anonymous person. "Youth Interviews Experience," 1950. PRC.

Echols, Evelyn. Interview by Mickey Crews, 8 July 1982, Cleveland, Tenn.

Hunter, Harold. Asst. Professor of Religion, COG School of Theology, Cleveland, Tenn. Interview by Mickey Crews, 13 Sept. 1983.

Jennings, Dorothy. Executive Director, COG Department of Ladies' Ministries. Interview by Mickey Crews, 8 Sept. 1986, Cleveland, Tenn.

Jones, Nora. Daughter of W.F. Bryant. Interview by Mickey Crews, 8 July 1982, Cleveland, Tenn.

Kinser, J.R. Archivist for Church of God of Prophecy. Interview by Mickey Crews, 1 Sept. 1982, Cleveland, Tenn.

Lauster, Bobbie. Interview by anonymous person. "Youth Interviews Experience," 1950, document 9A, PRC.

Lee, Flavius J., Jr. Interview by Mickey Crews, 3 Sept. 1982, Cleveland, Tenn.

Marshall, James. Interview by Mickey Crews, 25 Sept. 1982, Cleveland, Tenn.

Moorehead, Houston R. Interview by an anonymous person. "Youth Interviews Experience," 1950, document 9A, PRC.

Payne, T.S. Interview by anonymous person. "Youth Interviews Experience," 1950, PRC.

Robinson, Julian. Director of COG Records Department. Interview by Mickey Crews, 3 Nov. 1982, Cleveland, Tenn.

Smith, D.B. An early COG minister. Interview by Mickey Crews, 31 Oct. 1982, Auburn, Ala.

Spurling, James. Grandson of Richard G. Spurling, Jr. Interview by Mickey Crews, 25 Sept. 1982, Turtletown, Tenn.

Tharp, Zeno C. Interview by anonymous person. "Youth Interviews Experience," 1950, document 6, PRC.

Tomlinson, Milton A. Son of A.J. Tomlinson and general overseer, Church of God of Prophecy, Cleveland, Tenn. Interview by Mickey Crews, 1 Sept. 1982.

West, Georgia. Relative of Spurling family. Interview by Mickey Crews, 1 Sept. 1982, Turtletown, Tenn.

8. CHURCH OF GOD LITERATURE

Albert, Leonard C. *Give Me This Mountain*. Cleveland, Tenn.: Pathway Press, 1977.

Alford, Delton L. *Gospel Choir Arrangements*. Cleveland, Tenn.: Tennessee Music and Printing, 1966.

———. *Magnify the Lord*. Cleveland, Tenn.: Tennessee Music and Printing, 1963.

———. *Music in the Pentecostal Church*. Cleveland, Tenn.: Pathway Press, 1971.

Almand, Joan. *Establishing Values*. Cleveland, Tenn.: Pathway Press, 1976.

Arrington, French L. "A Critique of Good News for Modern Man." N.p., 1972.

———. "An Exegesis of Acts." N.p., 1968.

———. "An Exegesis of Hebrews 10:9–25." N.p., 1968.

———. "Apocalyptic Categories in Paul." N.p., n.d.

———. "Creation's Hopeful Expectation." N.p., 1972.

———. *Divine Order in the Church*. Cleveland, Tenn.: Pathway Press, 1978.

———. "Late Jewish Apocalyptic." N.p., n.d.

———. *Maintaining the Foundations*. Grand Rapids, Mich.: Baker Book House, 1982.

———. *New Testament Exegesis*. Washington, D.C.: Univ. Press of America, 1977.

———. "Paul's Aeon Theology in the First Letter to the Corinthians." N.p., 1973.

———. *The Ministry of Reconciliation*. Grand Rapids, Mich.: Baker Book House, 1980.

Aultman, Donald S. *A Guide to Family Training Hour*. Cleveland, Tenn.: Pathway Press, 1968.

———. *Guiding Youth*. Cleveland, Tenn.: Church of God, 1965.

———. *Learning Christian Leadership*. Cleveland, Tenn.: Pathway Press, 1960.

———. *Saved to Serve*. Cleveland, Tenn.: Pathway Press, N.d.

Baldree, J. Martin. *Sunday School Growth*. Cleveland, Tenn.: Pathway Press, 1971.

Battle, Lee H., Audit Company. "Audit Report: Church of God, Cleveland, Tenn., December 1, 1922." PRC.

Beach, Charles R. "Jim Crow or Jesus Christ?" N.p., 1947.

Beatty, Jerome. "Nile Mother." N.p., n.d.

Benz, Larry L. *Standards for Living*. Cleveland, Tenn.: Pathway Press, 1978.

Bible Training School. "Class Roll; First Six Terms, 1918–1920." N.p., n.d.

Bishop, David S. *Effective Communication*. Cleveland, Tenn.: Pathway Press, 1977.

Black, Hubert Perry. "The Teaching Success of Lee College Graduates in Cleveland and Bradley County Schools." N.p., 1970.

———. *Religious and Philosophical Foundations of Education*. Cleveland, Tenn.: Pathway Press, 1967.

Bock, Paul. *The Pentecostals*. Cincinnati, Ohio: P. Bock, 1973.

Bowdle, Donald N. "Epistle to the Phillipians." N.p., n.d.

———, ed. *The Promise and the Power*. Cleveland, Tenn.: Pathway Press, 1980.

Bowen, C.E. *The Lord's Supper and Feet Washing*. Cleveland, Tenn.: Pathway Press, 1955.

Bright, Jonathan D. *Chin Lifters for Ministers and Laymen*. Cleveland, Tenn.: COG PH, 1943.

——— . *The Baptism of the Holy Ghost*. Cleveland, Tenn.: COG PH, n.d.

Britt, George L. *The Bodily Resurrection*. Cleveland, Tenn.: COG PH, 1971.

——— . *The Hour Has Come*. Cleveland, Tenn.: Pathway Press, 1966.

Brock, Edith. *The Brighter Side*. Cleveland, Tenn.: Pathway Press, 1978.

Brock, Ronald E. *Overcoming Your Circumstances*. Cleveland, Tenn.: Pathway Press, 1979.

Broome, Connie. *Vessels Unto Honor*. Cleveland, Tenn.: Pathway Press, 1976.

Buxton, Clyne W. *The Bible Says You Can Expect These Things*. Old Tappan, N.J.: Revell, 1973.

——— . *What About Tomorrow?* Cleveland, Tenn.: Pathway Press, 1974.

Carey, Floyd D. *Campus Champion for Christ*. Cleveland, Tenn.: Pathway Press, 1963.

——— . *Involved*. Cleveland, Tenn.: Pathway Press, 1969.

——— . *Sunday School Basics*. Cleveland, Tenn.: Pathway Press, 1976.

——— . *Teenager's Treasure Chest*. Cleveland, Tenn.: Pathway Press, 1963.

Carroll, Dorothy P. "A Chosen Vessel." N.p., n.d.

Carroll, Ramon L. "That I May Know Him." N.p., n.d.

Church of God. *Encyclopedia on Evangelism*. Cleveland, Tenn.: COG PH, n.d.

——— . "General Instructions for the Ministry and Membership." N.p., n.d.

——— . *Ministerial Internship Program*. Cleveland, Tenn.: COG, 1978.

——— . *Pastoral Pointers*. Cleveland, Tenn.: Pathway Press, 1975.

——— . "Pictorial Review of the Church of God Orphanage, 1940, 20th Anniversary." N.p., n.d.

——— . "This We Believe: Church of God Declaration of Faith; What We Believe and Why We Believe It." 16 cassette tapes produced by COG Forward in Faith Radio and Television Department, and Lee College, 1976.

——— . Bible School. "The Harbinger." N.p., n.d.

——— . Elder's Council. "Report of Investigation." 12–21 June 1923.

——— . Evangelism and Home Missions Department. *Evangelism Breakthrough Lessons*. Cleveland, Tenn.: Pathway Press, n.d.

——— . Evangelism and Home Missions Department. *Perpetuation of Pentecost from the Upper Room, A.D. 36 to the Church Today*. Cleveland, Tenn.: Pathway Press, 1966.

——— . General Department of Education. *Ministerial Internship Program; Instructional Guide for Training Period November 1978–June 1979*. Cleveland, Tenn.: Pathway Press, 1978.

——— . General Executive Committee. *State Overseer's Manual*. Cleveland, Tenn.: COG, 1972.

——— . Ladies Auxiliary Department. *Study Courses for Young Ladies Auxiliary*. Cleveland, Tenn.: COG, n.d.

Church of God, Maryland. *Peninsular Pentecost 1919–1969*. Simpsonville, Md.: COG State Office, 1969.

Church of God, Southern California–Nevada. *A Challenging new Frontier: Presenting the Church of God in Southern California–Nevada*. Upland, Calif.: COG, 1970.

Clark, Elijah C. *Eloheim*. Cleveland, Tenn.: COG PH, 1929.

———. *The Baptism of the Holy Ghost and More*. Cleveland, Tenn.: COG PH, 1931.

———. *The Victory*. Cleveland, Tenn.: COG PH, 1944.

Colkmire, Lance. *Reasoning With Juniors For Christ's Sake*. Cleveland, Tenn.: Pathway Press, 1982.

Conn, Charles Paul. *The Man From Galilee*. Cleveland, Tenn.: Pathway Press, 1974.

———. *The Meaning of Marriage*. Cleveland, Tenn.: Pathway Press, 1977.

———. *The Music Makers*. Cleveland, Tenn.: Pathway Press, 1958.

———. *The Relevant Record*. Cleveland, Tenn.: Pathway Press, 1976.

Conn, Charles W. *A Guide to the Pentateuch*. Cleveland, Tenn.: Pathway Press, 1963.

———. *A Survey of the Epistles*. Cleveland, Tenn.: Pathway Press, 1969.

———. *Acts of the Apostles*. Cleveland, Tenn.: Pathway Press, 1965.

———. *Book of Books*. Cleveland, Tenn.: Pathway Press, 1961.

———. *Christ and the Gospels*. Cleveland, Tenn.: Pathway Press, 1964.

———. *Highlights of Hebrew History*. Cleveland, Tenn.: Pathway Press, 1975.

———. *Like A Mighty Army: A History of the Church of God*. 1955. Rev. ed. Cleveland, Tenn.: Pathway Press, 1977.

———. *Pillars of Pentecost*. Cleveland, Tenn.: Pathway Press, 1956.

———. *The Bible*. Cleveland, Tenn.: Pathway Press, 1961.

———. *The Pointed Pen*. Cleveland, Tenn.: Lee College Alumni Association, 1973.

———. *The Rudder and the Rock*. Cleveland, Tenn.: Pathway Press, 1960.

———. "Twelve Men and Their Message." N.p., n.d.

———. *Where the Saints Have Trod*. Cleveland, Tenn.: Pathway Press, 1959.

Coward, Parnell C. *Revelation Systematically Studied*. Cleveland, Tenn.: Pathway Press, 1974.

Cox, Clyde C. *Evangelical Precepts of the Revelation*. Cleveland, Tenn.: Pathway Press, 1971.

———. *Footprints of the Great Tribulation*. Cleveland, Tenn.: Pathway Press, 1961.

———. *Prophetical Events and the Great Tribulation*. New York: Exposition Press, 1957.

Cross, James A. *Healing in the Church*. Cleveland, Tenn.: Pathway Press, 1962.

———. *Sanctification*. Cleveland, Tenn.: Pathway Press, 1971.

Culpepper, Kohatha. *Everything You've Wanted To Know About the Equal Rights Amendment*. Cleveland, Tenn.: COG PH, 1979.

Daffe, Jerald J. "The Church of God in the Dakotas During the Depression."
N.p., n.d.

Davenport, R. Edward. *Person to Person Evangelism*. Cleveland, Tenn.:
Pathway Press, n.d.

Day, Ralph E. *Manual of Instruction in the Faith of the Church; for Children
(ages 4 through 11 years)*. Cleveland, Tenn.: Pathway Press, 1959.

————. *Manual of Instruction in the Faith of the Church; for Young People
(ages 12 through 24 years)*. Cleveland, Tenn.: Pathway Press, n.d.

Dirksen, Carolyn. "Let Your Women Keep Silent." Manuscript, PRC.

Dokter, Guy G. "Let Us Go Forward: A History of North West Bible College"
[Minot, North Dakota]. N.p., N.d.

Drake, H.M. *The Plan of God for the Ages*. Cleveland, Tenn.: Pathway Press,
1966.

Duncan, Paul E. *On Campus*. Cleveland, Tenn.: COG, 1977.

Echols, Evaline. *Climb Up Through Your Valleys*. Cleveland, Tenn.: Pathway
Press, 1980.

Fisher, Robert, ed. *The Challenge of the Ministry*. Cleveland, Tenn.: Pathway
Press, 1977.

————. *The Family and the Church*. Cleveland, Tenn.: Pathway Press, 1978.

Gause, R. Hollis. "A Study of the Doxology of Ephesians." N.p., n.d.

————. "A Critical and Exegetical Study of John 16:13." N.p., n.d.

————. "Acts 2:1–4." N.p., n.d.

————. "An Exegetical Study of 2 Timothy 3:6–13." N.p., n.d.

————. *Church of God Polity*. Rev. ed. Cleveland, Tenn.: Pathway Press,
1973.

————. *Living in the Spirit*. Cleveland, Tenn.: Pathway Press, 1980.

————. "St. Irenaeus, The Apostolic Preaching." N.p., 1964.

————. "The Lukan Transfiguration Account." N.p., 1975.

George, Bill. *His Story: The Life of Christ*. Cleveland, Tenn.: Pathway Press,
1977.

Gillum, Perry E. *Historical Annual Addressess*. Cleveland, Tenn.: White
Wing PH, 1970.

Green, Hollis Lynn. "Marching As to War." N.p., n.d.

————. *Understanding Pentecostalism*. Cleveland, Tenn.: Pathway Press,
1970.

————. *Why Churches Die*. Minneapolis: Bethany Fellowship, 1972.

Green, Peggy L. *The Way to Teen-Age Charm*. Cleveland, Tenn.: Pathway
Press, 1970.

Guffey, William A. "A History of Woodward Avenue Church of God at
Athens, Tennessee." N.p., n.d.

Guiles, Cecil R. *Ministering To Youth*. Cleveland, Tenn.: Pathway Press,
1973.

————. *The In Crowd*. Cleveland, Tenn.: Pathway Press, 1976.

————. *The Minister of Christian Education*. Cleveland, Tenn.: Church of
God, n.d.

Hammel, W.W. *How Shall We Escape If We Neglect.* Cleveland, Tenn.: Pathway Press, 1972.

Hargrave, Vessie D. *Moved By The Spirit.* San Antonio, Tex.: Evangelical PH, 1957.

Harrison, Alda B. *Child Training and Social Evangelism.* Cleveland, Tenn.: Pathway Press, n.d.

Heil, L.E. *The Double Portion.* Cleveland, Tenn.: Pathway Press, 1961.

Hickson, Peter C. "History of the Church of God (Colored Work)." N.p., n.d.

Horton, Virginia. *Many Songs for Mini People.* Cleveland, Tenn.: Tennessee Music and Printing, 1974.

Horton, Wade H. "Lectures on the Seven Churches." N.p., n.d.

———. *The Order of Church Discipline.* Cleveland, Tenn.: COG Executive Offices, n.d.

———. *The Seven Golden Candlesticks.* Cleveland, Tenn.: Pathway Press, 1974.

———. *Unto the Uttermost.* Cleveland, Tenn.: Pathway Press, 1973.

Hughes, Ray H. *Church of God Distinctives.* Cleveland, Tenn.: Pathway Press, 1968.

———. *Planning for Sunday School Progress.* Cleveland, Tenn.: Pathway Press, 1960.

———. *The Holy Spirit in Perspective.* Cleveland, Tenn.: Pathway Press, 1981.

———. *What is Pentecost?* Cleveland, Tenn.: Pathway Press, 1963.

Hunt, Sonjia L. *Shaping Faith Through Involvement.* Cleveland, Tenn.: Pathway Press, 1981.

Isbill, Walter H. "Survey Study: Tennessee New Field Churches." N.p., n.d.

Jernigan, John C. "Kentucky Favorites." N.p., n.d.

———. *Soul Stirring Songs With Ancient Proverbs.* Stone, n.d.

Juillerat, L. Howard, ed. *Book of Minutes: Annual Minutes, 1–13, 1906–1917.* Cleveland, Tenn.: COG PH, 1922.

Juillerat, Mrs. L. Howard, comp. *Gems of Religious Truth.* Cleveland, Tenn.: COG Evangel Press, 1919.

Knight, Cecil B. *Keeping the Sunday School Alive.* Cleveland, Tenn.: Pathway Press, 1959.

———. *Pentecostal Worship.* Cleveland, Tenn.: Pathway Press, 1974.

Land, Steven J. *Do-Tell.* Cleveland, Tenn.: Pathway Press, 1976.

Lane, G.W. "Doctrines of the New Testament in Ten Great Subjects." N.p., n.d.

———. "Program and Purpose: What We Do and Why We Do It." N.p., n.d.

Layne, James N. *Old Testament Study Simplified.* Cleveland, Tenn.: Pathway Press, 1978.

Lee College. "A Look at Lee College." N.p., 1968.

Lee College. Division of Education. "A Handbook for the Cooperation Teacher." N.p., 1968.

Lee College. Science Symposium. *Science and Theology*. Cleveland, Tenn.: Pathway Press, 1977.

Ledford, A.A. *Pathways to Prophetic Fulfillment*. Cleveland, Tenn.: Pathway Press, 1978.

Lemons, Frank W. *In Rememberance of Me*. Cleveland, Tenn.: Pathway Press, 1975.

———. *Looking Beyond*. Cleveland, Tenn.: Pathway Press, n.d.

———. *Our Pentecostal Heritage*. Cleveland, Tenn.: Pathway Press, 1963.

———. *Profile of Faith*. Cleveland, Tenn.: Pathway Press, 1971.

Lemons, M.S. "History of the Church of God." N.p., n.d.

———. "Questions Answered On Regeneration, Sanctification, Baptism With The Holy Ghost, the Church of God, and Speaking With Tongues." N.p., n.d.

Leroy, Douglas. *I Didn't Know That!* Cleveland, Tenn.: Pathway Press, 1973.

———. *We Believe: A Book For Children on the Church of God Declaration of Faith*. Cleveland, Tenn.: Pathway Press, 1974.

Llewellyn, Joseph Steele. *Bible Training for Children*. Cleveland, Tenn.: COG PH, 1924.

———. *Bible Training for Christian Workers*. Cleveland, Tenn.: COG PH, 1925.

———. *Summarized Bible Study*. Cleveland, Tenn.: COG PH, 1925.

Lowery, Thomas L. *The End of the World*. Cleveland, Tenn.: Lowery Publications, 1969.

———. *The Trends of Communism*. Cleveland, Tenn.: Lowery Publications, 1965.

Lyons, Bob E. *Kingdom of Priests*. Cleveland, Tenn.: Pathway Press, 1977.

Maxwell, John. *The Nature and Name of the Church*. Coimbatore, Ind.: Privately published, n.d.

May, F.J. "That We Might Have Life." N.p., n.d.

Maye, Aubrey D. *Pioneers For Christ, International*. Cleveland, Tenn.: COG, n.d.

McBrayer, Richard Terrell. "Lee College, Pioneer in Pentecostal Education, 1918–1968." N.p., n.d.

McClung, Floyd, Jr. *Just Off The Street*. Old Tappan, N.J.: Revell, 1975.

Mitchell, James N. *Messages on Church of God Doctrine*. Preached on WFPA Radio, Ft. Payne, Ala. N.p., n.d.

Morris, Phillip C. "The Humble Beginning: A First Year History of Lee College." N.p., 1960.

Noble, Jerry. *Really Rich*. Cleveland, Tenn.: Forward in Faith, 1977.

Parsons, C. Milton. *In Service*. Cleveland, Tenn.: Pathway Press, 1972.

Paulk, Earl P., Jr. *Sunday School Evangelism*. Cleveland, Tenn.: Pathway Press, 1958.

———. *Your Pentecostal Neighbor*. Cleveland, Tenn.: Pathway Press, 1958.

Payne, T.S. *The Church of God, Cleveland, Tennessee*. Cleveland, Tenn.: COG PH, 1929.

Perdue, Stanley W. *The Student*. Cleveland, Tenn.: Pathway Press, 1957.

Pettitt, Walter R. *The Evangelism Ministry of the Local Church*. Cleveland, Tenn.: Pathway Press, 1969.

Phillips, Allen A. *Nuggets for Happiness*. Cleveland, Tenn.: Pathway Press, 1959.

Polen, O.W. *Editorially Speaking*. Cleveland, Tenn.: Pathway Press, 1975.

————. *Promotion by Pen*. Cleveland, Tenn.: COG National Sunday School and Youth Department, 1956.

————. *The Sunday School Teacher*. Cleveland, Tenn.: Pathway Press, 1956.

Porter, Travis. "He Shall Direct Thy Paths." N.p., 1972.

Presenting the Church of God, America's Oldest Pentecostal Church, 1886–1961. Cleveland, Tenn.: COG PH, 1961.

Quinley, Rachel. *How To Plan and Conduct Kids Krusades*. Cleveland, Tenn.: Pathway Press, 1976.

Richardson, Carl H. *Divine Interruption*. Cleveland, Tenn.: Forward in Faith, 1976.

————. *Forecasts for the Future*. Cleveland, Tenn.: Pathway Press, 1973.

Roberts, Philemon. *Concerning Spiritual Gifts*. Temple Terrace, Fla.: New Life Ministries, n.d.

————. *God's Will for God's People*. Cleveland, Tenn.: Pathway Press, 1958.

Sanders, Kathleen. *Kids Klub Manual*. Cleveland, Tenn.: Pathway Press, 1974.

Scarborough, Peggy. *Hallelujah Anyway, Tim*. Cleveland, Tenn.: Pathway Press, 1976.

Simmons, E.L. *History of the Church of God*. Cleveland, Tenn.: COG PH, 1938.

Sisler, M. David. *Finished*. Cleveland, Tenn.: Pathway Press, 1977.

Slay, James L. *Rescue the Perishing*. Cleveland, Tenn.: Pathway Press, 1961.

————. *This We Believe*. Cleveland, Tenn.: Pathway Press, 1963.

Slocumb, Douglas W. *Church of God of North Carolina*. Charlotte, N.C.: H. Eaton, 1978.

Smith, Henry J. "Development of the Educational System of the Church of God." N.p., 1979.

Spence, G.H. "History of Northwest Bible College." N.p., n.d.

Stanley, W. Perdue. *The Student*. Cleveland, Tenn.: Pathway Press, 1957.

Stark, Pearl M. "History of the Work in Angola." N.p., n.d.

Steele, James E. *I Have a Ghetto in My Heart*. Cleveland, Tenn.: Pathway Press, 1973.

Stone, Hoyt E. *Living Right*. Cleveland, Tenn.: Pathway Press, 1982.

————. *Of Course You Can*. Cleveland, Tenn.: Pathway Press, 1973.

————. *The Inner Quest*. Cleveland, Tenn.: Pathway Press, 1979.

Tharp, Zeno C. *Favorite Stories and Illustrations*. Cleveland, Tenn.: COG PH, 1956.

The Church of God Orphans: A Historiette of and Code of Rules for the Church of God Orphans. Cleveland, Tenn.: COG PH, 1942.

Tomlinson, A.J. *God's Twentieth-Century Pioneer: A Compilation of Some of the Writings of A.J. Tomlinson*. Cleveland, Tenn.: White Wing PH, 1962.
————. *The Last Great Conflict*. Cleveland, Tenn.: Press of Walter Rodgers, 1913.
Tomlinson, Homer. *Shout of a King*. Queens Village, N.Y.: COG, 1968.
Triplett, Bennie S. *A Contemporary Study of the Holy Spirit*. Cleveland, Tenn.: Pathway Press, 1970.
Varner, Jeanne. *How To Make Children's Church Come Alive*. Cleveland, Tenn.: Pathway Press, 1979.
Vaught, Laud O. *Focus on the Christian Family*. Cleveland, Tenn.: Pathway Press, 1976.
Vest, Lamar. *The Church and Its Youth*. Cleveland, Tenn.: Pathway Press, 1980.
————. *What a Life—The Jesus Way*. Cleveland, Tenn.: Pathway Press, 1973.
Voorhis, George D. "The Gifts of the Spirit." N.p., n.d.
————. "One Hundred Difficult Bible Questions Answered." N.p., n.d.
————. "Revelation." N.p., n.d.
————. "The Course of This Present Age." N.p., n.d.
————. "The Gifts of the Spirit." N.p., n.d.
————. "The Truth About Catholicism." N.p., n.d.
Walker, John Herbert, Jr. *God's Living Room*. Plainfield, N.J.: Logos International, 1972.
Walker, Lucille. *What To Do When You Pray*. Plainfield, N.J.: Logos International, 1978.
Walker, Paul L. *Counseling Youth*. Cleveland, Tenn.: Pathway Press, 1967.
————. *Courage for Crisis Living*. Old Tappan, N.J.: Revell, 1978.
————. *Knowing the Future*. Cleveland, Tenn.: Pathway Press, 1976.
————. *Reaching With Records*. Cleveland, Tenn.: Pathway Press, 1967.
————. *The Ministry of Church and Pastor*. Cleveland, Tenn.: Pathway Press, 1965.
————. *Understanding the Bible and Science*. Cleveland, Tenn.: Pathway Press, 1976.
Williams, Edward L. "Be a Good Neighbor." N.p., n.d.
————. "Motivations in Crisis Situations of Divorce and Death." N.p., n.d.
————. "Preparing Persons for Church Memberships." N.p., n.d.
————. "The Church Discovers the Family." N.p., n.d.
————. "The Sect-Church Continuum: An Analysis of the Church of God." N.p., 1972.
————. "The Significance of Church Membership." N.p., n.d.
Willis, Lewis J. "Verbal Inspiration of the Bible." N.p., 1971.
Winters, William E. *Convert Conservation*. Cleveland, Tenn.: Pathway Press, 1970.

C. Secondary Sources

I. GENERAL HISTORIES

Cash, Wilbur J. *The Mind of the South*. New York: Knopf, 1941.

Divine, Robert A., ed. *American Foreign Policy*. New York: New American Library, 1960.

Durden, Robert F. *The Climax of Populism: The Election of 1896*. Lexington: Univ. of Kentucky Press, 1965.

Freel, Margaret Walker. *Our Heritage: The People of Cherokee County, North Carolina, 1540–1955*. Ashville, N.C.: Miller Printing, 1956.

Grattan, C. Hartley. *Why We Fought*. Edited by Keith L. Nelson. New York: Bobbs-Merrill, 1969.

Hicks, John D. *The Populist Revolt*. Minneapolis: Univ. of Minnesota Press, 1931.

Hofstadter, Richard. *The Age of Reform*. New York: Alfred A. Knopf, 1956.

Jensen, Richard. *The Winning of the Midwest: Social and Political Conflict, 1888–1896*. Chicago: Univ. of Chicago Press, 1971.

Kleppner, Paul. *The Cross of Culture: A Social Analysis of Midwestern Politics, 1850–1900*. New York: Free Press, 1970.

Miller, Charles A. *The Official and Political Manual of the State of Tennessee*. Spartanburg, S.C.: Reprint Co., 1974.

Nugent, Walter T. *The Tolerant Populists: Kansas Populism and Nativism*. Chicago: Univ. of Chicago Press, 1963.

Palmer, Bruce. *Man Over Money*. Chapel Hill: Univ. of North Carolina Press, 1980.

Parsons, Stanley B. *The Populist Context*. Westport, Conn.: Greenwood, 1973.

Peterson, H.C., and Gilbert C. Fite. *Opponents of War, 1917–1918*. Seattle: Univ. of Washington Press, 1957.

Pollack, Norman. *The Populist Response to Industrial America*. Cambridge, Mass.: Harvard Univ. Press, 1962.

Robinson, Daniel M. *Bob Taylor and the Agrarian Revolt in Tennessee*. Chapel Hill: Univ. of North Carolina Press, 1935.

Salutos, Theodore. *Farmer Movements in the South, 1865–1933*. Univ. of California Publications in History, 64. Berkeley: Univ. of California Press, 1960.

Schlesinger, Arthur M., ed. *The Rise of the City: 1878–1898*. New York: Macmillan, 1930.

Walters, Pat. *Coca-Cola: An Illustrated History*. Garden City, N.Y.: Doubleday, 1978.

Woodward, C. Vann. *The Burden of Southern History*. Baton Rouge: Louisiana State Univ. Press, 1962.

Youngdale, James M. *Populism: A Psychohistorical Perspective*. National

University Publications. Series in American Studies. Port Washington, N.Y.: Kennikat, 1975.

2. GENERAL RELIGIOUS HISTORIES

Abell, Aaron I. *The Urban Impact of American Protestantism, 1865–1900.* Hamden, Conn.: Archor, 1962.

Ahlstrom, Sidney E. *A Religious History of the American People.* New Haven: Yale Univ. Press, 1972.

Bailey, Kenneth. *Southern White Protestantism in the Twentieth Century.* New York: Harper & Row, 1964.

Beardsley, Frank Grenville. *A History of American Revivals.* Boston: American Tract Society, 1904.

Carter, Paul A. *The Spiritual Crisis of the Gilded Age.* DeKalb: Northern Illinois Univ. Press, 1971.

Cross, Robert D. *The Church and the City, 1865–1910.* Indianapolis, Ind.: Bobbs-Merrill, 1967.

Davenport, Frederick M. *Primitive Traits in Religious Revivals.* London: Macmillan, 1905.

Farish, Hunter D. *The Circuit Rider Dismounts: A Social History of Southern Methodism, 1865–1900.* Richmond, Va.: Dietz Press, 1938.

Gaustad, Edwin Scott. *Historical Atlas of Religion in America.* New York: Harper & Row, 1962.

———, ed. *The Rise of Adventism: Religion and Society in Mid-19th Century America.* New York: Harper & Row, 1974.

Handy, Robert T. *The History of the Churches in the United States and Canada.* New York: Oxford Univ. Press, 1977.

Harrell, David Edwin, Jr. *The Social Sources of Division in the Disciples of Christ, 1865–1900.* Vol. 2. Atlanta, Ga.: Publishing Systems, 1973.

———. *White Sects and Black Men in the Recent South.* Nashville: Vanderbilt Univ. Press, 1971.

Hudson, Winthrop. *American Protestantism.* Chicago: Univ. of Chicago Press, 1961.

———. *Religion in America.* New York: Scribner's, 1965.

McLaughlin, William G., Jr. *Modern Revivalism: Charles Grandison Finney to Billy Graham.* New York: Ronald Press, 1959.

McNeill, John T. *Modern Christian Movements.* Philadelphia: Westminster Press, 1954.

Marty, Martin E. *Righteous Empire: The Protestant Experience in America.* New York: Dial, 1970.

May, Henry F. *Protestant Churches and Industrial America.* New York: Harper & Bros., 1949.

Mead, Frank S. *Handbook of Denominations.* Nashville: Abingdon-Cokesbury, 1951.

Niebuhr, Helmut Richard. *The Kingdom of God in America*. Chicago: Willet, Clark and Co., 1937.
———. *The Social Sources of the Denominations*. New York: Henry Holt, 1929. Rptd. New York: Meridian Books, 1957.
Olmstead, Clifton E. *History of Religion in the United States*. Englewood Cliffs, N.J.: Prentice-Hall, 1960.
Robertson, Archie. *That Old-Time Religion*. Boston: Houghton Mifflin, 1950.
Salisbury, W. Seward. *Religion in American Culture: A Sociological Interpretation*. Homewood, Ill.: Dorsey, 1964.
Sechler, Earl T. *Our Religious Heritage: Church History of the Ozarks, 1806–1906*. Springfield, Mo.: Westport Press, 1961.
Spain, Rufus B. *At Ease in Zion: Social History of Southern Baptists, 1865–1900*. Nashville: Vanderbilt Univ. Press, 1967.
Sperry, Willard L. *Religion in America*. New York: Cambridge Univ. Press, 1946.
Stoeffler, F. Earnest. *The Rise of Evangelical Pietism*. Leiden: Brill, 1971.
Sweet, William Warren. *Revivalism in America*. New York: Scribner's, 1944.
Weisberger, Bernard A. *They Gathered At The River*. Chicago: Quadrangle, 1966.

3. WORKS CONCERNING THE HOLINESS MOVEMENT

Aitken, W. Hay. *The Highway of Holiness: Help to the Spiritual Life*. J.F. Shaw, n.d.
Atwood, Anthony. *The Abiding Comforter: A Necessity to Joyful Piety and Eminent Usefulness*. Philadelphia: Adam Wallace, 1874.
Boardman, Henry A. *The Higher Life of Sanctification as Tried by the Word of God*. Philadelphia: Presbyterian Board of Education, 1877.
Boardman, William E. *The Higher Christian Life*. Boston: Henry Holt, 1858.
Brooks, John R. *Scriptural Sanctification: An Attempted Solution of A Holiness Problem*. Nashville: Publishing House of the Methodist Episcopal Church, South, 1899.
Carradine, Beverly. *Sanctification*. Cincinnati, Ohio: God's Revivalists Office, 1890.
Chapman, J. Wilbur. *The Life and Work of Dwight L. Moody*. London: James Nesbet, 1900.
Cookman, Alfred. *The Higher Christian Life*. Boston: Witness Co., 1900.
Cross, Whitney R. *The Burned Over District*. New York: Harper & Row, 1965.
Cunningham, Raymond J. "From Holiness to Healing: The Faith Cure in America." *Church History* 43 (1974):499–513.
Dieter, Melvin E. *The Holiness Revival of the Nineteenth Century*. Metuchen, N.J.: Scarecrow, 1980.
Doty, Thomas K. *Lessons in Holiness*. Cleveland, Ohio: Privately published, 1881.

Dunn, Lewis Romaine. *Holiness—What Is It?* London: F.E. Langley, 1875.
———. *Relations of the Holy Spirit to the Work of Entire Holiness.* New York: W.C. Palmer, 1883.
Finney, Charles G. *Views on Sanctification.* Oberlin, Ohio: James Steele, 1840.
Godbey, William B. *Holiness or Hell.* Louisville, Ky.: Pentecostal Publishing Co., 1899.
Hoke, Jacob. *Holiness: Or The Higher Christian Life.* Dayton, Ohio: United Brethren Printing Establishment, 1870.
Johnson, Benton. "Do Holiness Sects Socialize in Dominant Values?" *Social Forces* 39 (1961):309–16.
Jones, Charles E. *Perfectionist Persuasion: The Holiness Movement and American Methodism, 1887–1936.* Metuchen, N.J.: Scarecrow, 1974.
Jones, R.B. *Rent Heavens: The Revival of 1904.* London: Pioneer Mission, 1948.
Lindsay, Gordon. *The Life of Alexander Dowie.* Shreveport, La.: Voice of Healing Publishers, 1951.
Pearse, Mark Gay. *Thoughts on Holiness.* Chicago: Christian Witness Co., 1884.
Peters, John Leland. *Christian Perfectionism and American Methodism.* New York: Abingdon, 1956.
Pickett, Leander L. *Entire Sanctification from 1799–1901.* Louisville, Ky.: Pickett Publishing, 1901.
———. *Christian Holiness: Its Philosophy, Theory, and Experience.* Brooklyn: Hope Publishing, 1882.
Roberts, Benjamin Titus. *Holiness Teachings.* North Chili, N.Y.: "Earnest Christian" PH, 1893.
Simpson, A.B. *Wholly Sanctified.* New York: Christian Alliance Publishing, 1893.

4. WORKS CONCERNING PENTECOSTALISM

Abell, Troy D. *Better Felt Than Said: The Holiness-Pentecostal Experience in Southern Appalachia.* Waco, Tex.: Markham Press, 1982.
Aikman, Duncan. "The Holy Rollers." *American Mercury,* 15 Oct. 1928.
Agrimson, J. Elmo, ed. *Gifts of the Spirit and the Body of Christ: Perspectives on the Charismatic Movement.* Augsburg, Ger.: Augsburg Publishing House, 1974.
Alland, Alexander. "Possession in a Revivalistic Negro Church." *Journal for the Scientific Study of Religion* 1 (1962):204–13.
Anderson, C. "Tongues of Men and Angels." *Lutheran Standard,* 16 May 1972.
Anderson, Robert M. *Vision of the Disinherited: The Making of American Pentecostalism.* New York: Oxford Univ. Press, 1979.

————. *Spirit Manifestations and "The Gift of Tongues."* New York: Loizeaux Bros., n.d.

Ansons, Gunars. "The Charismatics and Their Churches: Report on Two Conferences." *Dialog* 15 (1976):142–44.

Apostolic Faith. "The Apostolic Faith: Its Origin, Functions, and Doctrine." N.p., n.d.

Arnot, Gottfried. "The Modern 'Speaking With Tongues.'" *Evangelical Christian* 46 (Jan. 1950):23–25.

Bach, Marcus. *Strange Sects and Curious Cults.* New York: Dodd, Mead, 1961.

————. "Whether There Be 'Tongues.'" *Christian Herald* 87 (May 1964): 10–11.

Baker, D.L. "An Interpretation of 1 Corinthians 12–14." *Evangelical Quarterly* 46 (Oct.-Dec. 1974):224–34.

Baker, J.B. "A Theological Look at the Charismatic Movement." *Churchman* 86 (Winter 1972):259–77.

Bales, James D. *Miracles or Mirages?* Austin, Tex.: Firm Foundation PH, 1956.

Banks, R.M. "Speaking in Tongues: A Survey of the New Testament Evidence." *Churchman* 80 (1966):287–94.

Banks, William L. *Questions You Have Always Wanted to Ask About Tongues.* Chattanooga, Tenn.: AMG Publishers, 1978.

Barber, Theodore X. "Multidimensional Analysis of 'Hypnotic Behavior.'" *Journal of Abnormal Psychology* 74 (1969):209–20.

Barfoot, Charles H., and Shepard, Gerald T. "Prophetic vs. Priestly Religion: The Changing Role of Women Clergy in Classical Pentecostal Churches." *Review of Religious Research* 22 (1980):2–17.

Barnes, Douglas. "Charisma and Religious Leadership: An Historical Analysis." *Journal for the Scientific Study of Religion* 17 (Mar. 1978):1–18.

Barr, James. *Fundamentalism.* Philadelphia: Westminster, 1978.

Basham, Don. "I Saw My Church Come To Life." *Christian Life* 26 (Mar. 1965):37–39.

————. "They Dared to Believe." *Christian Life* 28 (Apr. 1967):28.

Bartleman, Frank. *How Pentecost Came to Los Angeles.* 2d ed. Los Angeles, Calif.: Privately published, 1925.

Bauman, Louis S. *The Tongues Movement.* Winona Lake, Ind.: Brethren Missionary Herald Co., 1963.

Beare, Frank W. "Speaking with Tongues." *Journal of Biblical Literature* 83 (Sept. 1964):229–46.

Bell, L. Nelson. "Babel of Pentecost." *Christianity Today* 4 (12 Oct. 1959): 19.

Bennett, Dennis. "Pentecost: When Episcopalians Start Speaking in Tongues." *Living Church* 142 (1 Jan. 1961):12–13.

————. "The Charismatic Renewal and Liturgy." *View* 2:1 (1965):1–6.

————. "They Spake With Tongues and Magnified God." *Full Gospel Business Men's Voice* 8 (Oct. 1960):6–8.

Berger, Peter L. "Sectarianism and Religious Sociation." *American Journal of Sociology* 64 (1958):41–44.

Bergoma, Stuart. *Speaking With Tongues: Some Physiological Implications of Modern Glossolalia.* Grand Rapids, Mich.: Baker Book House, 1965.

Bess, Donovan. "Speaking in Tongues—The High Church Heresy." *The Nation* 197 (28 Sept. 1963):173–77.

Bittlinger, Arnold. "Charismatic Renewal: An Opportunity for the Church?" *Ecumenical Review* 31 (July 1979):247–51.

Blackwelder, Boyce W. "Thirty Errors of Modern Tongues Advocates." *Vital Christianity* 94 (26 May 1974):9–10.

Blakemore, W.B. "Holy Spirit as Public and as Charismatic Institutions." *Encounter* 36 (Summer 1975):161–80.

Blaney, Harvey J.S. *Speaking in Unknown Tongues: The Pauline Position.* Kansas City, Mo.: Beacon Hill Press, 1973.

————. "St. Paul's Posture on Speaking in Unknown Tongues." *Wesley Theological Journal* 8 (1973):52–60.

Block-Hoell, Nils. *The Pentecostal Movement: Its Origin, Development, and Distinctive Character.* Translated from the Norwegian by the author. London: Allen & Unwin, 1964.

Bloesch, Donald G. "The Charismatic Revival." *Religion in Life* 35 (Summer 1966):364–80.

Boer, Harry R. "The Spirit: Tongues and Message." *Christianity Today* 7 (4 Jan. 1963):6–7.

Boisen, Anton T. "Economic Distress and Religious Experience: A Study of the Holy Rollers." *Psychiatry* 2 (May 1939):185–94.

————. *Religion in Crisis and Custom.* New York: Harper & Bros., 1945.

Bord, Richard J., and Joseph E. Faulkner. "Religiosity and Secular Attitudes: The Case of Catholic Pentecostals." *Journal for the Scientific Study of Religion* 14 (Sept. 1975):257–70.

————. *The Catholic Charismatics: Anatomy of a Modern Religious Movement.* College Park: Penn State Univ. Press, 1984.

Bradfield, Cecil D. "He's Not One of Us–Yet: Research in a Neo-Pentecostal Group." *Pnuema* 1 (Spring 1979):49–75.

Bradford, George C. "Are Presbyterians Post-Pentecostal?" *Presbyterian Life* 21 (1 June 1968):30.

Brandt, R.L. "The Case for Speaking in Tongues." *Pentecostal Evangel* 48 (5 June 1960):4, 29–30.

Brewster, Percy S. *The Spreading Flame of Pentecost.* London: Elim PH, 1970.

Britton, Francis M. *Pentecostal Truth.* Royston, Ga.: PH of the Pentecostal Holiness Church, 1919.

Brown, L.B. "Some Attitudes Surrounding Glossolalia." *Colloquim* 2 (1967): 221–28.

Brown, L.B. "The Structure of Religious Belief." *Journal for the Scientific Study of Religion* 5 (1966):259–72.

Bryant, Ernest, and Daniel O'Connell. "A Phonemic Analysis of Nine Samples of Glossolalic Speech." *Psychonomic Speech* 22 (1971):81–83.

Burke, Kathryn L., and Merlin B. Brinkerhoff. "Capturing Charisma: Notes on an Elusive Concept." *Journal for the Scientific Study of Religion* 20 (1981):274–84.

Brumbach, Carl. *A Sound From Heaven.* Springfield, Mo.: Gospel PH, 1977.

———. *Suddenly From Heaven: A History of the Assemblies of God.* Springfield, Mo.: Gospel PH, 1961.

Bruner, Frederick Dale. *A Theology of the Holy Spirit: The Pentecostal Experience and the New Testament Witness.* London: Hodder and Stoughton, 1971.

Burdick, Donald W. *Tongues: To Speak or not to Speak.* Chicago: Moody, 1969.

Burgess, W.J. *Glossolalia: Speaking in Tongues.* Little Rock, Ark.: Baptist Publications Committee, 1968.

Cannon, William S. *The Jesus Revolution.* Nashville: Broadman Press, 1971.

Campbell, Joseph E. *The Pentecostal Church, 1898–1949, Its History and Background.* Franklin Springs, Ga.: PH of the Pentecostal Holiness Church, 1951.

Carden, Karen W., and Robert W. Pelton. *The Persecuted Prophets.* Cranbury, N.J.: A.S. Barnes, 1976.

Carlson, Guy R. *Our Faith and Fellowship.* Springfield, Mo.: Gospel PH, 1977.

Carter, Charles W. *The Person and Ministry of the Holy Spirit, A Wesleyan Perspective.* Grand Rapids, Mich.: Baker Book House, 1974.

Carter, John. *Donald Gee: Pentecostal Statesman.* Nottingham, Eng.: Assemblies of God PH, 1975.

Carter, Richard. "That Old-Time Religion Comes Back." *Coronet,* Feb. 1958, 125–30.

Chandler, Russell. "Charismatic Clinics: Instilling Ministry." *Christianity Today* 17 (28 Sept. 1973):44–45.

———. "Fanning the Charismatic Fire." *Christianity Today* 18 (24 Nov. 1967):39–40.

Chinn, Jack J. "May We Pentecostals Speak?" *Christianity Today* 5 (17 July 1961):8–9.

Christenson, Laurence. "Speaking in Tongues." *Trinity* 2 (4 Nov. 1963):15–16.

———. *Speaking in Tongues.* Minneapolis: Bethany Fellowship Publishers, 1968.

Church of God of Prophecy. *These Necessary Things: The Doctrine and Practices of the Church of God of Prophecy.* 3d ed., Cleveland, Tenn.: White Wing PH, 1968.

Clanton, Arthur L. *United We Stand.* Hazelwood, Mo.: Pentecostal PH, 1970.

Clark, Elmer T. *Small Sects in America*. Rev. ed. New York: Abingdon Press, 1949.

Cocoris, G. Michael. "Speaking in Tongues: Then and Now." *Biblical Research Quarterly* 46:6 (Sept. 1981):14–16.

Coulson, Jesse E. "Glossolalia and Internal-External Locus of Control." *Journal of Psychology and Theology* 5 (1977):312–17.

Cunningham, Raymond. "From Holiness to Healing: The Faith Cure in America." *Church History* 43 (Dec. 1974):499–513.

Cutten, George B. *Speaking With Tongues: Historically and Psychologically Considered*. New Haven: Yale Univ. Press, 1927.

———. *The Psychological Phenomena of Christianity*. New York: Scribner's, 1908.

Dalton, Robert Chandler. *Tongues Like As of Fire*. Springfield, Mo.: Gospel PH, 1945. Rptd. Winona Lake, Ind.: Brethren Missionary Herald Co., 1963.

Damboriena, Prudencio. "Pentecostal Fury." *Catholic World* 202 (Jan. 1966):217–23.

Darrand, Tom C., and Anson D. Shupe. *Metaphors of Social Control in a Pentecostal Sect*. New York: Edwin Mellen, 1983.

Daughtry, Herbert. "A Theology of Black Liberation from a Pentecostal Prospective." *Spirit* 3:2 (1979):6–19.

Davies, Horton. "Pentecostalism: Threat or Promise?" *Expository Times* 76 (Mar. 1965):197–99.

———. *The Challenge of the Sects*. Philadelphia: Westminster, 1961.

Dayton, Donald W. "Doctrine of the Baptism of the Holy Spirit: Its Emergence and Significance." *Wesleyan Theological Journal* 13 (Spring 1978): 114–26.

———. "The Holiness and Pentecostal Churches: Emerging from Cultural Isolation." *Christian Century* 96 (15–22 Aug. 1979):786–92.

———. "The Theological Roots of Pentecostalism." *Pneuma* 2 (Spring 1980): 3–21.

———. *Three Early Pentecostal Tracts*. New York: Garland, 1985.

Dearman, Marion. "Christ and Conformity: A Study of Pentecostal Values." *Journal for the Scientific Study of Religion* 13 (Dec. 1974):437–53.

De Haan, Martin R. *Pentecost and After*. Grand Rapids, Mich.: Zondervan PH, 1964.

DeVol, Thomas I. "Ecstatic Pentecostal Prayer and Meditation." *Journal of Religion and Health* 13 (1974):285–88.

Dillow, Joseph C. *Speaking in Tongues*. Grand Rapids, Mich.: Zondervan PH, 1975.

Dominian, J. "Psychological Evaluation of the Pentecostal Movement." *Expository Times* 87 (July 1976):292–97.

Donovan, John J. "Religious Revivalism as Counterculture." *Spiritual Life* 18 (1972):47–57.

Douglas, J.D. "Tongues in Transition." *Christianity Today* 10 (8 July 1966): 34.

Duewel, Wesley L. *The Holy Spirit and Tongues.* Winona Lake, Ind.: Light and Life, 1974.

Durasoff, Steve. *Bright Wind of the Spirit: A Study of Pentecostal Glossolalia and Related Phenomena.* Englewood Cliffs, N.J.: Prentice-Hall, 1972.

Dynes, Russell R. "Church-Sect Typology and Socio-Economic Status." *American Sociological Review* 20 (1955):555–60.

Eddy, Norman G. "Store-Front Religion." *Religion in Life* 28 (Winter 1958): 68–85.

Edman, Raymond V. "Devine or Devilish?" *Christian Herald* 87 (May 1964): 14–17.

Elinson, Howard. "The Implications of Pentecostal Religion for Intellectualism, Politics, and Race Relations." *American Journal of Sociology* 70 (Fall 1965):403–15.

Ellison, Robert W. "Charismatic Renewal and Practical Usage." *Dialog* 13 (1974):33–39.

Ellswood, Robert S. *One Way: The Jesus Movement and Its Meaning.* Englewood Cliffs, N.J.: Prentice-Hall, 1973.

Ennis, Philip H. "Ecstacy and Everyday Life." *Journal for the Scientific Study of Religion* 6 (1967):40–48.

Enroth, Ronald M.; Erickson, Edward E.; and Peters, C. Breckenridge. *The Jesus People: Old-Time Religion in the Age of Aquarius.* Grand Rapids, Mich.: Eerdmans, 1972.

Ervin, Howard M. "As the Spirit Gives Utterance." *Christianity Today* 13 (11 Apr. 1969):7–8.

———. "Hermeneutics: A Pentecostal Option." *Pneuma* 3 (Fall 1981):11–25.

Ewart, Frank J. *The Phenomenon of Pentecost: A History of the Latter Rain.* St. Louis, Mo.: Pentecostal PH, 1947.

Failing, George E. "Should I Speak With Tongues?" *Wesleyan Methodist* 122 (20 Jan. 1965):6.

Farrell, Frank. "Outburst of Tongues: The New Penetration." *Christianity Today* 7 (13 Sept. 1963):3–7.

Faupel, David William. *The American Pentecostal Movement: A Bibliographic Essay.* Wilmore, Ky.: B.L. Fisher Library, Asbury Theological Seminary, 1972.

Fichter, Joseph H. "Liberal and Conservative Catholic Pentecostals." *Social Compass* 21 (1974):303–10.

———. "Pentecostals: Comfort or Awareness." *America* 129 (1 Sept. 1973): 114–16.

Ford, J. Massyngberde. *Baptism of the Spirit: Three Essays on the Pentecostal Experience.* Van Nuys, Calif.: Divine Word, 1971.

———. "The Catholic Charismatic Gifts in Worship." In *The Charismatic Movement,* ed. Michael Hamilton. Grand Rapids: Eerdmans, 1975.

————. *The Pentecostal Experience: A New Direction for American Catholics.* New York: Paulist Press, 1970.

————. "Tongues-Leadership-Women: Further Reflections on the New-Pentecostal Movement." *Spiritual Life* 17 (Fall 1971):186–97.

Foster, Fred J. *Think It Not Strange: A History of the Oneness Movement.* Hazelwood, Mo.: Pentecostal Publishing House, 1965.

Frank, Jerome D. *Persuasion and Healing: A Comparative Study of Psychotherapy.* Baltimore: Johns Hopkins Univ. Press, 1961.

Frodsham, Stanley H. *This Pentecostal Revival.* Springfield, Mo.: Gospel PH, 1941.

————. *With Signs Following: The Story of the Pentecostal Revival in the Twentieth Century.* Rev. ed. Springfield, Mo.: Gospel PH, 1946.

Fuller, Reginald H. "Tongues in the New Testament." *American Church Quarterly* 3 (Fall 1963):162–68.

Galanter, Marc. "Charismatic Religious Sects and Psychiatry: An Overview." *American Journal of Psychiatry* 139 (1982):1539–48.

Gaver, Jessyca. *Pentecostalism.* New York: Award Books, 1971.

Gee, Donald. *All With One Accord.* Springfield, Mo.: Gospel PH, 1961.

————. *The Pentecostal Movement.* London: Elim Publishing, 1941.

————. *Upon All Flesh: A Pentecostal World Tour.* Rev. ed. Springfield, Mo.: Gospel PH, 1947.

————. "Wheat, Tares and 'Tongues.'" *Pentecost* 67 (Dec. 1963–Feb. 1964): 17.

Gelpi, Donald L. *Experiencing God: A Theology of Human Experience.* New York: Paulist Press, 1978.

————. *Pentecostalism: A Theological Viewpoint.* New York: Paulist Press, 1971.

————. "Understanding Spirit-Baptism: As Catholic Pentecostals Practice It." *America* 122 (16 May 1970):520–21.

Gerlach, L.P., and Virginia H. Hine. "Five Factors Crucial to the Growth and Spread of a Modern Religious Movement." *Journal for the Scientific Study of Religion* 7 (Spring 1968):23–40.

Gerrard, Nathan Lewis. "The Snake-Handling Religions of West Virginia." *Transaction* (May 1968):22–30.

Gilmore, Susan K. "Personality Differences Between High and Low Dogmatism Groups of Pentecostal Believers." *Journal for the Study of Religion* 8 (1969):161–64.

Goldsmith, Henry. "The Psychological Usefulness of Glossolalia to the Believer." *View* 2 (2 Nov. 1965):7–8.

Goodman, Felicitas D. *Speaking in Tongues: A Cross-Cultural Study of Glossolalia.* Chicago: Univ. of Chicago Press, 1972.

Greathouse, William M. *Who Is the Holy Spirit?* Kansas City, Mo.: Nazarene PH, 1972.

Grislis, Egil. "The Challenge of the Charismatic Renewal to Lutheran Theology." *Concensus* 7 (Oct. 1981):3–25.

Gritsch, Eric W. *Born Againism: Perspectives of a Movement*. Philadelphia: Fortress, 1982.

Gunstone, John Thomas. *Pentecostal Anglicans*. London: Hodder and Stoughton, 1982.

Gustatis, Rosa. "The Pentecostals." *Jubilee* 15 (Jan. 1967):8–15.

Gutman, Herbert G. "Protestantism and American Labor." *American Historical Review* 72 (Oct. 1966):74–101.

Haley, Peter D. *The Idea of Charismatic Authority*. Ann Arbor: Univ. Microfilms, 1980.

Hamilton, Michael, ed. *The Charismatic Movement*. Grand Rapids, Mich.: Eerdmans, 1975.

Harper, Charles L. "Spirit-Filled Catholics: Some Biographical Comparisons." *Social Compass* 21 (1974):311–24.

Harper, Michael. *As At the Beginning: The Twentieth Century Pentecostal Movement*. London: Hodder & Stoughton, 1965.

Harrell, David Edwin, Jr. *All Things Are Possible: The Healing and Charismatic Revivals in Modern America*. Bloomington: Indiana Univ. Press, 1975.

———. *Oral Roberts: An American Life*. Bloomington: Indiana Univ. Press, 1985.

———. "The Roots of the Moral Majority: Fundamentalism Revisited." Occasional Papers, Institute for Ecumenical and Cultural Research, Univ. of Minnesota. May 1981, pp. 1–10.

———. *White Sects and Black Men in the Recent South*. Nashville: Vanderbilt Univ. Press, 1971.

Harrison, Irvine J. "A History of the Assemblies of God." N.p., 1954.

Harrison, Michael L. "Maintenance of Enthusiasm: Involvement in a New Religious Movement." *Sociological Analysis* 36 (Summer 1975):150–60.

———. "Sources of Recruitment to Catholic Pentecostalism." *Journal for the Scientific Study of Religion* 13 (1974):49–64.

Harrisville, Roy A. "Speaking in Tongues—Proof of Transcendence?" *Dialog* 13 (1974):11–18.

Hart, Larry D. "Problems of Authority in Pentecostalism." *Review and Expositor* 75 (Spring 1978):249–66.

Hayes, D.A. *The Gift of Tongues*. New York: Eaton and Main, 1913.

Hegy, Pierre. "Images of God and Man in a Catholic Charismatic Renewal Community." *Social Compass* 25 (1978):7–21.

Hine, Virginia H. "Bridge-Burners: Commitment and Participation in a Religious Movement." *Sociological Analysis* 31 (1970):61–66.

———. "Pentecostal Glossolalia: Toward a Functional Interpretation." *Journal for the Scientific Study of Religion* 8 (Fall 1968):21–26.

———. "Nonpathological Pentecostal Glossolalia: A Summary of Relevant Psychological Literature." *Journal for the Scientific Study of Religion* 8 (Fall 1969):211–26.

Hocken, Peter. "The Pentecostal-Charismatic Movement as Revival and Renewal." *Pneuma* 3 (Spring 1981):31–47.

Hoekema, Anthony A. *What About Tongue Speaking?* Grand Rapids: Eerdmans, 1966.

Hollenweger, Walter J. "A Black Pentecostal Concept: A Forgotten Chapter of Black History." *Concept* 30 (June 1969, Special Issue):4–9.

————. "Creator Spiritus: The Challenge of Pentecostal Experience to Pentecostal Theology." *Theology* 81 (Jan. 1978):32–40.

————. "The Pentecostal Movement and the WCC." *Ecumenical Review* 18 (July 1966):310–20.

————. *The Pentecostals: The Charismatic Movement in the Church.* Minneapolis: Augsburg PH, 1972.

————. "Pentecostalism and Black Power." *Theology Today* 30 (October 1973):228–38.

Holt, John B. "Holiness Religion: Cultural Shock and Social Reorganization." *American Sociological Review* 5 (May 1950):740–47.

Howard, Richard E. *Tongues Speaking in the New Testament.* Norway, Me.: Western Maine Graphics, 1980.

Howe, Claude L. "The Charismatic Movement in Southern Baptist Life." *Baptist History and Heritage* 13 (June 1978):20–27.

Hunter, Harold. "Spirit Baptism and the 1896 Revival in Cherokee County, North Carolina." *Pneuma* 5 (Fall 1983):1–17.

Hutch, Richard A. "The Personal Ritual of Glossolalia." *Journal for the Scientific Study of Religion* 19 (1980):255–66.

International Church of the Foursquare Gospel. *The Four Square Gospel.* Los Angeles, Calif.: Raymond L. Cox for the Heritage Committee of the Foursquare Gospel Church, 1969.

Jacobs, Hayes B. "Oral Roberts: High Priest or Faith Healer." *Harper's* 224 (Feb. 1964):37–43.

Jaquith, James R. "Toward a Typology of Formal Communicative Behavior: Glossolalia." *Anthropological Linguistics* 9 (1967):1–8.

Jensen, Peter. "Calvin, Charismatics, and Miracles." *Evangelical Quarterly* 51 (July–Sept. 1979):131–44.

Johnson, B. "Do Holiness Sects Socialize in Dominant Values?" *Social Forces* 39 (1961):309–16.

Johnson, C. Lincoln, and Andrew J. Weigert. "Emerging Faithstyle: A Research Note on the Catholic Charismatic Renewal." *Sociological Analysis* 36 (Summer 1978):165–72.

Jones, Charles E. *A Guide to the Pentecostal Movement.* 2 vols. Metuchen, N.J.: American Theological Library Association/Scarecrow Press, 1983.

Kantzer, Kenneth S. "The Charismatics Among Us: The Christian Today —Gallup Poll Identifies Who They Are and What They Believe." *Christianity Today* 24 (22 Feb. 1980):25–29.

Keeling, Alma Lauder. "Not by Faith Alone: A Pentecostal Account of a Pen-

tecostal Experience." *Journal of Religion and Psychical Research* 5 (Jan. 1982):50–53.
Kelsey, Morton T. *Speaking in Tongues: An Experiment in Spiritual Experience.* Garden City, N.Y.: Doubleday, 1965.
———. *Tongue Speaking.* New York: Doubleday, 1964.
Kendrick, Klaude. *The Promise Fulfilled: A History of the Modern Pentecostal Movement.* Springfield, Mo.: Gospel PH, 1961.
Kiev, Ari, ed. *Magic, Faith, and Healing.* New York: Free Press, 1964.
Kildahl, John P. *The Psychology of Speaking in Tongues.* New York: Harper & Row, 1972.
LaBarre, Weston. "Materials for a History of Studies of Crisis Cults: A Bibliographical Essay." *Current Anthropology* 12 (1971):3–44.
———. "Speaking in Tongues: Token Group Acceptance and Divine Approval." *Pastoral Psychology* 15 (May 1964):48–55.
———. *They Shall Take Up Serpents: Psychology of Southern Snake-Handling Cults.* Minneapolis: Univ. of Minnesota Press, 1962.
Lapsey, J.N., and J.M. Simpson. "Speaking in Tongues: Infantile Babble or Song of the Self?" *Pastoral Psychology* 15 (Sept. 1964):16–24.
———. "Speaking in Tongues: Token of Group Acceptance and Divine Approval." *Pastoral Psychology* 15 (May 1964):48–55.
Lane, Ralph, Jr. "Catholic Charismatic Renewal Movement in the United States: A Reconsideration." *Social Compass* 25 (1978):23–35.
Lang, G.H. *The Earlier Years of the Modern Tongues Movement.* Wimborne, England: Privately published, n.d.
Lenski, Gerhard. "Social Correlates of Religious Interest." *American Sociological Review* 18 (1953):533–44.
Lindberg, Carter. *The Third Reformation?: Charismatic Movements and the Lutheran Tradition.* Macon, Ga.: Mercer Univ. Press, 1983.
Lowe, Harry W. *Speaking in Tongues: A Brief History of the Phenomenon Known as Glossolalia, or Speaking in Tongues.* Mountain View, Calif.: Pacific Press Publishing Association, 1965.
MacDonald, William G. *Glossolalia in the New Testament.* Springfield, Mo.: Gospel PH, 1964.
Mackie, Alexander. *The Gift of Tongues.* New York: George H. Doran, 1921.
McDonnell, Kilian. "Catholic Charismatic Renewal: Reassesment and Critique." *Religion in Life* 44 (Summer 1975):138–54.
———. *Charismatic Renewal and the Churches.* Boston: Seabury Press, 1976.
———. "The Relationship of the Charismatic Renewal to the Established Denominations." *Dialog* 13 (1974):223–29.
McGaw, Douglas B. "Commitment and Religious Community: A Comparison of a Charismatic and a Mainline Congregation." *Journal for the Scientific Study of Religion* 18 (June 1979):146–63.
McGuire, Meredith B. "Testimony As a Commitment Mechanism in Catho-

lic Pentecostal Prayer Groups." *Journal for the Scientific Study of Religion* 16 (June 1977):165–68.

McLaughlin, William G. "Is There a Third Force in Christendom?" *Daedalus* 96 (Winter 1967):43–68.

Marsden, George M. *Fundamentalism and American Culture*. New York: Oxford Univ. Press, 1980.

Martin, Ira J. *Glossolalia, the Gift of Tongues: A Bibliography*. Cleveland, Tenn.: Pathway Press, 1970.

Marty, Martin E. *A Nation of Behavers*. Chicago: Univ. of Chicago Press, 1976.

McCone, Robert C. *Culture and Controversy: An Investigation of the Tongues of Pentecost*. Philadelphia: Dorrance, 1978.

McPherson, Aimee Semple. *The Foursquare Gospel*. Los Angeles, Calif.: Echo Park Evangelistic Association, 1946.

Mead, Margaret. "Holy Ghost People." *American Anthropologist* 58 (Feb. 1956):75–96.

Melton, J. Gordon. *Catholic Pentecostal Movement: A Bibliography*. Chicago: Institute for the Study of American Religion, 1976.

Menzies, William. *Anointed to Serve: The Story of the Assemblies of God*. Springfield, Mo.: Gospel Publishing House, 1971.

Metz, Donald. *Speaking in Tongues: An Analysis*. Kansas City, Mo.: Nazarene PH, 1964.

Mills, Watson E. *Charismatic Religion in Modern Research: A Bibliography*. Macon, Ga.: Mercer Univ. Press, 1983.

————. "Ecstaticism as a Background for Glossolalia." *Journal of the American Scientific Affiliation* 27 (1975):167–71.

————. *Speaking in Tongues—A Classified Bibliography*. Franklin Springs, Ga.: Society for Pentecostal Studies, 1974.

Morris, James. *The Preachers*. New York: St. Martin's, 1973.

Morris, John W. "The Charismatic Movement: An Orthodox Evaluation." *Greek Orthodox Theological Review* 28 (Summer 1983):103–34.

Muchlen, Heribert. *A Charismatic Theology*. New York: Paulist Press, 1978.

Newbold, W.R. "Spirit Writing and 'Speaking with Tongues.'" *Popular Science Monthly* 49 (Aug. 1986):516–22.

Nichol, John T. *Pentecostalism*. New York: Harper & Row, 1966.

Nouwen, Henri J.M. "The Pentecostal Movement: Three Perspectives." *Scholastic* 109 (22 Apr. 1967):15–17.

O'Connor, Edward D. "Charism and Institution." *American Ecclesiastical Review* 168 (Oct. 1974):507–25.

————. *The Pentecostal Movement in the Catholic Church*. Notre Dame, Ind.: Ave Maria Press, 1971.

————, ed. *Perspectives on Charismatic Renewal*. South Bend, Ind.: Univ. of Notre Dame Press, 1975.

Oates, Wayne E. "A Socio-Psychological Study of Glossolalia." In *Glossolalia: Tongue Speaking in Biblical, Historical, and Psychological Perspec-*

tive, edited by Frank E. Stagg, Glenn Hinson, and Wayne E. Oates, pp. 76–90. Nashville, Tenn.: Abingdon, 1967.

Oman, John B. "On 'Speaking in Tongues': A Psychological Analysis." *Pastoral Psychology* 14 (Dec. 1963):48–51.

Parham, Charles Fox. *The Everlasting Gospel*. Baxter Springs, Kansas: Privately published, 1942.

Paris, Arthur E. *Black Pentecostalism: Southern Religion in an Urban World*. Boston: University of Massachusetts, 1982.

Pattison, Mansell. "Behavioral Research on the Nature of Glossolalia." *Journal of the American Scientific Affiliation* 20 (Sept. 1968):73–86.

Pentecostal Church of God of America. *This We Believe*. Joplin, Mo.: N.d.

Pentecostal Fire Baptized Holiness Church. *Discipline and General Rules*. Toccoa, Ga.: 1919.

Pentecostal Holiness Church. *Discipline*. Franklin Springs, Ga.: 1925.

Pinnock, Clark H. "Opening the Church to the Charismatic Dimension." *Christianity Today* 25 (12 June 1981):16.

Poloma, Margaret M. "Toward a Christian Sociological Perspective: Religious Values, Theory, and Methodology." *Sociological Analysis* 43 (Summer 1982):95–108.

Pratt, James B. *Religious Consciousness: A Psychological Study*. New York: Macmillan, 1921.

Pridie, J.R. *The Spiritual Gifts*. London: Robert Scott, 1921.

Quebedeaux, Richard. *The New Charismatics: The Origins, Development, and Significance of Neo-Pentecostalism*. New York: Doubleday, 1976. Rev. ed., San Francisco: Harper & Row, 1983.

———. *The Worldly Evangelicals*. New York: Harper & Row, 1978.

Ranaghan, Kevin; and Ranaghan, Dorothy, eds. *Catholic Pentecostals*. New York: Paulist-Neuman Press, 1969.

Richards, William T. *Pentecost is Dynamite*. Nashville, Tenn.: Abingdon, 1972.

Richardson, James T. "Psychological Interpretations of Glossolalia: A Reexamination of Research." *Journal for the Scientific Study of Religion* 12 (1973):199–207.

Riggs, Ralph M. *We Believe*. Springfield, Mo.: Gospel PH, 1954.

Riss, Richard. "The Latter Rain Movement of 1948." *Pneuma* 4 (Spring 1982):32–45.

Roberts, Oral. *The Baptism with the Holy Spirit and the Gift of Speaking in Tongues Today*. Tulsa: Oral Roberts, 1964.

Robinson, Wayne A. *I Once Spoke in Tongues*. Atlanta, Ga.: Forum House, 1973.

———. *Oral*. Los Angeles: Action House, 1976.

Salisbury, William S. *Religion in American Culture: A Sociological Interpretation*. Homewood, Ill.: Dorsey, 1964.

Samarin, William J. "Forms and Functions of Nonsense Language." *Linguistics* 50 (July 1969):70–74.

———. "Language in Resocialization." *Practical Anthropology* 17 (1970): 269–79.

———. "Sociolinguistic versus Neurophysiological Explanations for Glossolalia." *Journal for the Scientific Study of Religion* 11 (Spring 1972):293–99.

———. "The Linguisticality of Glossolalia." *Hartford Quarterly* 8 (Apr. 1972):49–75.

———. *Tongues of Men and Angels: The Religious Languages of Pentecostalism*. New York: Macmillan, 1972.

Schwartz, Gary H. *Sect Ideologies and Social Status*. Chicago: Univ. of Chicago Press, 1970.

Seldes, Gilbert. *The Stammering Century*. New York: John Day, 1982.

Sherrill, John L. *They Speak With Other Tongues*. New York: McGraw-Hill, 1964.

Sholes, Jerry. *Give Me That Prime Time Religion*. New York: Hawthorne, 1979.

Simpson, George E. "Black Pentecostalism in the U.S." *Phylon* 35 (1974): 203–11.

Sirks, G.J. "The Cinderella of Theology: The Doctrine of the Holy Spirit." *Harvard Theological Review* 50 (Apr. 1957):77–89.

Snyder, Howard A., and Quincy Smith-Newcomb. "Servant Band: Prophets to the Rock Generation—The Jesus Movement Is Still Alive." *Christianity Today* 26 (26 Oct. 1982):76–77.

Spence, Othniel T. *Charismatism: Awakening or Apostacy?* Greenville, S.C.: Bob Jones Univ. Press, 1978.

Spittler, Russell P. *Perspectives on the New Pentecostalism*. Grand Rapids, Mich.: Baker Book House, 1976.

Starbuck, Edwin D. *The Psychology of Religion*. New York: Scribner's, 1914.

Stark, Rodney. "Psychopathology and Religious Commitment." *Review of Religious Research* 2 (1971):165–76.

Stones, Christopher. "Jesus People: Fundamentalism and Changes in Factors Associated with Conservatism." *Journal for the Scientific Study of Religion* 17 (June 1978):155–58.

Stagg, Frank E.; Hinson, E. Glenn; and Oates, Wayne E., eds. *Glossolalia: Tongue Speaking in Biblical, Historical, and Psychological Perspective*. Nashville: Abingdon Press, 1967.

Sullivan, Frances A. *Charisma and Charismatic Renewal: A Biblical and Theological Study*. Ann Arbor, Mich.: Servant Books, 1982.

Swatos, William H. "The Disenchantment of Charisma: A Weberian Assessment of Revolution in a Rationalized World." *Sociological Analysis* 42 (Summer 1981):119–36.

Synan, Vinson, ed. *Aspects of Pentecostal-Charismatic Origins*. Plainfield, N.J.: Logos International, 1975.

Synan, Vinson. *The Holiness-Pentecostal Movement in the U.S.* Grand Rapids, Mich.: Eerdmans, 1975.

————. *That Old-Time Religion: A History of the Pentecostal Holiness Church.* Franklin Springs, Ga.: Advocate Press, 1973.

Tinney, James S. "Black Origins of the Pentecostal Movement." *Christianity Today* 16 (1971):4–6.

Trigg, Joseph W. "The Charismatic Intellectual: Origen's Understanding of Religious Leadership." *Church History* 50 (March 1981):5–19.

Unger, Merrill F. *The Baptism and Gifts of the Holy Spirit.* Chicago: Moody, 1974.

United Pentecostal Church. *Manual.* St. Louis, Mo.: 1967.

Van Dusen, Henry A. "Third Force in Christendom: Gospel-Singing, Doomsday-Preaching Sects." *Life* 44 (9 June 1959):113–22.

Warburton, T. Rennie. "Holiness Religion: An Anomaly of Sectarian Typologies." *Journal for the Scientific Study of Religion* 8 (1969):130–39.

Warner, Wayne E., ed. *Touched by the Fire.* Plainfield, N.J.: Logos International, 1978.

Washington, Joseph R. *Black Religion: The Negro and Christianity in the United States.* Boston: Beacon, 1964.

————. *Black Sects and Cults.* Garden City, N.Y.: Doubleday, 1972.

Weaver, C. Douglas. *William Marrion Branham: A Study of the Prophetic in American Pentecostalism.* Macon, Ga.: Mercer Univ. Press, 1987.

Webster, Douglas. *Pentecostalism and Speaking with Tongues.* London: Highway Press, 1964.

Whalen, William J. *Minority Religions in America.* Staten Island, N.Y.: Alba House, 1972.

Williams, Cyril G. *Tongues of the Spirit: A Study of Pentecostal Glossolalia and Related Phenomena.* Cardiff: Univ. of Wales, 1981.

Williams, Melvin D. "Considerations of a Black Anthropologist Researching Pentecostalism." *Spirit* 3 (1979):20–26.

Wilmore, Gayraud S. *Black Religion and Black Radicalism.* Garden City, N.Y.: Doubleday, 1972.

Wilson, Bryan R. *Religious Sects: A Sociological Study.* London: Weidenfeld and Nicolson, 1970.

————. "The Pentecostal Minister: Role Conflicts and Status Contradiction." *American Journal of Sociology* 64 (1959):494–504.

Wilson, John, and Harvey K. Clow. "Themes of Power and Control in a Pentecostal Assembly." *Journal for the Scientific Study of Religion* 20 (Sept. 1981):241–50.

Wood, William W. *Culture and Personality Aspects of the Pentecostal Holiness Religion.* Paris: Mouton, 1965.

5. WORKS CONCERNING DIVINE HEALING

Allen, Asa A. *Does God Heal Through Medicine?* Miracle Valley, Ariz.: Allen, n.d.

————. *Can God?* Miracle Valley, Ariz.: Allen, n.d.

————. *God Will Heal You*. Miracle Valley, Ariz.: Allen, 1953.

————. *God's Guarantee To Heal You*. Miracle Valley, Ariz.: Allen, 1950.

————. *Is Your Sickness a Thorn in the Flesh?* Miracle Valley, Ariz.: Allen, n.d.

————. *Who Can Heal the Sick?* Miracle Valley, Ariz.: Allen, n.d.

Ballenger, A.F. *Power For Witnessing*. Minneapolis: Bethany Fellowship, 1963.

Banks, John Gayner. *Healing Everywhere*. San Diego, Calif.: St. Luke's Press, 1961.

Basham, Don. *Face Up with a Miracle*. Northridge, Calif.: Christian Voice Publishing, 1967.

Baur, Benjamin A. *The Great Physician*. Rochester, N.Y.: Glad Tidings Publishing Society, 1938.

Boggs, Wade H. *Faith Healing and the Christian Faith*. Richmond, Va.: John Knox, 1956.

Bostrom, Fred Francis. *Christ the Healer*. Springfield, Mo.: Gospel PH, 1948.

Branham, William. *Do You Fear Cancer?* Jeffersonville, Ind.: Branham Book Department, n.d.

Brooks, Noel. *Sickness, Health, and God*. Franklin Springs, Ga.: Advocate Press, n.d.

Caldwell, William. *Meet the Healer*. Tulsa, Okla.: Miracle Moments Evangelistic Association, 1965.

Coe, Jack. *Will Thou Be Made Whole?* Dallas, Tex.: Coe Foundations, n.d.

Culpepper, Richard W. *How You Too Can Receive Your Healing*. Bellflower, Calif.: Privately published, 1955.

Dake, Finis Jennings. *Bible Truths Unmasked*. Atlanta, Ga.: Bible Research Foundation, 1950.

Dove, William Felton. *The Calling of God, "Divine Summons."* Greenwood, S.C.: Privately published, n.d.

Dowell, Oscar B. *Divine Healing, Yes! Divine Healing, Yes!* San Diego, Calif.: Revival Time Evangelistic Campaigns, n.d.

Dowie, Alexander. *Divine Healing Vindicated*. Chicago: Divine Healing Association, 1893.

Ellithorpe, Milton Welch. *Death Unto Life*. Buena Park, Calif.: Privately published, n.d.

Ethridge, Hildreth. *Back from the Dark Valley*. Springfield, Mo.: Gospel PH, 1957.

Evangelical Action. Boston: United Action Press, 1942.

Fitch, Theodore. *Faith and Power Thru Fasting*. Council Bluffs, La.: Privately published, n.d.

Foot, David R.P. *Divine Healing in the Scriptures*. Springfield, Mo.: Assemblies of God PH, 1967.

Frodsham, Stanley H. *Smith Wigglesworth, Apostle of Faith*. Springfield, Mo.: Gospel PH, 1948.

Gardner, Velmer J. *The God of Miracles Lives Today*. Orange, Calif.: Velmer J. Gardner Evangelistic Association, 1954.
Gee, Donald. *Trophimus I Left Sick*. London: Elim Publishing, 1951.
Grant, Walter V. *Are You Sick and Tired of Feeling Sick and Tired?* Dallas, Tex.: Grant's Faith Clinic, n.d.
————. *Divine Healing Answers*. Dallas, Tex.: Voice of Healing Publisher, 1952.
————. *Exploits of Faith*. Dallas, Tex.: Grant's Faith Clinic, n.d.
————. *Faith Cometh: Or How To Get Faith*. Dallas, Tex.: Grant's Faith Clinic, n.d.
————. *Faith for Finance*. Dallas, Tex.: Grant's Faith Clinic, n.d.
————. *The Gift of Faith*. Dallas, Tex.: Grant's Faith Clinic, n.d.
————. *Gifts of Healing*. Dallas, Tex.: Grant's Faith Clinic, n.d.
————. *Healing in the Grant Campaigns*. Dallas, Tex.: Grant's Faith Clinic, n.d.
————. *The Last To Healing*. Dallas, Tex.: Grant's Faith Clinic, n.d.
————. *Power To Bind and Loose*. Dallas, Tex.: Grant's Faith Clinic, n.d.
————. *Power To Discern Disease*. Dallas, Tex.: Grant's Faith Clinic, n.d.
————. *Seven Reasons Why You Can't Receive Your Healing*. Dallas, Tex.: Grant's Faith Clinic, n.d.
————. *The Truth About Faith Healers*. Dallas, Tex.: Grant's Faith Clinic, n.d.
Hagin, Kenneth E. *How To Turn Your Faith Loose*. Tulsa, Okla.: Kenneth Hagin Evangelistic Association, n.d.
————. *The Key To Scriptural Healing*. Tulsa, Okla.: Kenneth Hagin Evangelistic Association, n.d.
Hall, Franklin. *Dynamic Gift of Faith Power*. Phoenix, Ariz.: Hall Deliverance Foundation, 1967.
————. *Our Divine Healing Obligation*. Phoenix, Ariz.: Hall Deliverance Foundation, 1964.
Hardy, Robert G. *The Blessings of Abraham Are Yours and Believe Against Hope*. Baltimore, Md.: Faith in Action, 1966.
Harrell, Irene Burk. *Lo, I Am With You*. Plainfield, N.J.: Logos International, 1970.
Hicks, Tommy. *Manifest Deliverance For You Now*. Dallas, Tex.: Healing Publishing, 1952.
————. *Millions Found Christ, Greatest Recorded Revival*. Hollywood, Calif.: Alberty Offset Printing, 1956.
Holdcroft, L. Thomas. *Divine Healing*. Springfield, Mo.: Gospel PH, 1967.
Iverson, Sylva F. *God's Deliverance*. Portland, Ore.: Bible Press, 1955.
Jeffreys, George. *Healing Rays*. London: Elim Publishing, 1932.
————. *The Miraculous Foursquare Gospel*. London: Elim Publishing, 1930.
Jenkins, Le Roy. *How You Can Receive Your Healing*. San Bernardino, Calif.: L.J. Evangelistic Association, 1966.

————. *Power for Abundant Living.* San Bernardino, Calif.: L.J. Evangelistic Association, 1956.

Jones, Pearl Williams. "A Minority Report: Black Pentecostal Women." *Spirit* 1 (1977):31–44.

Jones, Thea F. *God's Thief Who Never Got Caught.* Philadelphia: Philadelphia Evangelistic Centre, n.d.

Koch, Kurt E. *Occult Bondage and Deliverance.* Grand Rapids, Mich.: Kregel, 1970.

Kuhlman, Kathryn. *God Can Do It Again.* Englewood Cliffs, N.J.: Prentice-Hall, 1969.

————. *I Believe in Miracles.* Englewood Cliffs, N.J.: Prentice-Hall, 1962.

Lindsay, James Gordon. *All About the Gift of Faith.* Dallas, Tex.: Voice of Healing Publishing, 1963.

————. *Answers to the Difficult Questions Concerning Divine Healing.* Dallas, Tex.: Voice of Healing Publishing, 1960.

————. *Bible Days Are Here Again.* Dallas, Tex.: Voice of Healing Publishing, 1949.

————. *The Bible Secret of Divine Health.* Dallas, Tex.: Voice of Healing Publishing, 1960.

————. *Christ the Great Physician.* Dallas, Tex.: Voice of Healing Publishing, 1960.

————. *The Facts About the Seventh Day.* Dallas, Tex.: Voice of Healing Publishing, 1964.

————. *The Gifts of Healing.* Dallas, Tex.: Voice of Healing Publishing, 1963.

————. *God's Answer to the Puzzling Cases.* Dallas, Tex.: Voice of Healing Publishing, 1956.

————. *How To Receive Your Healing.* Dallas, Tex.: Voice of Healing Publishing, n.d.

————. *How You Can Be Healed, or All About Divine Healing.* Dallas, Tex.: Voice of Healing Publishing, n.d.

————. *How You Can Have Divine Health.* Dallas, Tex.: Voice of Healing Publishing, n.d.

————. *Is the Healing Revival from Heaven or of Men?* Dallas, Tex.: Voice of Healing Publishing, n.d.

————. *The Real Reason Why Christians Are Sick and How They May Get Well.* Dallas, Tex.: Voice of Healing Publishing, n.d.

————. *Thirty Reasons Why Christ Heals Today.* Dallas, Tex.: Christ for the Nations Publishing, 1968.

————. *True Visions of the Unseen World, and Other Visions.* Dallas, Tex.: Voice of Healing Publishing, n.d.

————. *World Evangelism Now by Healing and Miracles.* Dallas, Tex.: Voice of Healing Publishing, 1951.

Litell, Franklin H. "Free Churches and the Pentecostal Challenge." *Journal of Ecumenical Studies* 5 (Winter 1968):131–32.

Lovekin, Arthur A. and Newton Malony. "Religious Glossolalia: A Longitudinal Study of Personality Changes." *Journal for the Scientific Study of Religion* 16 (Dec. 1977):383–93.

Marlow, John D. *Faith That Worketh*. Silsbee, Tex.: Deeper Life Ministry, n.d.

——. *God's Word in Man*. Silsbee, Tex.: Deeper Life Ministry, n.d.

——. *It Is Written*. Silsbee, Tex.: Deeper Life Ministry, n.d.

——. *Redemption of the Body*. Silsbee, Tex.: Deeper Life Ministry, n.d.

——. *Secret of Divine Health*. Silsbee, Tex.: Deeper Life Ministry, n.d.

——. *So Be It Unto You*. Silsbee, Tex.: Deeper Life Ministry, n.d.

——. *What Is Faith?* Silsbee, Tex.: Deeper Life Ministry, n.d.

Martin, Bernard. *The Healing Ministry in the Church*. Richmond, Va.: John Knox, 1960.

McAlister, Robert E. *The Five Foundations of Healing*. South Bend, Ind.: Calvary Press, 1957.

McNutt, Francis. *The Gift of Healing*. Notre Dame, Ind.: Communication Center, 1971.

McPherson, Aimme Semple. *Divine Healing in the Word of God*. Los Angeles, Calif.: International Church of the Foursquare Gospel, n.d.

——. *Divine Healing Sermons*. Los Angeles, Calif.: International Church of the Foursquare Gospel, n.d.

Neal, Emily G. *The Lord is Our Healer*. Englewood Cliffs, N.J.: Prentice-Hall, 1956.

——. *A Reporter Finds God Through Spiritual Healing*. New York: Morehouse-Gorham, 1956.

Nee, Watchman. *The Spiritual Man*. New York: Christian Fellowship Publishers, 1968.

Nelson, Ernest. *Testimonies of Divine Healing*. East Peoria, Ill.: Lighthouse Publishing, 1961.

Norton, Mary C. *Life Sketch of Mary C. Norton; and Remarkable Healings on Mission Fields, by Irene E. Lewis*. Los Angeles, Calif.: Pilgrim's Mission, 1954.

Nunn, David O. *Holy Bible, The Confession of Faith*. Dallas, Tex.: Bible Revivals, n.d.

——. *The Life And Ministry of David Nunn*. Dallas, Tex.: Bible Revivals, n.d.

Osborn, T.L. *Christ in Siam*. Tulsa, Okla.: T.L. Osborn Evangelistic Association, 1956.

——. *Faith's Testimony: The Important Secret of Confession Unveiled and How to Keep Your Healing*. Tulsa, Okla.: T.L. Osborn Evangelistic Association, 1962.

——. *Healing From Christ*. Tulsa, Okla.: T.L. Osborn Evangelistic Association, 1955.

——. *Healing the Sick*. Tulsa, Okla.: T.L. Osborn Evangelistic Association, 1961.

———. *Healing the Sick and Casting Out Devils*. Tulsa, Okla.: T.L. Osborn Evangelistic Association, 1953.

———. *The Purpose of Pentecost*. Tulsa, Okla.: T.L. Osborn Evangelistic Association, 1962.

———. *Seven Steps to Receive Healing from Christ*. Tulsa, Okla.: T.L. Osborn Evangelistic Association, 1955.

Osteen, John H. *How To Be Healed*. Houston, Tex.: John H. Osteen Association, 1961.

———. *How to Release the Power of God*. Houston, Tex.: John H. Osteen Association, 1968.

———. *You Can Change Your Destiny*. Houston, Tex.: John H. Osteen Association, 1968.

Parr, J. Nelson. *Divine Healing*. Springfield, Mo.: Gospel PH, 1955.

———. *Healing Our Divine Heritage*. Corpus Christi, Tex.: Christian Triumph Press, 1952.

———. *The Power of Full Surrender*. Corpus Christi, Tex.: Christian Triumph Press, 1955.

———. *Wings of Victory*. Corpus Christi, Tex.: Christian Triumph Press, 1967.

Powell, Don. *Faith in the Fire, by Don Powell as Told to Maurice Berquist*. Daytona Beach, Fla.: World Evangelism Press, 1961.

Purkiser, W.T. *Spiritual Gifts: Healing and Tongues; an Analysis of the Charismatic Revival*. Kansas City, Mo.: Nazarene Publishing, 1965.

Reed, William S. *Surgery of the Soul*. Old Tappan, N.J.: Revell, 1969.

Roberts, Granville Oral. *Deliverance From Fear and From Sickness*. Tulsa, Okla.: Oral Roberts Evangelistic Association, 1954.

———. *Exactly How You May Receive Your Healing-Through Faith*. Tulsa, Okla.: Oral Roberts Evangelistic Association, 1958.

———. *Faith Against Life's Storms*. Tulsa, Okla.: Oral Roberts Evangelistic Association, 1957.

———. *God is a Good God, Believe It and Come Alive*. Tulsa, Okla.: Oral Roberts Evangelistic Association, 1960.

———. *Healing For the Whole Man*. Tulsa, Okla.: Oral Roberts Evangelistic Association, 1965.

———. *Healing Stream*. Tulsa, Okla.: Oral Roberts Evangelistic Association, 1959.

———. *How To Find Your Point of Contact With God*. Tulsa, Okla.: Oral Roberts Evangelistic Association, 1966.

———. *If You Need Healing Do These Things*. Tulsa, Okla.: Oral Roberts Evangelistic Association, 1950.

———. *My Story*. Tulsa, Okla.: Oral Roberts Evangelistic Association, 1961.

Roberts, Granville Oral. *Raising the Roof for Victory*. Tulsa, Okla.: Oral Roberts Evangelistic Association, 1964.

———. *Seven Divine Aids for Your Health*. Tulsa, Okla.: Oral Roberts Evangelistic Association, 1960.

———. *Ten Greatest Miracles of Oral Roberts' Ministry*. Tulsa, Okla.: Oral Roberts Evangelistic Association, 1961.

———. *This Is Your Abundant Life in Jesus Christ*. Tulsa, Okla.: Oral Roberts Evangelistic Association, 1962.

———. *Your Healing Problems and How To Solve Them*. Tulsa, Okla.: Oral Roberts Evangelistic Association, 1966.

Robinson, Reuben. *My Hospital Experience*. Kansas City, Mo.: Nazarene PH, n.d.

Sanford, Agnes Mary White. *The Healing Gifts of the Spirit*. Philadelphia: Lippincott, 1966.

———. *The Healing Gifts of the Spirit*. Philadelphia: Lippincott, 1966.

———. *The Healing Light*. London: London Healing Mission, 1963.

———. *The Healing Power of the Bible*. Philadelphia: Lippincott, 1969.

Simpson, Albert B. *The Lord For The Body*. Harrisburg, Penn.: Christian Publications, 1959.

Stewart, Alex. *Bodily Healing Since Pentecost and All Things*. New York: Loizeaus Brothers, n.d.

Torrey, Reuben A. *Divine Healing*. Grand Rapids, Mich.: Baker Book House, 1924.

Turner, William H. *Christ the Great Physician*. Franklin Springs, Ga.: Advocate Press, 1941.

———. *Five Thousand Years of Healing*. Franklin Springs, Ga.: Advocate Press, 1947.

———. *I Am The Lord That Healeth Thee*. Franklin Springs, Ga.: Advocate Press, 1947.

———. *Is It the Will of God To Heal All Who Are Sick?* Franklin Springs, Ga.: Advocate Press, 1947.

———. *Shall God's People Take Medicine?* Franklin Springs, Ga.: Advocate Press, 1947.

———. *What Must I Do To Be Healed?* Franklin Springs, Ga.: Advocate Press, 1947.

———. *Why Are Not All Healed?* Franklin Springs, Ga.: Advocate Press, 1947.

Ward, Charles M. *How Far Can a Mother's Prayer Reach?* Springfield, Mo.: Assemblies of God, 1963.

———. *The True Relationship Between a Pentecostal Believer and the Medical Doctor*. Springfield, Mo.: Revivaltime, n.d.

———. *What Are They Saying About Divine Healing? The Press, Doctors and Ministers*. N.p., n.d.

Whalley, W.E. "Pentecostal Theology." *Baptist Quarterly* 27 (July 1978): 282–89.

Wicks, Mildred. *The Dawn of a Better Day*. Tulsa, Okla.: Standard Printing, n.d.

Wiggins, Patrick. *The Pat Wiggins Story*. Tulsa, Okla.: Abundant Life Publisher, 1962.

Wigglesworth, Smith. *Ever Increasing Faith*. Springfield, Mo.: Gospel PH, 1924.

————. *Faith That Prevails*. Springfield, Mo.: Gospel PH, 1938.

Woods, William. *Claim Your Miracle*. Chicago: William Woods Evangelistic Association, 1962.

Woodworth-Etter, Maria B. *Marvels and Miracles God Wrought in the Ministry for Forty-Five Years*. Indianapolis, Ind.: Mrs. M.B. Woodworth-Etter, 1922.

————. *Acts of the Holy Ghost, or the Life, Work, and Experience of Mrs. M.B. Wordworth-Etter, Evangelist*. Indianapolis, Ind.: Mrs. M.B. Woodworth-Etter, 1912.

————. *Questions and Answers on Divine Healing*. Indianapolis, Ind.: Mrs. M.B. Woodworth-Etter, n.d.

Wyatt, Thomas. *Commanding Power*. Los Angeles, Calif.: Wings of Healing, 1956.

————. *Hidden Treasure*. Los Angeles, Calif.: Wings of Healing, 1957.

————. *Manna on the Ground*. Los Angeles, Calif.: Wings of Healing, 1958.

————. *Peace, Power, and Plenty*. Los Angeles, Calif.: Wings of Healing, n.d.

————. *A Study in Healing and Deliverance*. Los Angeles, Calif.: Wings of Healing, n.d.

————. *Then Jesus Came*. Los Angeles, Calif.: Wings of Healing, 1958.

————. *Wings of Healing*. Los Angeles, Calif.: Wings of Healing, 1955.

————. *Words That Work Wonders*. Portland, Ore.: Wings of Healing, 1951.

Yeomans, Lillian B. *Balm of Gilead*. Springfield, Mo.: Gospel PH, 1936.

————. *Divine Healing Diamonds*. Springfield, Mo.: Gospel PH, 1933.

————. *Healing From Heaven*. Springfield, Mo.: Gospel PH, 1926.

6. THESES AND DISSERTATIONS

Abell, Troy Dale. "The Holiness-Pentecostal Experience in Southern Appalachia." Vols 1 and 2. Ph.D. dissertation, Purdue Univ., 1974.

Allen Henry Dodson. "The Christian Conception of Holiness." Ph.D. dissertation, Univ. of Chicago, 1925.

Anderson, Robert. "A Study of the Theology of the Episcopalians, the Lutherans, and the Pentecostals of the Charismata of the Holy Spirit, Especially as Manifested in Speaking in Tongues and Healing." M.Div. thesis, Concordia Theological Seminary, 1964.

Anderson, Robert Mapes. "A Social History of the Early Twentieth-Century Pentecostal Movement." Ph.D. dissertation, Columbia Univ., 1969.

Baker, Cheryl D. "A Psycho-Political Comparison of Hallucinatory Phenomena Amongst Schizophrenics, LSD Users and Glossolalics." M.S. thesis, Univ. of Witwatersrand, South Africa, 1983.

Barnett, Maurice. "The Gift of the Spirit in the New Testament, with Special Reference to Glossolalia." Master's thesis, Univ. of Manchester, Eng., 1946.

Battle, Allen Overton. "Personal Status in a Negro Holiness Sect." Ph.D. dissertation, Catholic Univ. of America, 1961.

Beaman, Jay. "Pentecostal Pacificism: The Origin, Development, and Rejection of Pacific Belief Among Pentecostals." M.Div. thesis, North American Baptist Seminary, 1982.

Beeg, John Frederick. "Beliefs and Values of Charismatics: A Survey." Th.D. dissertation. Colgate Rochester Divinity School, 1978.

Black, Hubert Perry. "The Predictive Value of Selected Factors for Achievement of Lee College Freshmen." Ed.D. dissertation, Univ. of Tennessee, Knoxville, 1965.

Bond, J. Max. "The Negro in Los Angeles." Ph.D. dissertation. Univ. of Southern California, 1936.

Bradfield, Cecil David. "An Investigation of Neo-Pentecostalism." Ph.D. dissertation, American Univ., 1975.

Bruner, Frederick Dale. "The Doctrine and Experience of the Holy Spirit in the Pentecostal Movement and Correspondingly in the New Testament." Ph.D. dissertation, Univ. of Hamburg, 1963.

Chesire, C. Linwood. "The Doctrine of the Holy Spirit in Acts." Master's thesis, Union Theological Seminary, 1953.

Chordas, Thomas John. "Building The Kingdom: The Creativity of Ritual Performance in Catholic Pentecostalism." Ph.D. dissertation, Duke Univ., 1980.

Christenbury, Eugene Carl. "A Study of Teacher Education in Sixteen Pentecostal Colleges in the United States." Ed.D. dissertation, Univ. of Tennessee, Knoxville, 1972.

Cintron, Pedro. "American Denominational Revivalism and the Pentecostal Movement: A Comparative Study." Master's thesis, Union Theological Seminary, 1963.

Clow, Harvey Kennedy. "Ritual, Belief, and the Social Context: An Analysis of a Southern Pentecostal Sect." Ph.D. dissertation, Duke Univ., 1977.

Connelly, James Thomas. "Neo-Pentecostalism: The Charismatic Revival in the Mainline Protestant and Roman Catholic Churches in the United States, 1960–1971." Ph.D. dissertation, Univ. of Chicago, 1977.

Conway, Frederick James. "Pentecostalism in the Context of Haitian Religion and Health Practice." Ph.D. dissertation, American Univ., 1978.

Corvin, R.O. "History of Education Institutions of the Pentecostal Holiness Church." D.Div. dissertation, Southwestern Baptist Theological Seminary, 1956.

Dann, Norman Kingsford. "Concurrent Social Movements: A Study of the Interrelationships between Populists' Politics and Holiness Religion." Ph.D. dissertation, Syracuse Univ., 1974.

Dearman, Marion, Veurl. "Do Holiness Sects Socialize in Dominant Values?: An Empirical Inquiry." Ph.D. dissertation, Univ. of Oregon, 1972.

Delk, William Alexander. "Lee College and Its Relationship to the Community in Which It Is Located." M.S. thesis, Univ. of Tennessee, Knoxville, 1959.

Dieter, Melvin Easterday. "Revivalism And Holiness." Ph.D. dissertation, Temple Univ., 1973.

Eason, Gerald M. "The Significance of Tongues." Master's thesis, Dallas Theological Seminary, 1959.

Elliot, William Winston. "Sociocultural Change in a Pentecostal Group: A Case Study in Education and Culture of the Church Of God in Sonora, Mexico." Ed.D. dissertation, Univ. of Tennessee, Knoxville, 1971.

Engelsen, Nils Ivar Johan. "Glossolalia and Other Forms of Inspired Speech According to 1 Corinthians 12–14." Th.D. dissertation, Yale Univ., 1970.

Estes, Joseph Richard. "The Biblical Concept of Spiritual Gifts." Th.D. dissertation, Southern Baptist Theological Seminary, 1957.

Fischer, Harold A. "Progress of the Various Modern Pentecostal Movements Toward World Fellowship." Master's thesis, Texas Christian Univ., 1952.

Forbes, James A. "A Pentecostal Approach to Empowerment for Black Liberation." Ph.D. dissertation, Colgate Rochester Divinity School, 1975.

Gaddis, Merle E. "Christian Perfectionism in America." Ph.D. dissertation, Univ. of Chicago, 1928.

Gilbert, Earl Jean. "Some Personality Correlates of Certain Religious Beliefs, Attitudes, Practices, and Experiences in Students Attending a Fundamentalist Pentecostal Church College." Ed.D. dissertation, Univ. of Tennessee, Knoxville, 1972.

Gillespie, T.W. "Prophecy and Tongues." D.Div. dissertation, Claremont Graduate School and Univ. Center, 1971.

Gilmore, Susan Kay. "A Study of Differences in Personality Patterns Between Pentecostal Groups of Differential Religious Emphases." M.S. thesis, Univ. of Oregon, 1962.

Gonsalvez, Emma. "The Theology and Psychology of Glossolalia." Ph.D. dissertation, Northwestern Univ., 1978.

Greeley, Mary E. "A Study of the Catholic Charismatic Renewal." Ph.D. dissertation, Univ. of St. Louis, 1973.

Green, Hollis Lynn. "The Degree to Which the Church of God Remains Pentecostal in Experience." Th.D. dissertation, Luther Rice Seminary, 1968.

Harrison, Irvine John. "A History of the Assemblies of God." D. of Min. dissertation, Berkeley Baptist Divinity School, 1954.

Harrison, Michael Isaac. "The Organization of Commitment in the Catholic Pentecostal Movement." Ph.D. dissertation, Univ. of Michigan, 1971.

Hart, Larry Douglas. "A Critique of American Pentecostal Theology." Ph.D. dissertation, Southern Baptist Theological Seminary, 1978.

Heath, Robert Weaver. "Persuasive Patterns and Strategies in the Neo-Pentecostal Movement." Ph.D. dissertation, Univ. of Oklahoma, 1973.

Hiss, William C. "Shiloh: Frank W. Sanford and the Kingdom, 1893–1948." Ph.D. dissertation, Tufts Univ., 1978.

Hollenweger, Walter J. "Handbuch der Pringstbewegung." Ph.D. dissertation, Univ. of Zurich, Switzerland, 1965.

Horton, Gene E. "A History of Lee Junior College, Cleveland, Tennessee." Ed.M. thesis, Univ. of South Dakota, 1953.

Hughes, Ray A. "The Transition of Church-Related Junior Colleges to Senior Colleges with Implications for Lee College." Ed.D. dissertation, University of Tenn., Knoxville, 1966.

Johnson, Bobby G. "The Establishment and Development of Lee College, 1918–1954." M.A. thesis, Memphis State College, 1955.

Jones, Charles Edwin. "Perfectionist Persuasion: A Social Profile of the National Holiness Movement Within American Methodism, 1867–1936." Ph.D. dissertation, Univ. of Wisconsin, 1968.

Kane, Steven Michael. "Snake Handlers of Southern Appalachia." Ph.D. dissertation, Princeton Univ., 1979.

Keane, Roberta Catharine. "Formal Organization and Charisma in a Catholic Pentecostal Community." Ph.D. dissertation, Univ. of Michigan, 1974.

Keene, Gertrude B. "Distinctive Social Values of the Pentecostal Churches: A Social Field Study." M.A. thesis, Univ. of Southern California, 1938.

Kendrick, Klaude. "The History of the Modern Pentecostal Movement." Ph.D. dissertation, Univ. of Texas, 1959.

Kenyon, Howard Nelson. "An Analysis of Racial Separation Within the Early Pentecostal Movement." M.A. thesis, Baylor Univ., 1978.

Knight, Cecil B. "An Historical Study of Distinctives Among Divergent Groupings of American Pentecostalism." M.A. thesis, Butler Univ., 1968.

Lovekin, Arthur A. "Glossolalia: A Critical Study of Alleged Origins, the New Testament, and the Early Church." Master's thesis, Univ. of the South, 1962.

Lovekin, Arthur Adams. "Religious Glossolalia: A Longitudinal Study of Personality Changes." Ph.D. dissertation, Fuller Theological Seminary, 1975.

Lovett, Leonard. "Black Holiness-Pentecostalism: Implications for Ethics and Social Transformation." Ph.D. dissertation, Emory Univ., 1979.

Martin, Robert Francis. "The Early Years of American Pentecostalism, 1900–1940: A Survey of a Social Movement." Ph.D. dissertation, Univ. of North Carolina, 1975.

Masserano, Frank C. "A Study of the Worship Forms of the Assemblies of God Denomination." Master's thesis, Princeton Theological Seminary, 1966.

Mawn, Benedict Joseph. "Testing The Spirits: An Empirical Search for the Socio-Cultural Situational Roots of the Catholic Pentecostal Religious Experience." Ph.D. dissertation, Boston Univ., 1975.

Meeks, Fred E. "Pastoral Care and Glossolalia: Implications of the Contemporary Tongues Movement in American Churches." D.Min. dissertation, Southwestern Baptist Theological Seminary, 1976.

Menzies, William W. "The Assemblies of God, 1941–1967: The Consolidation of a Revival Movement." Ph.D. dissertation, Univ. of Iowa, 1968.

Micklethwaite, Kenneth. "The Numinous and the Ethical Dimensions Within Holiness." Ph.D. dissertation, Univ. of Ottawa, 1968.

Moonie, Peter Meredith. "The Significance Of Neo-Pentecostalism for the Renewal and Unity of the Church in the United States." Th.D. dissertation, Boston Univ. School of Theology, 1974.

Moore, Everett L. "Handbook of Pentecostal Denominations in the United States." M.A. thesis, Pasadena College, 1954.

Moore, John C. "A Critical Examination Of Neo-Pentecostalism Within the American Roman Catholic Church." Ph.D. dissertation, Dallas Theological Seminary, 1977.

Mortland, Carol Anne. "The Church of the Saints of the Last Days: An Interpretation of an American Pentecostal Group." Ph.D. dissertation, Univ. of Oregon, 1981.

Motley, Michael T. "Glossolalia: Analyses of Selected Aspects of Phonology and Morphology." Master's thesis, Univ. of Texas, 1967.

Nees, Thomas G. "The Holiness Social Ethic and Nazarene Urban Ministry." Ph.D. dissertation, Wesley Theological Seminary, 1976.

Nichol, John Thomas. "Pentecostalism: A Descriptive History of the Origin, Growth, and Message of a Twentieth-Century Religious Movement." Ph.D. dissertation, Boston Univ., 1965.

Olilia, James. "The Social Organization of the Pentecostal Movement." M.A. thesis, Univ. of Minnesota, 1968.

Oliver, John Bernard, Jr. "Some Newer Religions in the U.S.: Twelve Case Studies." Ph.D. dissertation, Yale Univ., 1946.

Palmer, Bruce. "The Rhetoric of Southern Populists: Metaphor and Imagery in the Language of Reform." Ph.D. dissertation, Yale Univ., 1972.

Palmer, Gary. "Trance and Dissociation: A Cross-Cultural Study in Psychophysiology." Master's thesis, Univ. of Minnesota, 1966.

Paris, Arthur Ernest. "Black Pentecostalism: World View, Society and Politics." Ph.D. dissertation, Northwestern Univ., 1974.

Paul, George H. "The Religious Frontier in Oklahoma: Dan T. Muse and the Pentecostal Holiness Church." Ph.D. dissertation, Univ. of Oklahoma, 1965.

Perrin, Steve W. "A Clanging Cymbal: Conflict Among Catholic Pentecostals." Ph.D. dissertation, Michigan State Univ., 1971.

Pike, Garnet Elmer. "The Rise of a Black Pentecostal Church in a Changing City: A Historical Case Study." D.Div. dissertation, Vanderbilt Univ. Divinity School, 1972.

Prosnitz, David Jerome. "Spirit in the Flesh: A Cultural Account of an Urban American Pentecostalism." Ph.D. dissertation, Univ. of Chicago, 1978.

Ranaghan, Kevin Mathers. "Rites of Initiation in Representative Pentecostal Churches in the United States, 1901–1972." Ph.D. dissertation, Notre Dame University, 1974.

Rarick, William J. "The Socio-Cultural Context of Glossolalia: A Comparison of Pentecostal and Neo-Pentecostal Religious Attitudes and Behavior." D.Div. dissertation, Fuller Theological Seminary, 1982.

Reed, David Arthur. "Origins and Development of the Theology of Oneness

Pentecostalism in the United States." Ph.D. dissertation, Boston Univ., 1978.

Rodriguez, Sylvia B. "Ecstasy: May and Threshold, A Cross-Cultural Study of Dissociation." Ph.D. dissertation, Stanford Univ., 1981.

Roth, Richard. "Social Structure in a Pentecostal Church." M.A. thesis, Univ. of Minnesota, 1967.

Sala, Harold James. "Investigation of the Baptizing and Filling Work of the Holy Spirit in the New Testament Related to the Pentecostal Doctrine of Initial Evidence." Ph.D. dissertation, Bob Jones Univ., 1966.

Saunders, Monroe R., Sr. "Some Historical Pentecostal Perspectives for a Contemporary Developmental Pentecost." D.Min. dissertation, Howard Univ., 1974.

Saxman, John H. "Schizophrenic Speech: Selected Fundamental and Rate Characteristics." Ph.D. dissertation, Purdue Univ., 1965.

Scott, Noel Wayne. "The Schools of the Church of God (Holiness)." Ph.D. dissertation, Univ. of Missouri, 1973.

Shopshire, James Maynard. "A Socio-Historical Characterization of the Black Pentecostal Movement in America." Ph.D. dissertation, Northwestern Univ., 1975.

Smeeton, Donald D. "Perfection or Pentecost: A Historical Comparison of Charismatic and Holiness Theologies." Master's thesis, Trinity Evangelical Divinity School, 1971.

Smith, Henry Jordan. "A History of West Coast Bible College, Fresno, California, 1949–1970." M.A. thesis, Fresno State College, 1970.

Sorem, Anthony M. "Some Secular Implications of the Pentecostal Denomination." Master's thesis, Univ. of Minnesota, 1969.

Speer, Blanche C. "A Linguistic Analysis of a Corpus of Glossolalia." Ph.D. dissertation, Univ. of Colorado, 1971.

Stephens, Raphael Weller, III. "A History of Governance at Lee College: A Study in Pentecostal Higher Education." Ed.D. dissertation, of William and Mary University, 1981.

Sorem, Anthony. "Some Secular Implications of the Pentecostal Denomination." M.A. thesis, Univ. of Minnesota, 1967.

Synan, Harold Vinson. "The Pentecostal Movement in the United States." Ph.D. dissertation, Univ. of Georgia, 1967.

Teeter, Floyd David. "Neo-Pentecostalism and Spiritual Deprivation." M.A. thesis, Pacific Lutheran Univ., 1978.

Underwood, James Lester. "Historical Development of Lee Junior College." M.S. thesis, Univ. of Tennessee, 1954.

Vivier, Lincoln Morse Van Eetveldt. "Glossolalia." M.D. thesis, Univ. of Witwaterstrand, South Africa, 1960.

Waldvogel, Edith L. "The 'Overcoming Life': A Study in the Reformed Evangelical Origins of Pentecostalism." Ph.D. dissertation, Harvard Univ., 1977.

Webb, Emma Sue. "The Limitations on Women Ministers in the Church of God." M.A. thesis, California Graduate School of Theology, 1981.
Wheelock, Ronald. "Spirit Baptism in American Pentecostal Thought." Ph.D. dissertation, Emory Univ., 1983.
Whiting, Albert N. "The United House of Prayer for All People: A Case Study of a Charismatic Sect." Doctoral dissertation, American Univ., 1952.
Williams, Melvin Donald. "A Pentecostal Congregation in Pittsburgh: A Religious Community in a Black Ghetto." Ph.D. dissertation, Univ. of Pittsburgh, 1973.
Womack, Sheila Ann. "Therapeutic Aspects of a Pentecostal Church on Alcohol and Drug Abusers." Ph.D. dissertation, Univ. of Texas, Austin, 1980.
Wood, William Woodhull. "Culture And Personality Aspects of the Pentecostal Holiness Religion." Ph.D. dissertation, Univ. of North Carolina, 1961.

Index

Allen, Asa A., 81
Allen, Dave, 117–18

Ball, Aaron, 135
Bachman School, 6
Baptism of Holy Ghost, 10–11; see also Baptism of Holy Spirit
Baptism of Holy Spirit, 9–11
Barnewall, P.F., 87
Barney Creek Meeting House, 9
Barney, Walter, 74–75
Barr, Edmund S., 165
Bayly, Joseph, 83
Beach, Charles, 163
Bennett, Father Dennis, 154
Boyd, Emma L., 99
Bradley, James, 75–77
Brazell, George, 163
Brewer, Hazel, 60
Bright, J.D., 152, 165
Britt, George L., 150
Broang, Paint, 17
Brouayer, George, 28–29
Bryant, Nettie, 5, 85
Bryant, William F., 10, 19, 85
Buckalew, J.W., 94
Burridge, Cecil, 55

Cain, Tom M., 123
Catholic Pentecostalism, 154
Chambers, Nora, 101

Charismatic Renewal, 154; see also Catholic Pentecostalism
Charismatic Revival, 82, 159–60; 175–76
Chesser, H.L., 148
Christian Perfectionism, 9–10; see also holiness, sanctification
"Christian Union," 10; see also Church of God
Church of God, 10, 13–14; see also "Christian Union"
Church of God: early stronghold, 7; eschatology, 16; list of teachings, 22; name change, 21; origins, 5–7; persecution of early members, 16–17; sacraments, 11
Church of God of Prophecy, 30; see also Tomlinson Church of God
Church of God transformation: attitude towards Civil Rights, 163; causes, 139; cooperation with other evangelicals, 146–48; effects of Charismatic Revival, 153–60; Human Rights Resolution, 167; opposition to Ecumenical movement, 148–51; political activism, 160–63; respectability, 151; secular humanism, 163; voting, 162
Churchill, C.A., 112
Clark, E.C., 89, 126, 146

Cole, C.W., 77
Conn, Charles W., 52, 55, 81, 90, 105–6; 145, 154–55; 167
controversy: charismatic movement, 154–55; dress code, 58–59; financial system, 23–24; jewelry, 62; "the Lattimer machine," 31–33; role of education, 141; Tomlinson's management of finances, 25–30
Cook, Robert A., 143
Crawford, Jennie, 91
Cross, James A., 38, 41–42, 60, 161
Cross, M.P., 49, 146–47
Crowley, Raymond E., 158–59

Dasher, Mrs. Frank, 89
Devore, J.E., 81
Dirksen, Carolyn, 95, 97
divine healing: effects of Healing Revival, 80–83; extreme position, 74–78; relaxation of extremism, 79–83; resolution of 1907, 70; role of faith, 72–74; sickness related to depravity of man, 72
Dixon, Rebecca, 77
Dorcas Society, 101
DuPlessis, David J., 149

Eason, Glen, 79–80
Eddy, Mary Baker, 98
education: attitude toward public education, 142–43; Bible Training School, 140; Christian day schools, 143–44; East Coast Bible College, 145; General Board of Education, 143; Graduate School of Christian Ministries, 145–46; Lee College, 140–42, 161, 163; Ministerial Internship program, 145–46; Northwest Bible School, 140; West Coast Bible College, 140–41

Ellis, J.B., 27, 50, 84, 118, 122–23

Finlay, James T., 119
French, Ellen, 104
Fry, Ella, 99

Gause, R. Hollis, 161
Gibson, Donald B., 83
Gillaspie, S.O., 28–29
glossolalic experience, 154; see also speaking in tongues
government: Body of Elders, 23; constitution, 25; Council of Eighteen, 37; Council of Seventy, 24, 31; Court of Justice, 24; Executive Committee, 37; first assistant general overseer, 31; first General Assembly, 20; General Council, 31; second assistant general overseer, 32; six regional assistant general overseers, 32; state overseer, 22; Supreme Council, 26, 62
Greene, Merle H., 80

Hagewood, Nannie Ruth, 100
Harrell, David Edwin, Jr., 70–71, 153
Harrison, Alda B., 45, 101
Hawes, H.A., 168
Haygood, Bishop Atticus, 8
Haynes, Efford, 28
Heath, S.J., 87
Hensley, George W., 83–85, 174
Hewett, Ottis, 137
Hicks, B.L., 77, 133
Hilsabeck, Ella, 100
Holcomb, Sam, 79
Holiness, 8–10, 39
Holiness Church, 11, 19; see also Church of God
Holiness doctrine, 7, 10
Holiness movement, 3, 173
Holiness standard, 12
Hollenweger, Walter, 95

Horton, Wade H., 42, 81–82, 155, 158, 168
Hughes, J.H., 140
Hughes, Ray H., 46, 142, 147, 150–51, 157–58

Ingram, Tracy, 68
Isaac, Rhys, 12

Jernigan, John C., 148, 151–52
Johnson, R.P., 34, 131–32
Johnson, W.E., 80
Juillerat, Howard, 52
Jussell, Roy, 162

Kennerly, W.T., 120
Kinsey, Lillian, 100
Knight, Cecil B., 106
Krutza, William J., 55

Lamb, Lou Etta, 94–95
Landmarkism, 7
Lattimer, S.W., 31, 33, 37, 128
Leatherman, Lucy M., 96
Lee, F.J., 27, 29, 31, 39, 56, 67, 79, 90–91, 125, 166
Lee H. Battle Co., 27
Lemons, David L., 168
Lemons, Frank W., 33
Llewellyn, J.S., 26–27, 57
Lowery, T.L., 164

McBrayer, Terrell, 162
McLain, Tom L., 85
McLuhan, M.G., 156
McNabb, Fred, 137
McNabb, Milton, 10
McPherson, Aimee Semple, 95
Mahan, Celia, 78
Martin, William, 10
Marty, Martin, 144
Moffet, Gale V., 82
Morehead, Houston R., 167
Moore, Ed, 135

National Association of Evangelicals, 143, 146–47, 160
Neopentecostalism, 154
Neopentecostals, 154
Nichols, John D., 170
Noble, C.F., 86

Osborne, James G., 132

Page, Barbara, 105
Pake, Margaret, 123
Paulk, Earl P., 32, 45, 59, 147
pentecostal blessing, 10; see also Baptism of Holy Spirit
Pentecostal Fellowship of North America, 146, 148, 151, 160
Perry, Sam C., 165
personal morality: alcoholic beverages, 48–51; "bobbing of hair," 63; cosmetics, 63; divorce and remarriage, 63–65; dress code, 55–61; jewelry, 61–63; labor unions, 66–68; moral asceticism, 38; movies, 42–44; secret societies, 65–66; sports, 40–41; television, 44–47; tobacco, 52–55
Phillips, D.G., 87
Pine Mountain Church of God, 90
Polen, O.W., 157
Pressgrove, H.A., 29

Richardson, Thomas F., 165
Roberts, J.T., 168–70
Roberts, Oral, 80, 151, 155
Roope, Belinda, 162
Rouse, L.G., 57, 85–86, 121–23
Rushin, Mrs. Brinson, 96–97
Ryder, F.L., 122–23

Samples, Edna, 76
sanctification, 3, 8, 10–11, 156
Sanders, Raymond, 135
Scott, J.L., 120

"second blessing," 3, 10; *see also* sanctification
"second work of grace," 8; *see also* sanctification
Shanks, Taylor, 54
Shipp, F.S., 120
Simmons, E.L., 56, 90, 129, 131, 146–47
Slay, James L., 135
snake-handling, 84, 89, 174
speaking in tongues, 10, 12, 154
Spurling, Richard G., 1, 6, 9, 10
Spurling, Richard G., Jr., 6, 9, 13, 19
Swiger, Avis, 45

Tapley, Earl M., 140
Tharp, Zeno C., 56, 153
The Lost Link, 6
The Willing Worker, 104
Thrash, Arnold D., 156–57
Thrasher, Lillian, 95–96
Tipton, Joe M., 10
Tomlinson, A.J., 3, 5, 21–22, 24, 26–29, 53, 65, 75–76, 83, 86–87, 97–99, 108–13, 115–17, 120, 125, 174
Tomlinson Church of God, 30; *see also* Church of God of Prophecy
Trimm, Flora, 75

Vinn, D.S., 119
Vore, J.C., 45

Walker, J.H., 34, 51, 130, 134, 140, 146–47

Walker, Paul H., 34, 51, 140
Wallace, George A., 166
war: anti-draft, 115; call for patriotism, 132; civil defense, 133–34; draftees, 132; investigation, 119–20, 175; *Lighted Pathway*, distributed on military posts, 133; members serve in combat, 135–36; new position on draft, 129–30; new ruling, 137; pacificism, 118, 174; ruling against going to war, 116; ruling removed temporarily, 125–26; service pastors, 135; telegram, 133
Webb, Emma Sue, 106–7
White, Robert, 143–44
Whitehead, Myrtle, 57
Williams, G.G., 86
Williams, H.D., 152
women: businesswomen, 105; church clerks, 98–99; educators, 100–1; exclusion from high office, 98; Ladies' Willing Worker Band, 32, 101, 103–5; male attitudes, 97–98; missionaries, 95–97; ordination denied, 94; orphanages, 100; participation, 93; pulpit ministry, 93; Sunday School, 99–100; traditional roles, 104–5
Wood, Mrs. S.J., 32, 101–2
World Pentecostal Fellowship, 146, 147, 151, 160